Perspectives on
Early Andean
Civilization in Peru

The Yale University Publications in Anthropology series, published by the Yale University Department of Anthropology and the Peabody Museum of Natural History at Yale University, is supported by the Theodore and Ruth Wilmanns Lidz Endowment Fund for Excellence in Scholarly Publications, dedicated to the dissemination of scholarly research and study of the world and its cultures.

The Yale University Publications in Anthropology series embodies the results of researches in the general field of anthropology directly conducted or sponsored by the Yale University Department of Anthropology and the Yale Peabody Museum of Natural History Division of Anthropology. Occasionally other manuscripts of outstanding quality that deal with subjects of special interest to the faculty of the Department of Anthropology may also be included.

Distributed by Yale University Press
NEW HAVEN AND LONDON

For quantity purchases or a complete list of available titles in this series visit www.yalebooks.com or yalebooks.co.uk

Perspectives on Early Andean Civilization in Peru

Interaction, Authority, and
Socioeconomic Organization
during the First and
Second Millennia BC

Edited by
Richard L. Burger
Lucy C. Salazar
Yuji Seki

NUMBER 94

Published by
the Yale University Department of Anthropology
and the Yale Peabody Museum of Natural History

Distributed by
Yale University Press
NEW HAVEN AND LONDON

Yale

YALE UNIVERSITY PUBLICATIONS IN ANTHROPOLOGY
NUMBER 94

Rosemary Volpe
Publications Manager

Cover design by Sally H. Pallatto
Index by Judy Hunt

Front cover: Excavation of the staircase leading up to the central plaza of Cardal, Lurín Valley, Peru. Photograph by Richard L. Burger.

Back cover: Monochrome frieze on the exterior of the Sector IIA summit building on the eastern arm of the complex at the archaeological site of Cardal, Peru. Photograph by Richard L. Burger.

Peabody Museum of Natural History, Yale University
P. O. Box 208118, New Haven CT 06520-8118 USA
peabody.yale.edu

Distributed by Yale University Press | NEW HAVEN AND LONDON
www.yalebooks.com | yalebooks.co.uk

ISBN 978-0-913516-30-0
ISSN 1535-7082
Printed in the United States of America

Library of Congress Control Number: 2019954871

∞ This paper meets the requirements of ANSI/NISO Z39.48-1992 (Permanence of Paper).
   10   9   8   7   6   5   4   3   2   1

Contents

Figures

TABLES

Preface

The International Congress of Americanists, founded in 1875, has played an important role in the development of Americanist archaeology. The ICA meets every three years, alternating its venues between Europe and the Americas. Some of the most important papers in this field, by pioneering figures such as Max Uhle and Julio C. Tello, were presented at ICA meetings. Throughout the history of the ICA investigators of many nations have participated in these gatherings, where the atmosphere always has been cosmopolitan, intentionally transcending narrow national boundaries.

At the Fifty-fourth Meeting of the International Congress of Americanists, held in Vienna, Austria, from 15–20 July 2012, we organized a session entitled "La Complejidad Social del Periodo Formativo en los Andes Centrales," in which participating scholars from four continents focused on emergent social complexity during the first and second millennia BC in the Central Andes. The session was so successful that the meeting organizers decided to publish future proceedings, agreeing that the Yale University Publications in Anthropology series produced by the Peabody Museum of Natural History and the Department of Anthropology at Yale University would be an appropriate venue. The present publication is the product of that decision. To create a book that more fully represented the exciting research being carried out on the Peruvian Formative, we also invited contributions from three young scholars who were unable to present papers at the original session: Ryan Clasby, Christopher Milan, and Jason Nesbitt. With the addition of these papers, this volume achieves a more comprehensive regional coverage of research on archaeological sites in southern, central, and northern Peru with geographic coverage of the early developments in coastal, highland, and cloud forest (*ceja de selva*) environments.

This book incorporates the activities of several academic centers that have a tradition of focusing on the Initial Period and Early Horizon, or what now is widely referred to as the Peruvian Formative. The Universidad Nacional Mayor de San Marcos has been involved in Formative research and training since Tello led his historic expeditions to the Marañon drainage in the early twentieth century. Seiichi Izumi, Kazuo Terada, and Yoshio Onuki from the University of Tokyo carried out research starting in the late 1950s at early sites in Peru, beginning with the work at Kotosh and Haldas. Their students are now based in museums and universities throughout Japan. Similarly, Yale University has a long history of archaeological research at early sites in Peru, from Wendell Bennett's work at Chavín de Huántar in 1938 and continuing with Thomas Patterson's investigations of the Ancón shell middens in the late 1960s. All the contributors to this volume are linked in some way to one of these three lineages of academic investigation.

These chapters attempt to provide new perspectives on early Andean civilization by focusing on patterns of interaction, authority, and socioeconomic organization during the first and second millennia BC. All the authors are involved in active investigations in the field and approach this challenging subject by emphasizing different bodies of evidence. Many chapters deal in detail with architectural layouts and how they change over time. These shifts in formal organization, scale, and technology are interpreted as expressing shifts in power, organization, and ideology. Other chapters emphasize alternative classes of evidence, such as animal bones, pottery style and technology, site orientation, and religious iconography. No one approach is sufficient for complete understanding, but all have insights to offer. At the request of anonymous reviewers, a concluding remarks section has been added.

Finally, we express our gratitude for the support provided by Yale University, New Haven, and the National Museum of Ethnology, Osaka, without which it would not have been possible to organize the ICA session or the publication of this volume. The ICA symposium was also supported by the Japan Society for the Promotion of Science Grants-in-Aid for Scientific Research (KAKENHI) number 23222003. Finally, we wish to acknowledge the assistance of Cynthia Dreier and Rosemary Volpe in the preparation of this manuscript for publication.

Richard L. Burger
Charles J. MacCurdy Professor of Anthropology,
Yale University, New Haven

Lucy C. Salazar
Research Associate, Department of Anthropology,
Yale University, New Haven

Yuji Seki
Professor, Department of Advanced Studies in Anthropology,
National Museum of Ethnology, Osaka

CHAPTER ONE

Wealth in People

An Alternative Perspective on Initial Period Monumental Architecture from the Caballo Muerto Complex

Jason Nesbitt

Monuments first appeared along the Peruvian coast during the Late Preceramic Period (2500–1700 BC; all dates in this chapter are calibrated using the 2013 Southern Hemisphere calibration curve [Hogg et al. 2013]) and proliferated significantly in the early part of the Initial Period (ca. 1700–1200 BC). Early settlements with monumental architecture functioned as temples and consisted of large terraced platform and plaza complexes (Williams 1985; Burger 1992). These first instances of public architecture represent the material manifestation of experiments in radically different ways of social, religious, and economic life than what came before. Perhaps the most important sociocultural innovation of this time were the first efforts in coordinating larger social groups that created the places and spaces for formalized religious practices. Thus, the first monuments would have had profound effects on their builder's perceptions of sociality, connection to place, and landscape (Bradley 1998; Joyce 2004; Dillehay 2007).

Yet, archaeologists have long been challenged by the problem of determining how the communities of the Late Preceramic Period and Initial Period actually organized themselves to produce large-scale public works. At issue is whether emergent leaders had the kinds of political and economic authority to coerce followers into constructing monuments (Haas 1987; S. Pozorski and T. Pozorski 1987, 1992; T. Pozorski and S. Pozorski 1993a, 1993b, 2005, 2018; Billman 1999, 2001; Haas and Creamer 2012), or whether more communal social and religious mechanisms were at play (e.g., Burger and Salazar-Burger 1991; Burger 2009a; Burger and Salazar 2012, 2014). To address these questions requires an understanding of how labor was mobilized. Here I discuss issues of early political economy through an examination of the first monument building societies dating to the early Initial Period at the Caballo Muerto Complex. I argue that, like other Initial Period complexes, Caballo Muerto's earliest monuments were built by societies lacking centralized political authority. Although leaders existed, they were unable to marshal labor through coercive political mechanisms such as control over economic or ideological "power bases" (e.g., Billman 2001, 2002; Haas and Creamer 2012). Instead, monumentalism at Caballo Muerto can be explained by shifting the focus toward determining how the social relations driving monument construction were constituted in the first place. I present a model of labor mobilization derived from sociocultural anthropology referred to as "wealth in people"

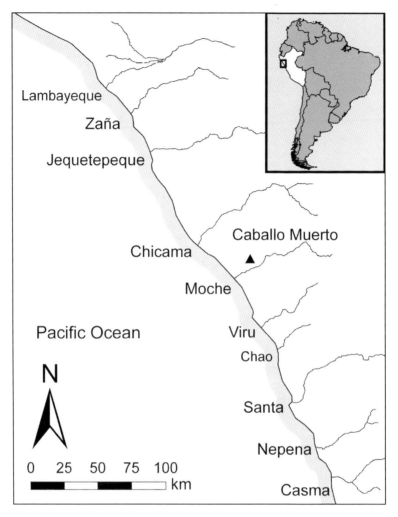

FIGURE 1.1. The location of Caballo Muerto in the lower Moche Valley of Peru.

(Guyer 1995), which places primacy on the accumulation of networks of social relationships as forming the critical elements of the political economy.

I use the first monuments at Caballo Muerto, a large Initial Period complex in the Moche Valley of northern Peru, to illustrate the wealth in people concept, by focusing on two of the earliest: Huaca Cortada and Huaca Herederos Grande. These two mounds are significant because they appear quite suddenly in the first half of the second millennium BC in an area without significant antecedent public architecture. By examining building sequence, I show that both buildings were constructed in stages over long periods. Although each required substantial labor investment, I argue that these early instances of monumentalism were not the product of elite direction or personal aggrandizement. Rather, I assert that the political economy can be more productively understood by seeing people as the critical unit of value.

The Caballo Muerto Complex

Unlike other coastal valleys, there is scant evidence for antecedent Late Preceramic public architecture in the Moche Valley (see Billman [1996:99–119] for a discussion of this). The lone exception is Alto Salaverry, a site with a small circular plaza, located on the Pacific coast at the mouth of the Moche Valley (S. Pozorski and T. Pozorski 1979a, 1990; Alto Salaverry was once considered to be an early Initial Period site that lacked pottery, but the sole radiocarbon date of 3430 ± 110 BP from the site [S. Pozorski and T. Pozorski 1979b, 1990] calibrates to a 2 sigma age range of 1964–1432 BC, and is therefore Late Preceramic Period in age). However, beginning around 1600–1500 BC there is a sudden increase in settlements with monumental architecture (compare Watanabe Matsukura 1976; T. Pozorski 1983; Billman 1999; Nesbitt, Gutiérrez, and Vásquez 2008). The spike in monument building in the Moche Valley parallels a proliferation of public architecture in other parts of the Peruvian coast in the first half of the second millennium BC (S. Pozorski and T. Pozorski 1987; Burger 1992:60–103). Concomitant with monument construction was a shift in settlement toward inland locations as part of a general trend of Initial Period irrigation and agricultural intensification (Farrington 1974, 1985; Moseley 1974; S. Pozorski and T. Pozorski 1979b; Moseley and Deeds 1982; T. Pozorski 1982; Burger 1992; Billman 1999, 2002; Burger and Salazar 2012). Initial Period monumental complexes are represented at sites such as the large adobe and stone platforms at Menocucho, tentatively dated to the early Initial Period (Gutiérrez 1998; see also Billman 1996:138–142; Prieto and Maquera 2015), as well as the first pulses of mound building at the Caballo Muerto Complex (T. Pozorski 1983; Nesbitt, Gutiérrez, and Vásquez 2008; Nesbitt 2012a).

The Geographic Setting of Caballo Muerto

The Caballo Muerto Complex is located in the lower Moche Valley of northern Peru, at an altitude of 150 masl, approximately 16 km from the Pacific shoreline (Figures 1.1 and 1.2). Caballo Muerto consists of eight terraced platform mounds dispersed over an area of roughly 200 ha (Figure 1.3). The clustering of mounds at Caballo Muerto is unusual for the Initial Period and is probably a result of the high agricultural potential of the north side of the lower Moche Valley (Farrington 1974, 1985; Moseley and Deeds 1982; Billman 1999, 2002; Gamboa and Nesbitt 2012).

Caballo Muerto is just below a restricted valley neck where the Moche Valley expands into a broad alluvial plain, which encompasses considerably more potential area for agricultural land than other valleys to the south (Moseley and Deeds 1982:27). The valley neck has a steep gradient that was ideal for the first simple gravity canals of the Initial Period (Moseley 1974; Moseley and Deeds 1982:27–29). Two canal systems on the north side of the Moche Valley, Vichansao and Moro, irrigated the lands around Caballo Muerto during the Initial Period (Moseley and Deeds 1982:35–36; Farrington 1985:633; Billman 2002:378–380; see also T. Pozorski 1982). Other nearby irrigation systems were present that collectively permitted 1,300 to 1,500 ha of land, mostly located along the north side of the valley, to be reclaimed for agricultural production during the Initial Period (Farrington 1985:634–637; Billman 2002:379–380). A significant proportion of this land is within a few kilometers of the Caballo Muerto Complex. Furthermore, the amount of usable land on the north side of the lower Moche Valley is at least twice what is available for irrigation in the middle section of the valley (Billman 2002:380).

It is likely that these agricultural advantages stimulated the kinds of demographic

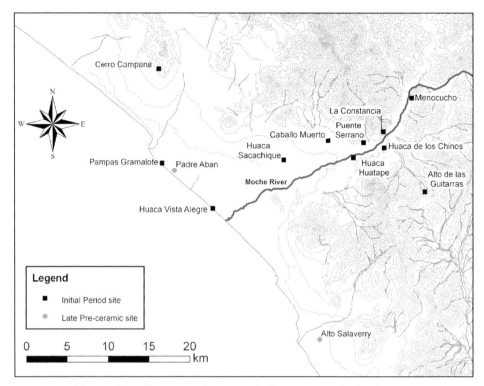

FIGURE 1.2. The Moche Valley region showing Caballo Muerto and other key Late Preceramic Period and Initial Period settlements.

concentration needed for the construction of many buildings in a relatively circumscribed area during the Initial Period. Archaeological surface survey has had limited success in locating Initial Period villages (Billman 1996, 1999), because many of the nonmonumental settlements are buried under deep deposits of alluvium (Nesbitt 2012b). Nevertheless, Billman (2002:394) estimates that 1,800 to 2,600 people lived in the lower Moche Valley during the Initial Period. This population was more than enough from which to draw labor.

Initial Period Architecture at Caballo Muerto

Caballo Muerto is perhaps best known in the archaeological literature for Huaca de los Reyes, a low platform and plaza complex dating to the late Initial Period (ca. 1100–800 BC). Huaca de los Reyes is decorated with anthropomorphic friezes executed in an art style sometimes referred to as Cupisnique (Moseley and Watanabe 1974; T. Pozorski 1975, 1982, 1995; Watanabe 1976; Conklin 1985). However, Huaca de los Reyes dates relatively late in the Caballo Muerto sequence. Far less is known about the much earlier and larger mounds at Caballo Muerto that dominate the surrounding landscape.

Thomas Pozorski (1983) and I (Nesbitt 2012a) present two chronological sequences for the Caballo Muerto Complex. Though there are differences in specifics, both chronologies agree that the first phases of public building began sometime around 1600–1500 BC, or what I refer to as the Cortijo Phase (ca. 1600–1100 BC). As will be outlined below, it is during the early part of the Cortijo Phase that Huaca Cortada and Huaca Herederos

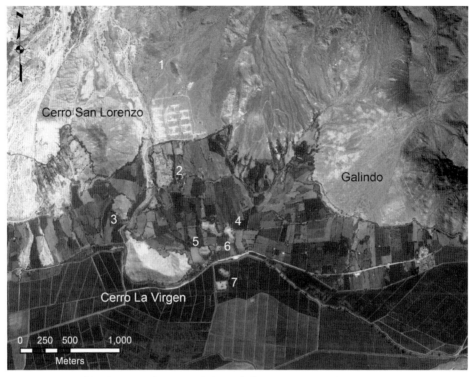

FIGURE 1.3. Satellite (IKONOS) image of the Caballo Muerto Complex. 1. Huaca San Carlos. 2. Huaca de los Reyes. 3. Huaca de la Cruz. 4. Huaca Guavalito. 5. Huaca Cortada. 6. Huaca Curaca. 7. Huaca Herederos Grande Chica. Image courtesy of the GeoEye Foundation.

Grande were first established. In addition to the Cortijo Phase monuments, there were also examples of deeply buried architecture, such as small room complexes at the base of Huaca Herederos Grande (Watanabe 1976; Chauchat, Guffroy, and Pozorski 2006), as well as two large isolated square rooms known as the Hall of the Niches (T. Pozorski 1976:25–28) and Unit 5 (Nesbitt, Gutiérrez, and Vásquez 2008) at the base of Huaca Cortada. Though space here prohibits a detailed description, these structures were probably ceremonial in nature.

There is also evidence for domestic occupation at the base of Huaca Cortada, which was characterized by wattle-and-daub structures with earthen floors and associated hearths (Nesbitt 2012b). Additional evidence for possible domestic occupations occur in the spaces between Huaca de la Cruz and Huaca de los Reyes, and on the slopes of Cerro la Virgen (T. Pozorski 1976:135). Taken together, it is apparent that Caballo Muerto was not a vacant ceremonial center, but was instead an early type of settled village. The following section provides an overview of the evidence for Cortijo Phase monument building at Caballo Muerto.

Huaca Cortada

Most detail regarding Cortijo Phase monument construction comes from Huaca Cortada, located approximately 300 m to the north of the somewhat larger and contemporary Huaca Herederos Grande, and 75 m west of the much later Huaca Curaca (Figure 1.4). After Huaca Herederos Grande, Huaca Cortada is the second largest monument at Ca-

FIGURE 1.4. Huaca Cortada, Huaca Curaca, Huaca Herederos Grande, and Huaca Herederos Chica.

ballo Muerto by volume (Figures 1.5 and 1.6). Huaca Cortada is oriented to the east and consists of a large central mound flanked by two low platforms that enclose a central plaza that measures 50 by 60 m (T. Pozorski 1976:299). These platforms are today largely destroyed as a result of agricultural and construction activities.

At its base the main mound of Huaca Cortada measures approximately 100 by 80 m. Today, the main mound is 17–18 m in height. However, excavations in the agricultural fields to the south of the main mound show that the early Initial Period ground surface was approximately 2 m lower than today (Nesbitt 2012b). Therefore, in antiquity, Huaca Cortada was probably 20 m high (Nesbitt, Gutiérrez, and Vásquez 2008:265). The main mound of Huaca Cortada is a large platform of at least four superimposed terraces. Each terrace wall consists of rows of quarried boulders that alternate with flatter stones set horizontally, a masonry technique similar to the façade walls at contemporary Initial Period monuments such as Sechín Alto in the Casma Valley (T. Pozorski and S. Pozorski 2005). The boulders that make up the exterior sides of the terrace walls were likely extracted from Cerro La Virgen, a rocky hill 150 m to the west of Huaca Cortada. In places where there is good preservation, the terrace walls were covered in multiple layers of white-painted plaster.

The original investigations suggested that Huaca Cortada contained 192,000 m³ of fill thought to belong to a single building phase (T. Pozorski 1976:455; T. Pozorski and S. Pozorski 1993b:390). This estimate was used to argue for the "coordinated direction of substantial amounts of corporate labor over a relatively short period of time" (T. Pozorski and S. Pozorski 1993b:390; compare T. Pozorski 1980:104). However, my more recent mapping and excavation of Huaca Cortada indicate that it was actually composed of between roughly 65,000 and 75,000 m³ of fill (Nesbitt, Gutiérrez, and Vásquez 2008; compare Billman 1996:171; Thomas Pozorski's [1976] estimates of volume were calculated by multiplying width by length by height, without taking into account the shape of the mound, but here the formula for calculating the volume of a truncated pyramid is used). Although the quantity of fill is still quite substantial, excavations reveal stratigraphic evidence that Huaca Cortada was built in several phases over a long period.

For instance, clearing of the eastern façade of Huaca Cortada exposed a large, partially destroyed, central platform that abuts the main mound and covers the two lowest terraces of the mound. Oriented to the east, the platform measures 12 m in width and,

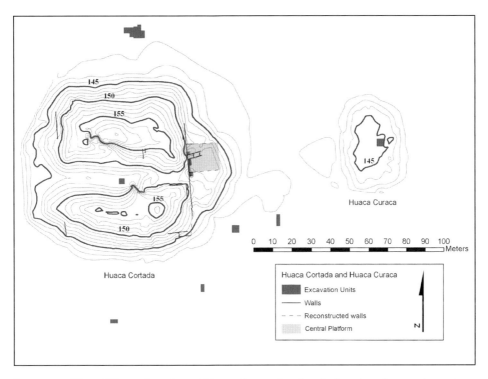

FIGURE 1.5. Plan of Huaca Cortada and Huaca Curaca showing the location of excavation units.

in some sections, more than 4 m in height. Radiocarbon dating results indicate that the platform was added to the façade of the mound around 1600–1500 BC (Nesbitt 2016), corresponding to one of the earliest phases of monument building. Although its length is difficult to determine, clearly the construction of the central platform was part of an outward expansion of the temple, complementing evidence for the vertical raising of the height of the building over time (see below).

Additional evidence for architectural transformation comes from excavations on both sides of the looter's trench that bisects Huaca Cortada (Figure 1.7). Despite considerable damage to the architecture, this trench afforded an opportunity to conduct profile cleaning just behind the eastern façade, as well as near the mound summit. Each of these excavations provided important information for understanding construction technique and building sequence.

Excavations on the trench's north side revealed deposits of ordered fill that comprise the hearting of the eastern façade. Layers of rounded boulders alternating with thick layers of gray clay characterize this fill. The ordered patterning of the rubble seems to conform to a variation of building "segmentation" defined by Moseley (1975:193) as "the division of an otherwise homogenous construction project into repetitive modular units." Moseley argues that segmented building activities are archaeological correlates for the presence of distinct labor parties that specialize in specific tasks (the implications of this observation are discussed below).

On the opposite side of the looter's trench excavations cleared a distinct profile from the north, revealing a long, low 15 m wall of quarried stones (Figure 1.8). Beneath this wall

FIGURE 1.6. View of Huaca Cortada looking to the east.

was another layer of clay with a fill of large stones set in mud mortar. The wall was likely part of a structure used to contain stone fill, similar to the "chamber-and-fill" technique described from the Moche site of Pampa Grande (Shimada 1994:160–162).

Clearing near the mound summit showed that Huaca Cortada's height increased through time (Figure 1.9A). Excavations exposed two clearly superimposed walls corresponding to at least three different phases of mound growth. Although much of the architecture that would have been on top of the mound was destroyed, these walls clearly corresponded to some kind of summit room complex common to all Initial Period architecture. The earliest structure is referred to as Wall A and the later Wall B (Figure 1.9B).

Wall A was constructed in a masonry style similar to the eastern façade. The height of the wall was at least 1.45 m. Directly behind the wall was an ordered, layered fill identical to that described from the fill behind the terrace walls of the eastern façade. Wall B is separated from Wall A by a rubble fill that raised the height of the mound by at least 1 m. The masonry technique is identical to Wall A. At the base of the wall was a plaster floor, which would have corresponded to the surface of a poorly defined summit structure. Covering Wall B and the associated floor was another layer of boulder fill, suggesting that there was another, unexcavated structure that was superimposed over Walls A and B.

More minor instances of rebuilding include the superposition of terrace floors exposed along the eastern façade, which were periodically renovated over the course of Huaca Cortada's history. Interestingly, each renovation of the floors relates to replastering of the corresponding terrace wall. Replastering events are characterized by the application of thin layers of white-painted plaster that correlate with cyclical periods of temple renewal.

The latest floor showed an important change in the architecture of Huaca Cortada. Two large circular columns were found along the exposed portion of the floor. The columns were lined with clay with cane imprints and a wrapped cane core. Similar examples of columns were found on the summit of Mound F at Huaca de los Reyes (T. Pozorski 1976:393). No dates are currently available for this late transformation; however, the pottery found on the floor, as well as the overlying fill, was composed of stirrup-spout bottle fragments and red-and-black bichrome pottery diagnostic of the late Initial Period (or San Lorenzo Phase, ca. 1100–900 BC; Nesbitt, Gutiérrez, and Vásquez 2008). Similar pottery styles were found at the late Initial Period site of Huaca de los Reyes at Caballo Muerto (T.

FIGURE 1.7. The north profile of the looter's trench of Huaca Cortada showing ordered fill.

Pozorski 1976, 1983). Taken together, the excavations along the eastern façade suggest that occupation of the mound spanned at least five centuries.

Huaca Herederos Grande

Huaca Herederos Grande (Figure 1.10A) is close to Huaca Cortada, making comparison between the two buildings important. At its base, the mound measures 120 by 100 m. Thomas Pozorski's (1976:16–17) excavations revealed that Huaca Herederos Grande was comprised of at least four or five stepped terraces and was oriented to the east. The exterior of the mound is made up of rounded cobbles set in mud mortar and was covered by thick plaster with traces of white paint.

Today the "summit" of the mound is approximately 16 m above the contemporary ground surface, but the original height is more difficult to determine. In the early 1960s, at least 3 m of the top of the mound was destroyed by bulldozing activity (T. Pozorski 1976:16). Furthermore, excavations and geomorphological study suggest the original ground surface may be as deep as 6 m below its present elevation (T. Pozorski 1976:171; Feldman and Kolata 1978; Chauchat, Guffroy, and Pozorski 2006:242). Therefore, a height of 20–24 m is a more accurate estimate of the maximum size of the mound in the Initial Period (compare T. Pozorski 1976:17–18; Billman 1996:171). Despite this uncertainty, a conservative estimate for the total mound volume falls between 90,000 and 100,000 m³ (compare Billman 1996:171).

There is compelling evidence that Huaca Herederos Grande and Huaca Cortada were contemporary (T. Pozorski 1983). Excavations at the base of Huaca Herederos Grande

FIGURE 1.8. The south profile of the looter's trench of Huaca Cortada showing the long wall enclosing fill.

uncovered a square enclosed chamber (Huaca Herederos Chica) that seems to have been a small-scale religious structure. The pottery associated with this structure is similar to early Initial Period pottery from Huaca Cortada and Huaca de la Cruz (T. Pozorski 1983; Chauchat, Guffroy, and Pozorski 2006; see also Nesbitt 2012a). In addition, two carbon samples taken from a refuse deposit associated with this building yielded two calibrated radiocarbon dates averaging around 1500 cal BC. Thomas Pozorski (1983) persuasively argued that Huaca Herederos Chica dates to the same time as the initial construction of Huaca Herederos Grande.

There is other evidence that suggests that Huaca Herederos Grande had a similar long-term history to Huaca Cortada. Because of the destruction in the 1960s, little can be said about the final phases of architecture that would have been present on the mound's summit. However, during surveys of the mound summit in 2006 and 2007–2008, a looter's pit revealed the presence of probable room walls constructed from quarried stone. This confirms the existence of construction phases that predate the final building stages of the now destroyed mound summit (Figure 1.10B). Lastly, limited test excavations by Luis Watanabe uncovered pottery corresponding to the later phases of the mound. The ceramic assemblage consisted of red-slipped and graphite wares with decorative and formal aspects that are quite similar to pottery recovered from the final phases of Huaca Cortada (Watanabe 1976:216). As discussed above, this pottery style dates to the late Initial Period. Taken together, the evidence as it exists from Huaca Herederos Grande suggests that it was first built around 1500 BC (T. Pozorski 1983) and lasted until sometime around 1100–1000 BC.

Early Initial Period Monument-building at Caballo Muerto

Building Sequence and Labor

The data from Huaca Cortada and Huaca Herederos Grande suggest that these mounds developed contemporaneously. Building sequence shows that Huaca Cortada was built in a series of relatively small construction phases over several centuries. This also seems to be the case for Huaca Herederos, where data are more limited.

As outlined earlier, the total mound volume of Huaca Cortada is somewhere between 65,000 and 75,000 m^3 (Nesbitt, Gutiérrez, and Vásquez 2008; see also Billman 1996:171). Ethnographic and experimental data on quarrying and transportation of stone and clay, manufacture of plaster, and the planning and layout of the architecture suggest that the labor invested in Huaca Cortada was probably in the range of 800,000 to 1 million person days (see Erasmus 1965; Abrams 1994; Murakami 2015; see also T. Pozorski 1980; Patterson 1985). A somewhat greater estimate can be made for Huaca Herederos Grande from its larger overall dimensions. Collectively, a conservative approximation of at least 2 million person days were invested in the construction of Huaca Cortada and Huaca Herederos Grande. Though this represents an impressive labor investment, recall that the occupations of Huaca Cortada and Huaca Herederos spanned approximately five centuries, or some twenty generations. To build either of these monuments over this long period may have only required the periodic organization of one to two hundred people.

A labor pool of this size could easily have been provided from the inhabitants that lived around Caballo Muerto. There are also indications that people were drawn from the larger lower valley population as a whole. Support for this hypothesis comes from the ubiquity of marine fishes and mollusks found in midden deposits at Huaca Cortada and Huaca Herederos Chica (e.g., S. Pozorski 1983; Víctor F. Vásquez Sánchez and Teresa E. Rosales Tham, 2009 unpublished report, "Análisis de restos de fauna de Huaca Cortada y Huaca la Cruz," Centro de Investigaciones Arqueobiológicas y Paleoecológicas Andinas ARQUEOBIOS, Trujillo; see also Nesbitt 2012b). These products were brought to Caballo Muerto from coastal communities such as the contemporary fishing village of Pampas de Gramalote (S. Pozorski and T. Pozorski 1979b; Prieto 2014). Possibly members of coastal communities came to Caballo Muerto to contribute labor toward monument construction and participate in religious ceremonies.

Political Organization

Despite the high investment of person days in construction, the duration of occupation coupled with the presence of different construction episodes suggests that leaders were only able to marshal relatively few people over short periods. Labor was likely divided into work parties drawn from the local communities of the lower Moche Valley.

Like its contemporaries of the early Initial Period, Caballo Muerto shows little indication that it was built by communities with institutionalized hierarchical social arrangements. Although situated in a productive landscape, there is no evidence that land or agricultural resources were controlled by any single paramount or group of elite individuals. There are no storage facilities and no evidence that any mound was used as a focal point for redistribution. Correlates for individualized social ranking at Caballo Muerto are largely absent.

On the other hand, there is no doubt that religion was a critical component of so-

Figure 1.9. Excavations at Huaca Cortada. **A.** Excavation near the summit. **B.** The two superimposed terrace walls that show how the height of the mound summit was raised over time.

cial organization. All Initial Period monuments, including those at Caballo Muerto, have architectural patterns that emphasize processions (Moore 1996a) into spaces that become increasingly restricted as people approach the main mound's summit (see T. Pozorski [1982] for a discussion of the access patterns of Huaca de los Reyes). Room complexes on the mound summits were enclosed and emphasize seclusion for probable religious leaders, who had access to specialized ritual knowledge. Although much of the summit architecture has been destroyed, this kind of architecture was undoubtedly present at Huaca Cortada and Huaca Herederos Grande. As a result, it is likely that some level of authority during the Initial Period at Caballo Muerto was rooted in specialist canonical religious knowledge (see Moore [2005] for a discussion).

Emergent religious leaders aided in the recruitment and coordination of labor for the construction of monuments like Huaca Cortada and Huaca Herederos Grande. That said, the evidence suggests that their power was limited. In this regard, the nature of political organization was structured quite similarly to what is postulated for the contemporary Manchay culture of the central coast (Burger and Salazar-Burger 1991; Burger 1992, 2009a; Burger and Salazar 2008, 2012, 2014; this volume). Though the evidence at Caballo Muerto and elsewhere suggests decentralized social organization, the motivations for how and why labor was mobilized remains to be explained.

Wealth in People

The concept of "structural power" provides productive insight into thinking about ancient political economy at Caballo Muerto. As defined by Eric Wolf (1990:587), structural power "rephrases the older notion of social relations of production, and is intended to emphasize power to deploy and allocate social labor. These governing relations do not come into view when you think of power primarily in interactional terms. Structural power shapes the social field of action so as to render some kinds of behavior possible, *while making others less possible or impossible*" (emphasis added). Little explanation has been put forth to explain how and why labor was mobilized and accumulated in conditions in which coercive power was impossible or unthinkable.

To look at the motivations for monument building requires a recasting of the political economy toward thinking about how people conceived of wealth and value. I contend that the political economy of Caballo Muerto was based on people and social relationships, not the concentration of resources by a group of elites. Cultural anthropologists working in Africa coined the term "wealth in people" to describe just these sorts of political economies (Guyer 1993, 1995; Guyer and Belinga 1995). At the broadest level, this concept refers to the means through which leaders were able to enlarge social networks and ritual knowledge "in a context where indirect controls through land, capital, and the threat of superior force are either absent altogether or intermittently realizable" (Guyer 1995:86). Power in this type of political economy does not necessarily rest in individual leaders, but rather in the people that made up society (Clastres 1987:207). In fact, personhood itself is created, developed, and defined by the acquisition of social relationships (Comaroff and Comaroff 2001).

In his discussion of the construction of Archaic Period monuments in the American Southeast, Gibson (2004:257) stated that leaders were "only a small part of the overall mound building process, not the source of power," and instead authority was vested in "the

FIGURE 1.10. Huaca Herederos Grande. **A.** The site as seen looking toward the south. **B.** Looter's pit on the destroyed summit with part of a stone building that corresponds to an earlier construction phase.

power of all people who labored in unison for a common goal." Emergent leaders would have been unable to achieve large-scale collective goals without the consent of people who would constitute the bulk of the labor. Ethnographers studying "big-men" in New Guinea point out the paradox that the creation of extended social networks also served as an impediment to political centralization (Strathern 1971; Wiessner 2002). These kinds of sociopolitical arrangements seem to be broadly similar to the situation described for Caballo Muerto.

In the case of Caballo Muerto the energies of people were clearly directed toward the construction of temples. Monuments like Huaca Cortada or Huaca Herederos Grande were highly visible places on the landscape and likely embodied symbols, both religious and social, that shaped the formation of community identities. As community symbols, the construction of the temples was the product of collective efforts, not the result of individual aggrandizing individuals. One can conceive of labor being provided freely by community members who hoped to benefit in "practical" (e.g., agricultural productivity) and cosmological terms (see Gibson 2004). As a result, wealth in people models require us to reconsider what actually constitutes "work" in early monument building societies like those of Initial Period Caballo Muerto (Guyer 1993; see also Burger 2009a; Topic 2009). Spielmann (2002:197) points out that ritual practice itself requires substantial amounts of work and makes up a substantial portion of the economy in "small-scale" societies.

Labor groups recruited to work at Caballo Muerto fulfilled a multiplicity of cosmological, religious, and community obligations. Gibson (2004) refers to this as "beneficent obligation," which involves civic and religious responsibilities to give labor as part of reciprocal gifting relationships that would yield spiritual or cosmological benefits to the community (sensu Mauss 1990). There are ethnographic accounts of this type of practice for public architecture. For instance, Evans-Pritchard (1935:61–63) discussed the construction of a conical earthen mound of about 17 m in Nuer territory of eastern Africa. Evans-Pritchard notes that the labor was voluntary from throughout the countryside "as an act of piety" (Evans-Pritchard 1935:63).

Although seemingly speculative, the concept of beneficent obligation makes a great deal of sense if framed in the cultural logics of the communities that built the monuments in the first place. The relatively high labor estimates presented earlier make it clear that much work was put into Huaca Cortada and Huaca Herederos Grande. These types of energetic estimates are typically used to think about how much labor, people, and coordination were involved in monument production (T. Pozorski 1980). An alternative interpretation, however, can be provided. Figures of quantity of person days invested in early Caballo Muerto can instead be used not as an index of work, but rather of value (Graeber 2001:55). That is, the many person days expended is an excellent proxy for the importance placed on ritual architecture and temples. As a result, archaeologists can productively rethink notions about "energetics," not only in the sense of labor costs and investment, but also as a kind of "ritual energetics" that takes seriously questions about how much time was actually spent in the pursuit of ceremony (see also Spielmann 2002, 2007). The time dedicated to religious and community activity is difficult to estimate from an archaeological standpoint. However, a perusal of Amazonian ethnography reveals the complexity of ceremonial calendars, which indicate that significant parts of the year were dedicated to ritual performance (e.g., Nimuendajú 1946). Regardless, this is an issue that archaeologists should consider before immediately leaping to the conclusion that monuments were conglomerations of rubble built for the personal aggrandizement of a chief or other elite. The creation of temples also signals a common community social identity formed and maintained through collective action and shared religion. The construction of monuments at Caballo Muerto represented the periodic pooling of communal labor in cyclical events of temple construction. It is possible that the episodic nature of the building phases and replastering of floors and temple walls at Huaca Cortada and Huaca Herederos Grande could relate to cyclical patterns of ritual time and long-term ideological continuity with respect to perceptions of monument construction (Burger and Salazar-Burger 1985, 1991).

Patterson (1983) and Dillehay (2004) have hypothesized that ritualized episodic construction phases also served as a social mechanism used by members of local commu-

nities to intentionally slow down tendencies toward social hierarchy and political centralization. In other words, there may have been contradictions in sociopolitical organization,
in which incipient leaders may have established their status through esoteric ritual
knowledge while their power was counterpoised by repetitive ceremonial acts (monument
building) that "memorialized a community and, presumably, equality" (Pauketat and Alt
2003:156).

The Significance of Caballo Muerto as a Multi-mound Center

Earlier I outlined the evidence for the presence of other large mounds at Caballo Muerto
that were contemporary with Huaca Cortada, namely Huaca Herederos Grande. Two observations about the relationship between these two large buildings are key. The first is that
Huaca Herederos Grande is located only 300 m to the south of Huaca Cortada. Second,
the two mounds share the same orientation, but are not architecturally integrated. That is,
they have no shared plaza spaces or other features that link the two buildings. This kind of
multi-mound settlement is found at several Initial Period North Coast archaeological sites,
including Purulen (Alva 1988) and San Luis (Dillehay 2008). Taken together, I hypothesize
that Huaca Cortada and Huaca Herederos Grande were built by different, possibly competing, social groups with similar "wealth in people" economies.

Accepting the premise that each mound was the symbolic expression of a different
community, we still need to explain the relationship between different social groups. Both
Huaca Cortada and Huaca Herederos Grande have evidence of cyclical building over
long stretches of time in the Initial Period. Semi-autonomous communities participated
in the construction of the different ceremonial buildings in a way analogous to Renfrew's
concept of competitive emulation among peer polities (Renfrew 1986). Burger and Salazar
(2008) have made a similar argument in their analysis of the monumental complexes of
the Manchay culture. Incipient leaders may have tried to outdo other leaders, by attract-
ing more religious followers to their specific temple in a kind of religious clientelism
(sensu Guyer 1995; Guyer and Belinga 1995). Competition may also have emerged when
communities sought to outdo one another through the creation of larger and larger
buildings through time during seasonal "potlatch-like" events. These kinds of "material
extravaganzas" could have had unintended consequences. They may have decreased the
access of other potential competitors to labor and resources (Rathje 2002). In other words,
the syphoning off of labor for construction of different monuments may have prevented
already politically weak religious leaders from accumulating larger groups of people and
hence slowed any trajectory toward political centralization.

Conclusions

A central contention of this chapter is that monument building created, and was the
product of, new ideas of social organization. One can therefore argue that there is no
reason, empirical or theoretical, to conclude that the societies of the Initial Period (or Late
Preceramic Period) were organized like ethnographically abstracted social types such as
chiefdoms or states (David and Sterner 1999; see also McIntosh 1999; Yoffee 2005; Pauketat 2007). Instead, archaeologists working on the Late Preceramic Period and Initial Period can benefit by thinking more carefully about the mechanisms of how and why labor
was mobilized. I suggest that focusing on how social relationships were created is a more

profitable avenue of inquiry than focusing solely on aggrandizers to explain the pooling of large labor forces (e.g., Spielmann 2002; Inomata, MacLellan, and Burham 2015).

Caballo Muerto falls within a pattern of communal organization that characterizes the Peruvian coast during the Initial Period (see Burger 1992, 2009a). During this time, the accrual of human social relationships was the key unit of wealth and value in the political economy. However, I do not discard the possibility of political economic "mosaics" (Stahl 2004). The patterns displayed at Caballo Muerto contrast with Initial Period sites in Casma, such as Pampa de las Llamas-Moxeke, where there is a clearly planned architectural layout in which a long central axis unites aligned mounds to create a much more formal integrated pattern (S. Pozorski and T. Pozorski 1986). It is therefore possible that entirely different ways of mobilizing human labor may have been at play in the Casma Valley during the second millennium BC (T. Pozorski and S. Pozorski 1993a, 2012, among others).

Examination of the archaeological record suggest that the ideas put forth here can also be applied to the monuments of the Late Preceramic Period. Archaeological evidence from many of the late Preceramic Period monuments of the Norte Chico indicate that they were built in many stages (Haas and Creamer 2012:296), suggesting smaller social groups laboring over long periods. Recent work at one Norte Chico complex, Cerro Lampay, shows that discrete building phases were associated with feasting events (Vega-Centeno Sara-Lafosse 2007). Feasting for labor parties suggests that early monumental building was a festive and communal process. There is currently insufficient evidence for the process of monument construction at Late Preceramic Period sites such as the multi-mound complex at Caral (e.g., Shady Solis, Haas, and Creamer 2001). That said, interestingly, like Caballo Muerto (or Purulén), the layout of Caral as a whole does not show centralized planning. Each platform mound instead had its own circular plaza, suggesting each temple was associated with its own particular social group or community. Monument building at Caral may therefore have had elements of communalism coupled with competition similar to Caballo Muerto during the early Initial Period.

The concepts of communalism and wealth in people is not "minimizing-the-monumental" (Clark 2013:235), but rather an explanation of the empirical data on the operation of the political economy of the earliest Peruvian monumental centers. Archaeologists working on early manifestations of public architecture in other parts of the world have reached similar conclusions, arguing that access to people rather than the accrual of things was the principal unit of value (e.g., Pauketat 2004; Clark, Gibson, and Zeidler 2010). Rethinking the political and economic along these lines permits archaeologists to move beyond neoevolutionary mechanisms and instead consider how human economies were created during the formative moments of Peruvian civilization.

CHAPTER TWO

EARLY SETTLEMENT AND CULTURAL LANDSCAPE IN THE TEMBLADERA AREA OF THE MIDDLE JEQUETEPEQUE VALLEY

Eisei Tsurumi

In the middle Jequetepeque River Valley (Figure 2.1), around a village called Tembladera, there are many monumental buildings, such as platforms and sunken courts, dated to the Initial Period (ca. 1500–800 BC). Most of these buildings of the Tembladera area are concentrated in the Hamacas Plain, which extends between the modern villages of Chungal and Montegrande along the north bank of the river (Figure 2.2). Notably, on this plain there are considerable numbers of masonry burial towers of the same time period. Such a densely clustered concentration of early monumental buildings and conspicuous tombs is uncommon in the Central Andes. These cultural remains are highly visible and situated in a relatively narrow zone so that from one we often can see the others. They seem to have been planned to form a cultural landscape in this sector of the valley.

I launched the Tembladera Archaeological Project in collaboration with Peruvian archaeologists to investigate these monumental buildings of the Hamacas Plain. We focused on a site called Las Huacas to clarify the chronological and functional relationships among them. Formerly they had been registered as twenty-three discrete archaeological sites (Ravines 1981), but after our investigations in 2003, 2004, and 2005, I came to realize that they should be divided into only eight clusters of architectural complexes, each one consisting of multiple buildings serving as nuclei of civic-ceremonial centers. Furthermore, on the opposite bank of the Hamacas Plain I found another architectural complex that belongs to the same period. Including the latter, I regard these nine civic-ceremonial center sites as remains of a local community that lasted for more than seven centuries during the Initial Period. I have named this the Hamacas Complex site (see Figures 2.2, 2.3).

Moreover, during our subsequent investigations in 2009 I found another monumental building of the Initial Period on the south bank of the river. Named Platform A (of Mosquito), it presents different features from those of the Hamacas Complex in terms of its geographic context, architectural configuration, and associated materials.

The discussion here of the chronological and functional relationships among these monumental buildings will give special consideration to the landscape composed of cultural remains and geographical characteristics. First, the chronological sequence of the nine civic-ceremonial centers of the Hamacas Complex will be presented, and the sequence will be explicated according to environmental setting, ritual practices, and social

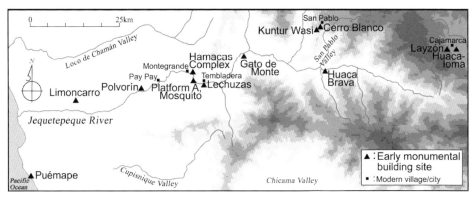

FIGURE 2.1. The archaeological sites of the Jequetepeque River Valley, Peru.

organization during the Initial Period. Second, Platform A (of Mosquito) and its associational rock art dated to the Initial Period will be introduced. Finally, a comparison of the Hamacas Complex and Platform A will reveal the nature of Initial Period settlement in the Tembladera.

The Hamacas Complex

Research Problems

Today many of the archaeological sites of the Hamacas Plain have been totally or partially destroyed by the Gallito Ciego Reservoir and roads constructed during the 1980s. The early monumental buildings in the Hamacas Plain were reported by Richard Keatinge (1980), who warned of their impending destruction. The sites were subsequently investigated by two major archaeological projects before and during construction on the reservoir. The Proyecto Rescate Arqueológico del Valle de Jequetepeque produced an inventory and maps of archaeological sites between the villages of Tembladera and Pay Pay (Ravines 1981) and carried out test excavations at some sites on the Hamacas Plain (Ravines 1982, 1985a, 1985b). Another project, Kommission für Allgemeine und Vergleichende Archäologie des Deutschen Archäologischen Instituts, excavated some architectural complexes (Carcelén 1984; Paredes 1984; Tam and Aguirre 1984; Tellenbach 1986; Ulbert 1994), most notably the monumental buildings at the North Complex of Plateau 2 of Montegrande and the surrounding residential area. This research is well known for its discussion of social organization (Tellenbach 1986:295) and detailed analysis of pottery (Ulbert 1994). After the completion of the reservoir, no archaeologists returned to explore this zone until the Japanese Archaeological Mission in 1999 (Sakai et al. 2000), through which we rediscovered some sites on the shores of the reservoir.

The two research problems proposed at the beginning of this archaeological project was to establish a chronological sequence for such an unusually large number of monumental buildings, and to clarify of the functional relationship among them. The two projects in the 1980s had focused on these to some extent, but their results had not been reconsidered in an integral way, nor reevaluated in light of advances of studies on the Initial Period.

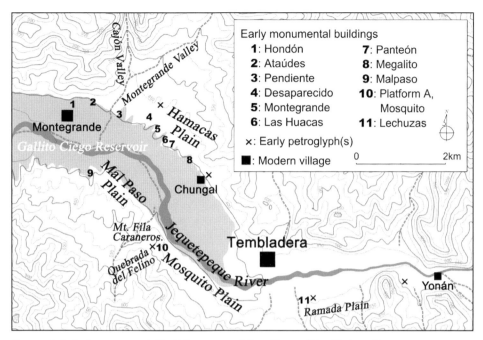

FIGURE 2.2. Early monumental buildings around the village of Tembladera, Peru.

Chronological Sequence

The chronological sequence of the development of the Hamacas Complex can be divided into two phases: the Hamacas Phase (ca. 1500–1250 BC) and the Tembladera Phase (ca. 1250–800 BC). These chronologically correspond, respectively, to the early Initial Period and late Initial Period occupations of Jequetepeque Valley (Figure 2.4). Each can be divided in two subphases by radiocarbon dating and according to differences in the stylistic features of pottery (Tsurumi 2008).

The investigators of the Montegrande site argued that the pottery classified as Alfar A was introduced before Alfar B (Ulbert 1994), on the basis of the architectural sequence (Tellenbach 1986). I support their discussion, because I confirmed the same sequence at Las Huacas through stratigraphic excavations. Applying this chronological change of the pottery to the Hamacas Complex sites, the time period when only Alfar A pottery was used as Hamacas 1 (sub-)Phase, ca. 1500–1350 BC, and the period after the introduction of Alfar B as Hamacas 2 (sub-)Phase, ca. 1350–1250 BC. At Las Huacas I also confirmed the chronological sequence of the Tembladera Phase potteries (Tsurumi 2008:165–166) and established two subphases as Tembladera 1 (subphase), ca. 1250–1000 BC, and Tembladera 2 (subphase), ca. 1000–800 BC. I will refer to these chronological subdivisions as necessary.

Furthermore, I have assigned certain time spans to each architectural complex, according to the data below. First, the stylistic difference of pottery excavated or collected from the surface of each site suggests differences of chronological position among them (Tsurumi 2008:148–154). Second, a wide variety of architectural features (number and direction of staircases attached to the platforms, configuration of the sunken court, and others) of each architectural complex enable a seriation analysis. I demonstrated gradual change of the architectural configuration of Initial Period sites of the Hamacas Complex

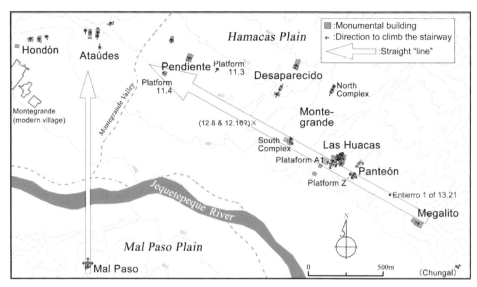

FIGURE 2.3. The nine civic-ceremonial centers of the Hamacas Complex site.

(Tsurumi 2008:154–157). Third, radiocarbon dating from two of the nine civic-ceremonial center sites embodies the time span among them (Tsurumi 2008:157–159). Finally, large masonry tomb "burial towers" constructed beside the architectural complexes suggest that the buildings had not functioned permanently, but had "opened" and "closed" at certain times in association with funeral practice. I will show that the construction sequence of the Hamacas Complex explains the problem of the funeral practice.

Five architectural complexes (Hondón, Ataúdes, Pendiente, Desaparecido, and Montegrande) correspond to the Hamacas Phase, but I do not believe that all functioned as civic-ceremonial centers simultaneously. They seem to have been built sequentially from the western to eastern areas of the plain, and were abandoned one by one in the same order. Because each of these sites is accompanied by burial towers, it suggests that each of them was intentionally abandoned. The previous investigators of Montegrande concluded that after the abandonment of the monumental buildings some burial towers were constructed (Paredes 1984; Tellenbach 1986). Interestingly, the other four centers of the Hamacas Phase also present burial towers on or beside their monumental buildings (Ravines 1981). I believe that this shows that these centers were ritually closed. The closing of an old civic-ceremonial center by the addition of one or more burial towers and the opening of a new one could be part of a chain of events, so that only one (or two) of the centers functioned at a given moment. All five centers opened during the Hamacas 1 Phase, but only Desaparecido and Montegrande have architectural components of the Hamacas 2 Phase as well. At Las Huacas some terraced platforms were built during the Hamacas 2 Phase and I suggest that they had a residential character rather than a ceremonial one. This is because they were not accompanied by any sunken court and the retaining walls of the terraces were too low to be considered characteristic of a civic-ceremonial center.

During the Tembladera 1 Phase three architectural complexes (Las Huacas, Panteón, and Megalito) were constructed, but none of the centers built during the former phase continued to function. Las Huacas was renovated more frequently than the others and consequently became the largest center among them. Such prominence among contemporary centers was related to an altered practice of burial. Las Huacas was never closed with the addition of a burial tower inside of its architectural complex. Outside of Las Huacas many burial towers were built for the individuals who needed to be interred in a culturally acceptable manner. Several of the large burial towers (Ravines 1982:171–180, 181–182) formed important parts of the architectural complex of Panteón and another large burial tower (referred to by Ravines as the Entierro 1 of the 13.21 site) was constructed between Panteón and Megalito (Ravines 1982:136–138). Malpaso, the only center situated in the Malpaso Plain of the south bank, seems to have appeared after the three centers on the Hamacas Plain, possibly during the Tembladera 2 Phase.

With the chronological question addressed, I will consider its implications for understanding the formation of the cultural landscape of the Hamacas Complex.

Visibility among Monumental Buildings and Ancestor Worship

During the Hamacas Phase, the local inhabitants constructed burial towers near monumental buildings to "close" them. This architectural change was a mechanism that resulted in a dense concentration of architectural complexes, and its underlying principle was to construct a landscape based on ancestor worship (compare Zoubek 1998). It is likely that a closed center lost its pragmatic function and was transformed into a memorial for ancestor worship, a monument composed of a mound and one or more burial towers. The buried persons could well have been the dominant figures among the local community (Tellenbach 1986). From the new buildings founded to the east their descendants could see the monuments associated with memories of the deceased. The burial towers were located in such a way that they do not block the view from the east. Considering that there are later style pottery fragments on the surface, the descendants seem to have occasionally visited the closed buildings and burials, and left some offerings (Ulbert 1994, pl. B3).

The repetition of such ritual practices can be inferred from the configuration and location of the monumental buildings. Each platform has at least one stairway that serves as a main access and indicates its architectural axis. Hondón and Ataúdes, the two earliest centers, only featured stairways oriented to the north and south, thereby corresponding to the geographic inclination. In contrast, Pendiente and Montegrande, the later centers, are characterized by platforms with stairways oriented to the east and west (more precisely, west–northwest and east–southeast) in addition to those of north and south. Although the platforms of Desaparecido are totally destroyed, I hypothesize that the site of Desaparecido also had a building with an east–west stairway directed toward Ataúdes, possibly at sites 12.8 and 12.16 below the architectural components of later periods (Ravines 1981:25–26). Thus, I infer that the civic-ceremonial centers built late in the sequence featured buildings whose axis was intentionally directed toward the closed centers. As a result, the buildings with east–west stairways formed an almost straight line across the plain on the map (see Figure 2.3). The local community of the Hamacas Complex was characterized by the succession of public centers based on kinship throughout the entire Initial Period. This line related to ancestor worship continued during the following period, the Tembladera Phase, with three centers and a burial tower, Entierro 1 of the 13.21 site, in the eastern half of Hamacas Plain.

Naturally, the perceptual relations among monumental buildings depended in part

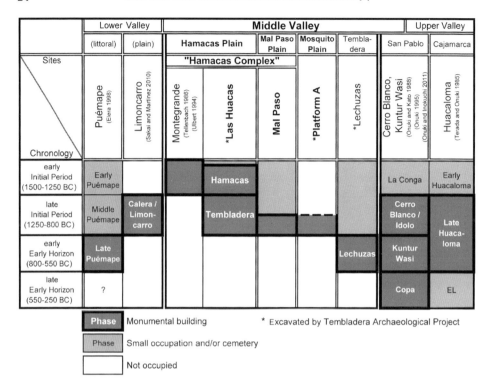

FIGURE 2.4. Chronological relationship among the early sites in the Jequetepeque River Valley.

on the topography of the Hamacas Plain. I have developed a three-dimensional digital model from survey maps, which represents the local landforms before they were altered by the massive reservoir and road system, and studied it using geographic information system (GIS) spatial analysis (Viewshed tool in ArcGIS 9 [ESRI 2004] with the Spatial Analyst extension; Tsurumi 2008:163–164, 2014:212–213).

The western half of the plain is a gentle slope and the eastern half is a fluvial terrace divided by many ravines. The earliest two centers without east–west stairways are placed clinging to the steep slope at the base of the mountain. Hondón, which could be rather earlier than Ataúdes considering the whole chronological sequence described above, was located inside a hollow, so that it cannot be viewed from any other civic-ceremonial centers except Ataúdes. Ataúdes is on higher ground to the east of Hondón and thus has such high visibility that it can be seen from the other centers. Furthermore, only Ataúdes among the centers of the Hamacas Complex is accompanied by a conspicuous natural landmark, a small hill to its eastern side. The spatial axis of monumental buildings between Pendiente and Megalito were set toward Ataúdes with its high visibility. Each of the buildings built after Ataúdes permits a view of the greater part of Ataúdes and the whole of the neighboring small hill.

Malpaso, on the opposite bank, displays continuity with the former civic-ceremonial centers in the Hamacas Plain in regard to ancestor worship. This architectural complex is situated on the gentle slope of the Malpaso Plain and consists of a sunken court and terraced platforms. The stairways between them correspond to the geographic inclination and face toward the Ataúdes complex across the river at the same time.

From Frequent Location Shift to Long-term Coexistence

As evident from the preceding discussion, ancestor worship was a shared practice among the inhabitants of Hamacas Complex over many centuries. But it is necessary to explain why the nine civic-ceremonial centers, which embodied ritual practices, differ in location, architectural configuration, and time span. The centers built during the Hamacas Phase functioned only for around one century, yet those of the Tembladera Phase were maintained for several centuries. Roughly speaking, in the former phase many centers were built as a result of repeated "location shifts" originated by closing and opening events, whereas the latter phase was characterized by multiple coexisting centers.

The location shift of civic-ceremonial centers does not seem to be a unique practice among Initial Period sites of the Central Andes. For example, the abandonment of Cerro Blanco Phase architecture at the Cerro Blanco site (Onuki and Kato 1988) and the founding of Idolo Phase architecture at the Kuntur Wasi site (Onuki, Kato, and Inokuchi 1995; Inokuchi 2008) in the San Pablo Basin seem to be linked events, which resulted in a location shift of centers over a distance of 1.5 km (Tsurumi 2014:218). There are also other similarities to the Hamacas Phase. Inhabitants of the Idolo Phase at Kuntur Wasi left a burial with offerings, including Idolo Phase pottery, on the Cerro Blanco site and then set the architectural axis of their new center toward it. However, the shift in the San Pablo Basin occurred only one time during the Initial Period, whereas in the Hamacas Complex it occurred five times just during the early Initial Period (Hamacas Phase).

As I consider next, the high frequency pattern of location shifts launched the long sequence of the Hamacas Complex. Second, I will discuss the switch from short-term to long-term and the newer pattern of the coexistence of centers, paying attention not only to chronological position but also to the spatial locations of the centers, because the Hamacas Complex sequence was a continuous expansion or multiplication over a specific area. Thus the topographic features of the Hamacas Plain and Malpaso Plain also need to be studied as a unique setting, different from other regions, such as the San Pablo Basin.

Hamacas Phase Centers

Probably the three earliest civic-ceremonial centers in the western half of the Hamacas Plain (Hondón, Ataúdes, and Pendiente) were arranged next to the cultivated field on the riverbed (like the modern farming village of Montegrande that once occupied this zone and is submerged today). It is known that during the Hamacas Phase agriculture had already started. I confirmed manioc starch on the surface of Hamacas Phase pottery sherds of Las Huacas (Tsurumi 2008:163) and Platform 11.3 of Pendiente was accompanied by a terraced field for cultivation (Ravines 1985a:133, 1985b:213). These centers were situated on the riverbed of the Montegrande Valley, which runs from the northern mountains and joins with the Jequetepeque River and Cajón Valley (see Figure 2.2). This zone is richer in water resources than the fluvial terraces of the eastern half. GIS analysis (the specific

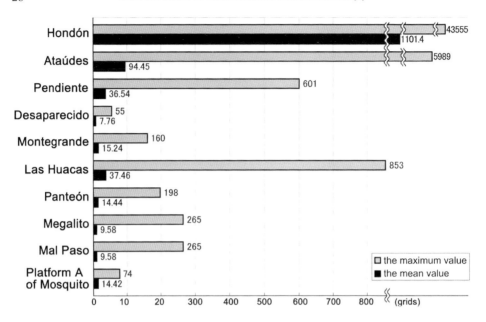

FIGURE 2.5. A relative comparison of the maximum and average volume of water brought by *huaycos* to ten architectural complexes, computed by GIS specific catchment area analysis. The watershed of the middle Jequetepeque Valley was divided into 2 by 2 m grids. Numbers indicate how many grids gathered water inside each site, according to topographic inclination.

catchment area analysis using ArcGIS 9 with the Spatial Analyst extension [ESRI 2004]) also supports this interpretation.

At the same time, this part of the plain is in peril of flash floods (*huaycos*) that in times of El Niño events run down along the Montegrande Valley and the Cajón Valley. For example, the huayco in 1998 deeply hollowed out the land in spite of the large modern drain, and even washed away the asphalt road. Such natural disasters have destroyed the masonry buildings of Montegrande and Las Huacas many times on the eastern half of the plain, but GIS analysis indicates that the centers in the western half must have suffered even more severely (Figure 2.5). The most dangerous location among the nine centers of Hamacas Complex is Hondón, and the second most in peril is Ataúdes. This difference, resulting from topography, suggests that refuge from huaycos may have been one motivation behind location shift. This would explain at least the three shift events: from Hondón to Ataúdes, from Ataúdes to Pendiente, and from Pendiente to Desaparecido. These shifts are the result of a locational strategy in search of refuge (Figure 2.6).

The earliest location shifts were motivated by the desire for refuge, but through those events people came to be conscious of the creation of a cultural landscape in relation to ancestor worship. Through a study of the chronology, I infer that during the Hamacas Phase two centers could have functioned at the same time, assuming some decades of time lag (Tsurumi 2008, 2014), and people intended to build a new center offering a view of the anterior center. Such an interest was clearly embodied in Platform 11.4 of Pendiente with its east–west stairway (Figure 2.6). Stepping up to the platform by this stair, they could see Ataúdes directly ahead. When Ataúdes was closed by the addition of burial towers, it became the commemorative monument of the ancestors. Hondón was out of view because

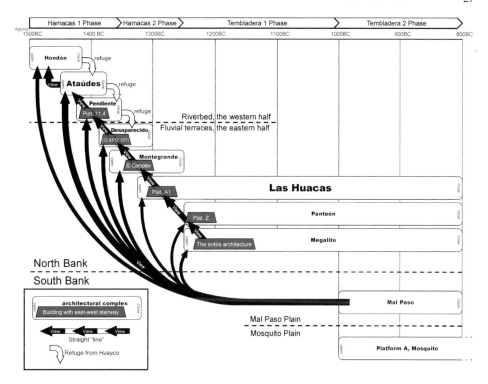

FIGURE 2.6. Schematic drawing of the chronological and functional relationships among monumental buildings of nine civic-ceremonial centers of the Hamacas Complex.

of its geographic condition, so Ataúdes came to be the principal one. Above I mentioned two intentions to manage the water—as resource and as risk—but the former can only explain the shifts inside the western half of the plain. By the opening of Desaparecido on the fluvial terrace of the eastern half, people acquired safety from huaycos when compared to the former occupations. At the same time, they gave up the opportunity to construct their civic-ceremonial center, the symbolic core of the village, next to the cultivated land on the floodplain. As mentioned above, I hypothesize that Desaparecido also possibly had an east–west oriented stairway. If this assumption is correct, then concerns about ancestor worship became more important than those of agricultural production in determining architectural practice.

Furthermore, the shift from Desaparecido to Montegrande did not make any sense as protection against huaycos. On the contrary, the platforms of Las Huacas opened in the Hamacas 2 Phase occupied an even more dangerous location than Montegrande (see Figure 2.5). After the opening of Montegrande, people apparently were not concerned about protection from huaycos until the Tembladera Phase. Even on the fluvial terraces, huaycos repeatedly damaged buildings at Montegrande and Las Huacas. However, these were less severe than the tragic incidents that had formerly occurred on the floodplain, so the inhabitants only took small measures, such as the construction of terraces, to support dwellings and walls to protect against the water flow (Tsurumi 2008:163, 2014:211). Probably the main motivation of opening Montegrande and Las Huacas was the location shift event itself. By the Hamacas 2 Phase the location shift came to be recognized as a standard ritual practice. Toward this end they constructed with the goal of viewing the closed centers with memories of their ancestors from the South Complex of Montegrande, and from Platform A1 of Las Huacas (see Figure 2.6).

Tembladera Phase Centers

The coexistence of multiple civic-ceremonial centers, their long-term maintenance, and the appearance of a new center on the south bank are distinctive characteristics of the Tembladera Phase centers and contrast with the former ones of the Hamacas Phase.

I hypothesize that the role of the centers and the relationship between them had transformed, considering the prominent scale and spatial position of Las Huacas and the placement of the other centers and burial towers. Platform Z of Panteón and the entity of Megalito were situated on the almost straight line toward the closed centers of the Hamacas Phase, so from these platforms one could view those monuments with memories of the deceased, but only over the huge Platform A1 of Las Huacas. For this reason, I infer that Las Huacas had played a special role in the worship by the people of the Tembladera Phase for the ancestors of the former phase, and that Panteón and Megalito functioned especially for worshipping the more recently deceased during the Tembladera Phase (Tsurumi 2008:159–161, 2014:214–216). This interpretation is suggested by the absence of tombs inside of the Las Huacas site and the existence of larger burial towers than those of the former phase situated around Panteón and Megalito.

We can observe changes not only in the monumental buildings, but also in the residential areas. In the case of the Hamacas Phase, in Montegrande there were a few dwellings on the terraces next to the monumental buildings that were surrounded by many more simple dwellings constructed directly on the natural plateau surface. The former dwellings might be able to survive a huayco to some extent, but the latter residences could not. Such a difference is one of the reasons to believe that the local society of the Hamacas Phase was organized hierarchically (Tellenbach 1986). As to the Tembladera Phase in Las Huacas, I confirmed a wide residential area, but it was characterized by a series of low terraces sustaining a few dwellings. Unlike Montegrande, there were no simple ones constructed directly on natural ground. In the eastern outskirts of the Hamacas Plain, near the now submerged village of Chungal (see Figure 2.2), I also excavated architectural remains of the Tembladera Phase and found only a low platform supporting a few dwellings (Tsurumi 2016). The investigations of Tembladera Phase dwellings on the Hamacas Plain indicate that all were strongly built, and there was no evidence of simpler ones. I suggest that during the Tembladera Phase the residential area was divided geographically by the steep cliff that exists there. Only a few small human groups had lived near the monumental buildings on the fluvial terrace, whereas other community members were distributed among the cultivated land in the bottom of the valley. Although this idea cannot be tested because of the reservoir, I believe that it is plausible because the twentieth century farming villages of Montegrande and Chungal were similarly located on the riverbed.

Such differences between Hamacas and Tembladera Phases show that the dominant figures of the social organization, namely, elite religious authorities, aimed to reinforce their power by emphasizing continuity derived from worshipped ancestors, possibly on the basis of kinship. By constructing three civic-ceremonial centers, and placing Las Huacas in the principal position among them, they altered the whole of the landscape of the

FIGURE 2.7. Petroglyph "Felino" and a winged anthropomorphic being.

Hamacas Plain. From a broad setting that memorialized their ancestors, they shifted to construct a landscape that represented a more hierarchical social organization. This new approach functioned over several centuries, at least during the Tembladera 1 Phase, possibly because they intended to maintain such a new order.

Finally, I wish to consider the circumstances underlying the appearance of Malpaso on the Malpaso Plain along the south bank. It is likely that this occurred later than at other sites. Three features of Malpaso attracted my attention. First, from Malpaso one can see all the centers on the north bank, including the five centers of the Hamacas Phase and the three of the Tembladera Phase. Because Malpaso's architectural axis is directed toward Ataúdes, it also suggests that Malpaso shared with Ataúdes a special interest with contemporaneous centers. Second, the sunken court of Malpaso has a special configuration resembling those of Las Huacas: the four sides are delimited by two unevenly parallel walls, like a bench with a back. It suggests that the ritual practice at sunken courts was shared between two sites. Finally, Malpaso was intentionally placed to have a direct view of the Hamacas Phase centers on the opposite bank, but not to view them over the monumental buildings of Las Huacas. Considering such features, I suppose that Malpaso insisted on an equal role with Las Huacas in the landscape.

The common features between monumental buildings of Las Huacas and Malpaso, like the architectural axis and the configuration of a sunken court, can be considered an "idiosyncratic architectural practice" (Bandy 2004:325) that the founders of Malpaso derived from the original community controlled by Las Huacas after a fissioning event of occupation. I suppose that such an event could be a consequence of the population increase in this area, although, as Bandy (2004:324–325) pointed out, it is difficult to identify village fissioning archaeologically, and in our case, the Gallito Ciego Reservoir has only made matters worse. Because of this evidence, I suggest that the social organization of the Tembladera Phase became more complex than during the former phase.

Platform A, Mosquito Plain

Research Questions

The monumental construction situated on the Mosquito Plain of the south bank (see Figure 2.2) is quite different from that of the Hamacas Complex already discussed. The Mosquito Plain is an arid alluvial fan that is currently unpopulated. Its eastern end, just to the south of Tembladera village, is separated from Ramada Plain by a steep ravine and the western side is separated from Malpaso Plain by Mount Fila Caraneros. Before my investigations, no remains of early occupations were reported for this area, with the exception of petroglyphs (Pimentel Spissu 1986; Falcón and Suárez 2009). The western end of the plain narrows to an arid valley, and there are many rocks with petroglyphs inside and along the mouth of this valley.

Víctor Pimentel Spissu (1986) documented a huge image of a feline, 3 m in height, that was carved on a large rock (Rock 3; Figure 2.7). This boulder is located inside the valley, and Pimentel therefore called this valley, with its concentration of petroglyphs, *Quebrada del Felino*. Most of these petroglyphs are considered to have been carved after the Early Intermediate Period, although a few of the images, including the feline, present earlier stylistic features. Henning Bischof (1994) argued that the Felino and a bird inside its body were carved in a Late Preceramic Period artistic style, but identifying the chronological position of a petroglyph based only on its style is not reliable (Bischof 2009). I include this site in my study of the early landscape because, whether an example of genuine Late Preceramic art or an imitation carved during the Initial Period, it would have been visible to the inhabitants of the Hamacas Complex as an element of the landscape.

When I began an archaeological project on the Mosquito Plain in 2009, I proposed two research problems. The first was to verify the presence of some remains dating to the Late Preceramic Period in addition to this putative late Preceramic Felino petroglyph. The second was to consider the relationship between the Hamacas Complex and the Felino petroglyph during the Initial Period. The results of the first research problem will be reported in detail elsewhere. Suffice it to say that some monumental buildings in the Mosquito Plain were found to be earlier than the introduction of pottery, so it is likely that Felino also was carved during the Late Preceramic Period. Here I discuss the second research focus.

Chronological Sequence

During our research on the Mosquito Plain I encountered a large monumental building, about 20 m east of the Felino petroglyph, and named it Platform A (Figure 2.8). The site is located at the bottom of the valley along the steep slope of the northern bank, and consists of two levels of terraced platforms. The Lower Terrace faces south and is sustained by a masonry retaining wall that connects a stairway on the east end and a large rock referred to as Rock 5 on the west end. The Upper Terrace extends to the west of Rock 5, sustaining a rectangular room. Another retaining wall that sustained the Upper Terrace must have connected Rock 5 and Rock 3, but at present no remains of it are visible because of natural erosion. The details of the excavation are given elsewhere (Tsurumi and Morales Castro 2012).

Platform A seems to have been built during the Tembladera Phase, according to a few pottery sherds unearthed from the fill beneath the floor. Furthermore, among the offerings left with the two bodies buried at the time of construction was a sodalite

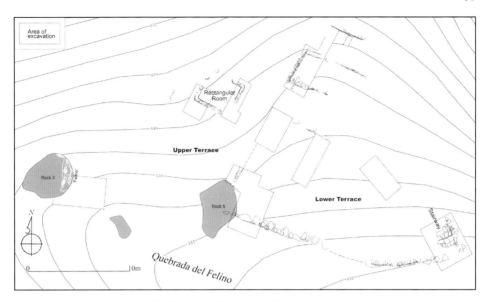

FIGURE 2.8. The monumental building Platform A on the Mosquito Plain.

bead. Sodalite is a typical exotic material associated with late Initial Period burials of the Jequetepeque Valley (Onuki and Kato 1988:6–8; Elera 2009:74; see also Shimizu et al. 2007). In addition, two petroglyphs support this tentative chronological position. The first imagery is carved on Rock 5 and depicts a profile of a jaguar-like human head seen frequently on Classic Cupisnique art (Elera 1998, 2009) of the late Initial Period. The second one is another anthropomorphic being carved on Rock 3 (Tsurumi and Morales Castro 2013), which can be included as an example of the Yurayaku-type proposed by Bischof (2008:131–133). The motif has wings carved over the buttock of a feline. The combination of winged anthropomorphs on the upper level and jaguars on the lower level could be an "iconographic complex" (Shibata 2008) similar to some late Initial Period mural decorations, which can be seen at the Chavín de Huántar (Lumbreras 1977) and Huaca Partida sites (Shibata 2008). I consider that Felino was carved during the Late Preceramic Period and that some centuries afterward, during the late Initial Period, Platform A was built beside it. I have not obtained data dating either to the early Initial Period or Early Horizon at Platform A, but after the Early Intermediate Period some narrow terraces were added to the Platform A.

Platform A and Buildings of the Hamacas Complex

In this section I describe features of Platform A and compare them with the buildings of the Hamacas Complex. This requires first a discussion of the differences in architectural features between both sites. The Lower Terrace of Platform A is an amorphous platform sustained by a curved wall that has no similarity among the platforms of the Hamacas Complex. Rock 5 is a prominent architectural feature of Platform A, but there are no other examples of a huge natural rock used as part of wall among Hamacas Complex centers.

It is also important to point out that the petroglyphs that exist on the Hamacas Plain are distant from the Initial Period centers previously described.

Second, the location of Platform A needs to be considered from a broader point of view. As mentioned above, none of the buildings of the Hamacas Complex was built within such a rocky, steep, and narrow valley as the Quebrada del Felino, where Platform A is situated. Because of the location, the land near Platform A could never have been cultivated nor would it have been possible to live without anxiety about huaycos during the rainy season. Moreover, from the area of Platform A it would not have been possible to see the monumental buildings and burial towers of the Hamacas Complex.

On the threat of huaycos, additional comments are necessary. The GIS analysis indicates that most of the platform has not suffered serious damage (see Figure 2.5) and is still intact today. However, a strong current of water (17,879 grids; see Figure 2.5) flows down several meters to the south of the platform and another (2,649 grids; see Figure 2.5) runs from the northern slope over the edge of the stairway. From several perspectives, this spot is not suitable for permanent occupation.

Considering these factors, I concluded that Platform A was not a civic-ceremonial center similar to those of the Hamacas Complex, in spite of its large scale. It did not function as the center of a village, and the rarity of cultural and natural remains associated with the structure seems to support this idea. The focus of the founders and users of Platform A seemed to be on the Felino, which had been there for many centuries. In this spirit, they added some carvings and modified the environmental setting to form an architectural complex as an expression of their interest in the huge boulder bearing the petroglyph of the Felino.

As has been observed by some researchers (e.g., Guffroy 1999:70), the relationship between rock art and interregional routes may hold the key to understanding the nature of Platform A. On the bank opposite that where the Felino is located, there was a platform designated 14.14 by Ravines (1982:90) that is said to be connected to a rock carved with a petroglyph of an agnatic head (Ravines 1982:60; Pimentel Spissu 1986:22). This motif in the Jequetepeque Valley has been interpreted as the head of an anthropomorphized spider (Salazar-Burger and Burger 1983; Pimentel Spissu 1986:38–39, fig. 13), a motif dated to the late Initial Period, as are the two additional carvings on the boulder with the Felino. The topographic features of the banks and riverbed between the two platforms associated with petroglyphs permit one to cross the river on foot more easily than at other locations (Tsurumi and Morales Castro 2012). Furthermore, the restricted visibility of the site (see Figure 2.6) suggests that the founders of Platform A on the Mosquito Plain were unrelated to the inhabitants of Hamacas Plain by blood, recalling that the burial practice and formation of landscape in the Hamacas Complex were based on kinship. Thus I consider Platform A to be a building founded by a group foreign to those responsible for the Hamacas Complex, and I would suggest that these outsiders visited this spot only intermittently. This idea needs to be tested in the field, not only using local archaeological evidence, but also from an interregional viewpoint.

Conclusions

I have compared the architectural features and location of the monumental buildings in the Hamacas Plain, considering them in relation to the Malpaso site on the opposite bank of the Jequetepeque River, and discussed these archaeological complexes in relation to

Platform A on the Mosquito Plain. This review is an attempt to understand the process by which the cultural landscape around Tembladera in the mid-Jequetepeque Valley developed during the Initial Period. On another occasion, I will integrate the data on the monumental buildings of the Late Preceramic Period and the Early Horizon into this picture to consider the dynamics over a longer time scale. I also plan to consider the relationships between the Tembladera populations with communities of the other regions.

Finally, I want to emphasize the importance of chronological study in my research. I was able to discuss the formation process of landscape with a consideration of the role of memory thanks only to my knowledge of the local chronological sequence. It is through this chronological control that continuity can be demonstrated. A "sacred space" can be reused through ritual practices, such as the construction of buildings and burials, despite temporal and conceptual discontinuity (Moore 2010). However, the cases in which monumental buildings present continuous sequence, as in the Tembladera area, permit us to study the social background of architecture as elements of landscape (McFadyen 2008) on the basis of the supposed continuity of memory. Especially in local ancestor worship, different ideas among founders of the architectural complexes were embodied as elements of the landscape: between the civic-ceremonial centers of the Hamacas Phase and those of the Tembladera Phase, between the Hamacas Plain and the Malpaso Plain, and between the Hamacas Complex and Platform A of Mosquito. The diachronic and synchronic comparison among monumental buildings based on the subdivision of the Initial Period into four time periods enables such detailed considerations. Tembladera is exceptional to study because of its abundance of monumental buildings in a narrow area.

Clearly the construction of monumental buildings throughout the northern Peruvian Andes from the Late Preceramic Period until the Early Horizon was continuous in spite of regional differences. As seen here, further study of local chronology to clarify the continuous sequence will be a great help in discussing the early settlements with monumental buildings and the communities that sustained them.

Acknowledgments. The Tembladera Archaeological Project has been supported by JSPS KAKENHI (grants 05J03077, 23720380, 23222003, and 25300036) and the Takanashi Foundation for Arts and Archaeology (Takanashi Foundation, Japan). I deeply appreciate the Peruvian archaeologists and students who participated in my excavations as co-directors and field assistants: Regina Abraham (co-director in 2003), Anyanett Mora (co-director in 2004), Raúl Cholán (2004, director in 2005), Nelly Martell (2003), Carlos Morales (2004, 2005, co-director in 2009), José Peña (2005), Moira Novoa (2005), Abraham Quispe (2009), and Alfredo Fernández (2009). Thanks also go to the Ministerio (Instituto Nacional) de Cultura Cajamarca for facilitating my study.

Many researchers kindly collaborated with me: radiocarbon dating by Kunio Yoshida (Radiocarbon Lab of the University Museum, University of Tokyo); bioarchaeological analysis by Víctor Vásquez (Arqueobios; Andean Center of Archaeological and Paleontological Research) and Teresa Rosales (National University of Trujillo); and GIS analysis by Yuko Ito and Yuta Kaneko. I am extremely thankful to Richard Burger and Lucy Salazar (Yale University), and Yuji Seki (The National Museum of Ethnology, Japan), for the opportunity to publish.

I would also like to express my debt to Yoshio Onuki (The Little World Museum of Man, Japan) and Yasutake Kato (Saitama University, Japan) for supporting my investigations. Finally, I express gratitude to Gentaro Miyano for proofreading my English text and making very useful comments.

CHAPTER THREE

INTRAREGIONAL COMPETITION AND INTERREGIONAL RECIPROCITY

Formative Social Organization in the Lower Nepeña Valley on the North-central Coast

Koichiro Shibata

The primary objective of this chapter is to test an emergent model of social organization in the Formative Period, at a local and interregional scale, on the basis of data from recent excavations in the lower Nepeña Valley. In contrast to some later cases as shown for the Mochica culture (Swenson 2006; Quilter and Castillo 2010), searching for the social organization of the Formative Period is like groping in the dark, unless it rests on the traditional and static neoevolutionary models of state or chiefdom. To adapt a priori these models to fit the Andean Formative, however, can conceal peculiarities of the specific societies. Therefore, leaving aside this "imported" image, as well as its problematic definition, this brief essay will explore and illustrate some ceremonial communities and their constituency in the Formative Period, being aware of "how they were" and "what they did" (compare Yoffee 2005). Some of our archaeological findings from Formative ceremonial areas are useful in approaching the theme, with the help of ethnohistoric information. Note, however, that part of this problem is caused by the difficulty of finding residential areas associated with the ceremonial centers, and this is one of the tasks we too have to face in the future.

We scarcely have data for social organization in a site or a polity in the Formative Andes, but studies on interregional relationships have been well developed, often referring to people on the move in trading caravans, exiled migrants, warfare, pilgrimages, and priests sent from the center to the provinces (S. Pozorski and T. Pozorski 1987; Burger 1992; Lumbreras 1993; Elera 1997; Onuki 2001), or carefully examining the world-system approach focused on the south-central highlands (Burger and Matos 2002; Matsumoto 2010). The recent archaeological researches on the lower Nepeña Valley provide evidence for a hypothetical model not necessarily incompatible with the previous arguments.

Setting

We investigated two ceremonial centers, Cerro Blanco and Huaca Partida, in the lower Nepeña River Valley on the north-central coast of Peru (Figure 3.1). Three seasons of excavation at both archaeological sites allowed us to establish the local chronology of

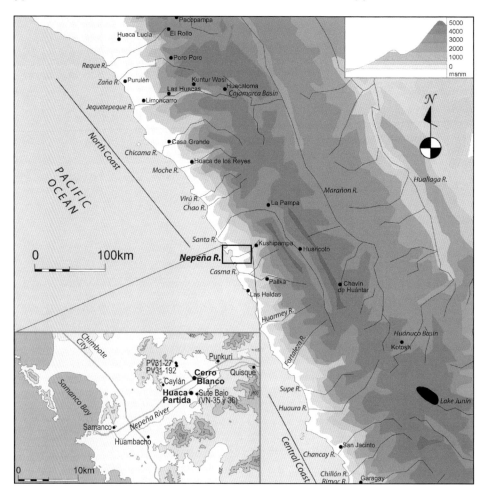

FIGURE 3.1. Map of northern Peru showing the location of the lower Nepeña River Valley.

the lower Nepeña Valley (Figure 3.2) from Huambocayan Phase (Early Formative) to Samanco Phase (Late or Final Formative), though this essay focuses on the Cerro Blanco Phase (Middle Formative Period) and the earlier part of the Nepeña Phase (Late Formative Period), during which the Peruvian coast witnessed the prosperity of the Cupisnique culture on the North Coast (Elera 1997) and the Manchay culture on the Central Coast (Burger and Salazar 2008). Note that the period does not include much of the Late Formative (i.e., Early Horizon), during which the decadence of the ceremonial centers of these cultures occurred.

Cerro Blanco

Cerro Blanco is one of the best known Formative Period ceremonial centers in the lower Nepeña Valley. Located on the right bank of the river, it consists of three artificial mounds that extend over an area 250 m (west–east) by 200 m (north–south). The central mound reaches 14 m high from the cultivated surface around the site. After a casual discovery of polychrome friezes during construction of a railway, Peruvian archaeologists

Local Phase	BC	cal BC	Sites of Cerro Blanco and Huaca Partida	Other Sites in the Lower Nepeña valley	Andean Sequences		
					A	B	C
Samanco (SM)	500–250	450–150	Reutilization	Huambacho Samanco Caylán	Late Formative	Final Formative	Early Horizon
Nepeña (NP)	700–500	800–450	Ceremonial center with megalithic wall			Late Formative	
Cerro Blanco (CB)	1000–700	1100–800	Ceremonial center with polychrome frieze	PV31-27 and PV31-192 (?)	Middle Formative	Middle Formative	Initial Period
Huambocayan (HC)	1300–1000	1500–1100	Earliest ceramics in lower Nepeña valley		Early Formative	Early Formative	

FIGURE 3.2. Chronology for the Formative Period of the lower Nepeña River Valley. Local phases are based on Shibata (2008).

excavated the northwestern corner of the south mound (Tello 1943, 2005). Our project has completed two seasons of excavation at all mounds (north, central, and south) revealing a well-defined cultural sequence through architectural superposition, associated ceramics, and contextualized radiocarbon dates (Ikehara and Shibata 2008; Shibata 2008).

Huaca Partida
Located 2.2 km south of the site of Cerro Blanco, Huaca Partida is the second largest prehispanic monument on the left bank of the lower Nepeña Valley. Unlike Cerro Blanco, there seems to be only a main mound, which measures 50 by 60 m and 10 m in height. Though it was registered by Proulx (1985) in his systematic survey of the valley, no archaeological excavation had been conducted until 2004, when our project started after the excavation of Cerro Blanco. Its architectural and ceramic sequences resemble those of Cerro Blanco (Shibata 2011, 2014).

Formative Chronology of the Lower Nepeña Valley
Though found only at the Cerro Blanco site, the Huambocayan Phase is the earliest ceramic occupation known in the lower Nepeña Valley. No architectural feature has been confirmed, but the characteristics of the pottery suggest close relations to the Haldas Phase ceramic group found in the lower Casma Valley (T. Pozorski and S. Pozorski 2005).

The Cerro Blanco Phase witnessed the first monumental construction at the site. Conical and slightly smaller rectangular adobe used with cut stones is a diagnostic construction technique that distinguishes this phase from the next. The most noteworthy characteristics are the polychrome friezes, showing Cupisnique–Chavin related iconography, decorating some exterior walls. The associated ceramics suggest a Cupisnique-like tradition with narrow incisions.

In the subsequent Nepeña Phase almost all the previous constructions were buried and covered by a larger terraced platform that we named "Megalithic Temple." No adobe is used as material for wall construction, but huge cut stones characterize this phase. Some ceramic forms and decorations follow the earlier phase, but their variation clearly increases, and incision lines tend to be broader. Circle and dot stamping are some of the new features distinguishable from the previous phase.

Megalithic temples at both sites seem to have been abandoned with the beginning of the Samanco Phase. The main staircase was blocked with coarse walls, and layers of architectural rubble and organic residue accumulated on and around the platform.

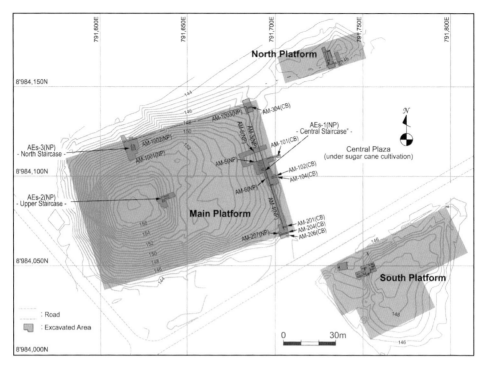

FIGURE 3.3. Plan of the Cerro Blanco site.

Though some large vessels share morphological characteristics with the Nepeña Phase, new decoration techniques are notable. They include textile imprint, showing a close relationship to the emerging centers of Caylán, Huambacho, and Samanco in the lower valley (Chicoine 2008).

Evidence and Implications

A careful review of the archaeological materials and information that we unearthed from the lower Nepeña Valley allows us to reveal a series of past activities that the members of both ceremonial centers carried out, and to eventually propose a model for a Formative Period society.

Commoners
Our excavations did not detect any residential area and related structures of the Formative Period, as was often the case with the coastal sites of this period. However, some features and our analysis of them allowed us to speculate about communal members, that is, followers of a ceremonial center and possibly of a leader.

Local Ceramics in a Feasting Context
At the Cerro Blanco site we uncovered a sealed small precinct with deposits of "rubbish" from feasting activities carried out probably at the central plaza. Among the materials recovered, semicomplete vessels, animal bones with cut marks, shellfish remains, and

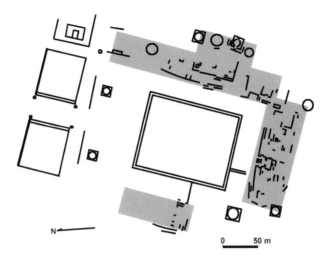

FIGURE 3.4. Plan of Cardal (Middle Formative Period). Redrawn with modifications after Burger and Salazar-Burger (1991).

obsidian flakes are prominent. Large vessels such as neckless jars show distinct pottery varieties that, despite being produced locally (Ikehara 2007), suggest that many production groups supplied these vessels to the ceremonial center.

Construction Materials
In both of the ceremonial centers under consideration, the retaining walls were constructed with a variety of materials. For example, during the Cerro Blanco Phase, the Cerro Blanco site had walls of conical adobe and cut stone in the North Platform and Central Platform, whereas some walls of conical adobe and others of rectangular adobe and cut stone were incorporated in a structure of the South Platform. On the other hand, truncated pyramidal adobes and cut stone were used at the contemporaneous Huaca Partida site. A well-known study of the heterogeneity of the adobes and their markings at the Huaca del Sol (Hastings and Moseley 1975) interprets the morphological and material differences as indicating that not only one but many groups contributed to the construction. If this interpretation is applied here, then many groups were involved in the construction of Cerro Blanco and Huaca Partida.

Leaders
Although we have not found so far any prominent funeral context at either site, a comparative analysis of architecture and iconography gives us a picture of the appearance of local leaders.

Architecture
Today the Cerro Blanco site has three artificial mounds arranged to form an asymmetric U. Our excavations have confirmed that these three architectural features already existed in the Cerro Blanco Phase (Figure 3.3). This asymmetric U arrangement is a common characteristic of the contemporaneous ceremonial centers on the Central Coast (Figure 3.4), but are rarely observed along the north and north-central coasts (Williams 1985; Burger and Salazar 2008).

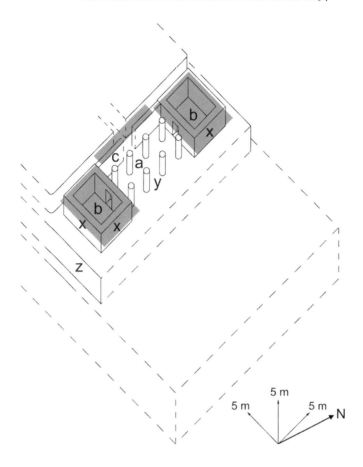

FIGURE 3.5. Hypothetical reconstruction of the Huaca Partida platform, Cerro Blanco phase (Middle Formative Period). Features shown are (**a**) an atrium, (**b**) a rectangular room, (**c**) a double-faced wall, (**x**) a polychrome mural painting with incised black outline, (**y**) a polychrome column (front row only), and (**z**) a bichrome high-relief.

Once again, the architectural plan of the Huaca Partida site during the Cerro Blanco Phase is quite different from the coeval Cerro Blanco site. Composed of a single massive platform (Figure 3.5), the plan shows a clear symmetry as far as revealed by the excavation, including a columned atrium (Figure 3.5a) located between the two lateral rectangular rooms (Figure 3.5b) and in front of the rear double-faced wall (Figure 3.5c). This complex is a typical architectural feature of the North Coast during the Middle Formative Period (Figure 3.6).

The distribution of ceremonial centers with these characteristics does not show any contiguous territory; they are instead scattered like an archipelago. Moreover, the nearby centers of Cerro Blanco and Huaca Partida, with their mutually distinct architectural features, seem to have interacted during the Cerro Blanco Phase with their counterparts in different regions.

Now, what or who was the interregional vehicle that connected these ceremonial centers? In considering this, architectural data from the Nepeña Phase are suggestive.

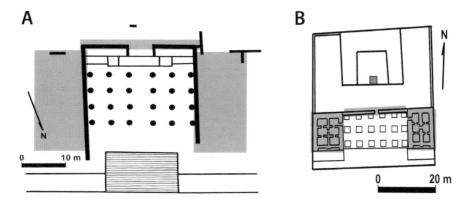

FIGURE 3.6. Typical architectural features of the Middle Formative Period. **A.** Plan of Huaca Lucía. Redrawn with modifications after Shimada, Elera, and Shimada (1982). **B.** Partial plan of Huaca de los Reyes. Redrawn with modifications after T. Pozorski (1975).

It is often assumed that access to the esoteric knowledge embodied in the ceremonial architecture was rigidly restricted during the Formative Period. Although we have not unearthed any of the staircases of the Cerro Blanco Phase, we did register four staircases dating to the Nepeña Phase at both centers. They are quite steep and of similar length (with 27, 39, 40, and 43 steps). One of the staircases is hidden (semisubterranean) and three were gradually narrowed or closed during the Formative Period. These lead to the highest part of the main building, the only spot with a panoramic view of the entire center. If only selected people had access to the upper structure, as in the ethnohistorical case of Pachacamac, this suggests that such people should have been the vehicle conveying the esoteric knowledge of ceremonial architecture, crossing valleys, hills, and deserts.

Iconography

The archaeological site of Cerro Blanco is well known for the polychrome frieze excavated at the South Platform by Tello's team eight decades ago (Tello 1943, 2005; Bischof 1997). One of the prominent iconographic conventions is the "kenning" (Figure 3.7), a literary metaphor introduced to Peruvian archaeology by Rowe (1967). In this imagery the vertebra is composed of a row of teeth and fangs; in other words, these teeth visually convert into a vertebra. This kind of kenning is known only from the Cerro Blanco (Figure 3.7A) and Huaca Partida (Figure 3.7B) sites in the lower Nepeña Valley, and from Chavín de Huántar (Figure 3.7C), and a few nearby sites in highland Ancash.

Another important kenning convention is that of a "foot converting into monstrous head" (Figure 3.8), found at Huaca Partida (Figure 3.8A). Outside the Nepeña Valley, this kenning appears on immovable or difficult to move materials only at the Middle Formative ceremonial center of Huaca de los Reyes in the North Coast (Figure 3.8B), though slightly later or almost at the same time it was engraved at Chavín de Huántar (Kembel 2008; see also Burger 1983) and painted on the textiles of the South Coast (Cordy-Collins 1976).

An iconographic combination from Huaca Partida is peculiarly noteworthy. Engraved and painted clay friezes representing a winged anthropomorphic figure are part of the two rectangular rooms on top of the terraced platform. The south retaining wall

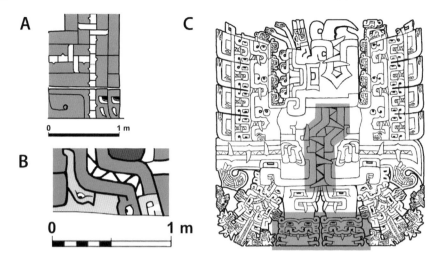

FIGURE 3.7. Examples of kenning showing vertebra composed of teeth. **A.** Relief from Cerro Blanco, Cerro Blanco Phase (Middle Formative Period). Redrawn with modifications after Bischof (1997). **B.** Mural painting from Huaca Partida, Cerro Blanco Phase (Middle Formative Period). **C.** Kenning (gray areas) on a column from Chavín de Huántar (beginning of the Late Formative Period). Redrawn with modifications after Rowe (1967).

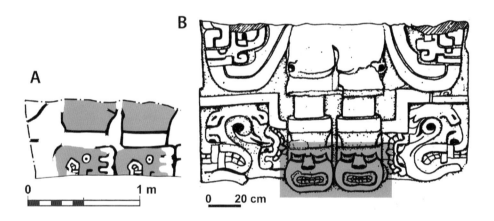

FIGURE 3.8. Examples of kenning. **A.** A mural painting from Huaca Partida, Cerro Blanco Phase (Middle Formative Period). **B.** Kenning (gray area) in a relief from Huaca de los Reyes (Middle Formative Period). Redrawn with modifications after T. Pozorski (1975).

(and probably the others) of the middle terrace on which those rooms are located features a row of supernatural felines in profile (Figure 3.9). Although further research will be required, it is assumed so far that both these elements—the ornithopomorphic and anthropomorphic figure on the upper section and the feline on the lower section—are an iconographic pair shared exclusively between Huaca Partida and Chavín de Huántar (Figure 3.10).

In turn, some differences between the neighboring centers should not be over-

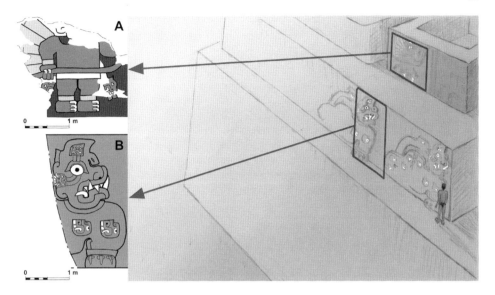

FIGURE 3.9. Winged anthropomorphic figure (**A**) and supernatural felines (**B**) from friezes at Huaca Partida, Cerro Blanco Phase (Middle Formative Period).

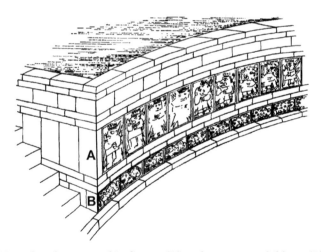

FIGURE 3.10. Winged anthropomorphic figures (**A**) and supernatural felines (**B**) at Chavín de Huántar, beginning of Late Formative Period. Redrawn with modifications after Lumbreras (1977).

looked. The frontal agnathic faces found at Cerro Blanco show three fangs, with the central one in triangular form (Figure 3.11A, B), that can be seen at many contemporaneous sites (compare Roe 1974). However, the frontal agnatic faces at Huaca Partida are unique and have four fangs (Figure 3.11C).

In sum, the information on iconography suggests that, in spite of their geographic proximity (only 2 km apart), Cerro Blanco and Huaca Partida used considerably different artistic conventions and that each had its own connection with specific distant ceremo-

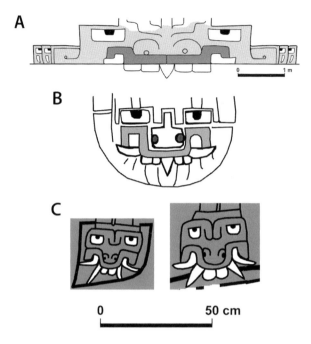

Figure 3.11. Frontal agnathic faces. **A.** A relief from Cerro Blanco, Cerro Blanco Phase (Middle Formative Period). Redrawn with modifications after Bischof (1997). **B.** A relief Cerro Blanco, Cerro Blanco Phase (Middle Formative Period). Redrawn with modifications after Tello (2005). **C.** A relief Huaca Partida, Cerro Blanco Phase (Middle Formative Period).

nial centers. Considering the complexity and sophistication of its iconography, it is not unreasonable to suggest that the vehicle for these links was not the common people. If true, did artists in charge of the religious friezes, or the communal or ceremonial leader, travel long distances, visit other ceremonial centers reaching the most sacred areas, and, eventually, incorporate foreign features into their local religious conventions? Before presenting an explanation, it is crucial to review an ethnohistoric study on the Peruvian coast that will allow us to interrelate the disparate archaeological data.

Discussion and Conclusions

Competing Leaders: Ramírez's Model

This section will summarize three intertwined characteristics of the late prehispanic communities on the Peruvian North Coast (Ramírez 1996, 2001) to better interpret the fragmented archaeological data. In late prehistoric times on the North Coast, subjects did not necessarily live close to their leader, and in fact sometimes lived nearer other chiefs (Figure 3.12). There was a complex pattern of exploiting certain resources and sharing between the two chiefdoms. There was no fixed territory because, in addition to separate land use, the relationship between a leader and his subjects was not stable. So, in other words, they had no fixed geographical borders but rather changing social boundar-

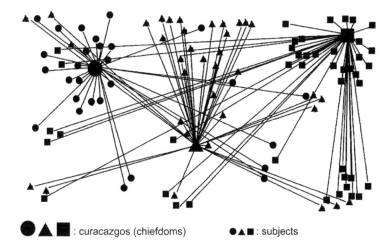

● ▲ ■ : curacazgos (chiefdoms)   ● ▲ ■ : subjects

FIGURE 3.12. Representation of late prehispanic scattered occupation for three chiefdoms (*curacazgos*) and their subjects in the North Coast of Peru. Redrawn with modifications after Ramírez (2001).

ies. Subjects were able to leave their leader for the protection of other chiefs who could provide a better living, or in such circumstances as environmental crisis. This "scattered occupation" could be one factor behind this betrayal of loyalty.

Because commoners were able to leave their leader, competition arose among the leaders to increase the number of their subjects, since without this labor force no one could exploit natural resources. The chiefs, then, competed with each other for better governance, redistribution, and hospitality.

A Tentative Model for the Formative Period

We will now interrelate our data from the lower Nepeña Valley, filling the void of archaeological evidence with ethnohistoric information, and thus present a tentative model for the Formative Period. In this model (Figure 3.13), between a leader (X, Y, and Z) and his subjects (a, b, d) in the same region, even if they reside near other leaders, there should be a reciprocal relationship (c), as many researchers have been proposing. New evidence from the Nepeña Valley has allowed us to propose that there was also a long-distance relationship between some leaders in different regions (e), and it is assumed that this interregional relationship could be peaceful and reciprocal (h), as explained below. One of the factors that allowed the leaders to intercommunicate without any tension derives from interregional barriers (f) such as physical distance, and environmental and linguistic differences (Torero 1986, 1990). Such obstacles did not easily permit the subjects of one leader to migrate far to be under the patronage of other leaders. As a consequence, it is likely that the contact between a leader and commoners of other regions was limited. On the other hand, it is expected that there was significant competition (g) between neighboring leaders (Y1, Y2, and Y3) to increase their subjects, as Ramírez (1996) has proposed for the later prehistoric period.

Although we have not yet found any residential area associated with either of the ceremonial centers discussed here, we understand some reasons why commoners gathered at the centers, and indeed there is much evidence for this. Yet while our excavations

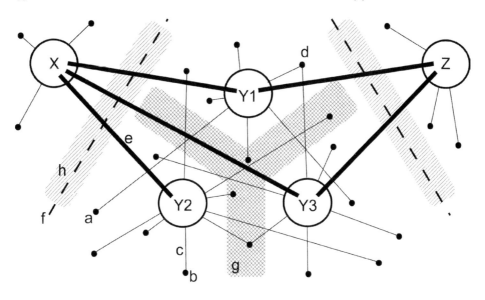

FIGURE 3.13. Schematic diagram of Formative Period social organization. Open circles are ceremonial centers with their own leaders, dots represent subjects. **X** is leader in the North Coast (or Highlands of Cajamarca); **Y1, Y2,** and **Y3** are neighboring leaders in the North-Central Coast; **Z** is leader in the Central Coast (or Highlands of Ancash); **a** is a subject of Y1; **b** is a subject of Y2; **c** is a reciprocal connection; **d** is a subject who supports both Y1 and Y3; **e** is a reciprocal connection between leaders; **f** (dotted lines) are interregional boundary obstacles (such as distance, environment, and language,); **g** indicates areas of significant competition among leaders to increase the number of subjects; **h** signifies the difficulty of competition between leaders.

have revealed important footprints that suggest interregional contact among leaders, we need to examine how and why they engaged in long-distance communication.

Returning to the body of Formative Period iconographic data, one easily realizes that there are no cases in which friezes or monoliths found in different regions were designed by a single artist or skilled group. There are, however, several features not shared among nearby centers, but rather among centers separated by a great distance. Moreover, foreign features are generally incorporated into local motifs or styles. As anticipated, it has been necessary to study the esoteric iconography of the friezes in situ to make another observation. It is inferred that the artist-priest of a center visited other centers and, after returning, designed a fused iconography. Thus, we propose that leaders in the Formative Period traveled, observed, returned, and then assimilated.

We have some archaeological and ethnohistorical evidence to support this proposal. At the Formative ceremonial center of Kuntur Wasi, in the northern highlands, some special burials have been found. One of them contains a priest whose skull shows pathological alteration linked to a coastal lifestyle (Onuki 1995:212). This confirms the existence of at least one example of the one-way interregional transfer of a religious leader. Tsurumi (2012) notes that Formative Period petroglyphs are often located along presumed intervalley routes. Who was responsible for these drawings, some of which contain iconography so complex that commoners would have hardly been able to execute it successfully? Moreover, some ethnohistorical information indicates the frequent travel of leaders (including Inca) and commoners (e.g., Ramírez 1996:19–21). This communication network is presumed to have been intertwined with the interregional identity of the leaders in scattered regions, which is just reflected in the symbolic materials, unlike commoner's daily materials (Schortman 1989:58–59; DeMarrais, Castillo, and Earle 1996:31), as we can observe in the case of the lower Nepeña Valley with other regions.

Assuming that the above argument is correct, why did Formative leaders travel such long distances? There must have been advantages to justify these efforts. For example, through travel and obtaining exotic objects, the leaders were able to increase their local authority (Helms 1993; Goldstein 2000; Ikehara and Shibata 2008). Leaders who resided far away would be considered less negative when they arrived at distant centers, since they were not in direct competition with local leadership (Helms 1988:42).

Finally, it should be understood that this proposal is not incompatible with the well-known Pachacamac model and its application to the Formative Period (e.g., Burger 1988, 1992; Lumbreras 1993), and we can consider the possibility that the link between distant leaders was established on the basis of religious kinship. It should be kept in mind, however, that Chavín de Huántar was not necessarily the religious "father."

CHAPTER FOUR

New Insights into the Architecture and Organization of Cardal

Richard L. Burger and Lucy C. Salazar

At least forty-seven public centers of the Manchay culture were built in the Lurín, Rimac, Chillón, Chancay, and Huaura drainages of Peru's Central Coast during the Initial Period (ca. 1800–800 BC). We estimate that over twenty-four million person-days were required for their construction. These mound complexes all have a north–northeast orientation and a common layout characterized by a flat-topped pyramid flanked by longer asymmetric lateral platforms or "arms" surrounding a massive central open space on three sides (Williams 1980; Burger 1992; Burger and Salazar 2008, 2014).

The core conventions shared by these U-shaped civic-ceremonial centers were identified by Carlos Williams (1985) several decades ago, but most aspects of this public architecture and its organization remain poorly understood. This is not surprising considering that the monumental architecture has been seriously degraded over the last three millennia by torrential El Niño rains, wind erosion, and more than a few earthquakes. Moreover, after the abandonment of the complexes many of the sites were badly damaged by canals, construction projects, and looting. As a result, these monumental centers today appear to the casual viewer as undifferentiated piles of earth and stone, with little architectural detail, above and beyond the large volume and layout of the platform mounds (Figure 4.1).

Aerial and satellite photographs and surface exploration sometimes reveal wall fragments and depressions corresponding to buried rooms, but such evidence is more suggestive than definitive. Our excavations at Cardal, Mina Perdida, and Manchay Bajo and those by other investigators, such as Rogger Ravines and William Isbell at Garagay in Rimac and Jorge Silva at Huacoy in Chillón, have resulted in the description of some subsurface constructions (Ravines and Isbell 1976; Silva 1998; Burger and Makowski 2009; compare Ludeña Restaure 1973; Carrión Sotelo 1998). Until recently, investigations usually have been confined to the central mounds of the U-shaped complexes and largely ignored the arms of the U and the open central area of the complex.

Here we summarize the findings of four months of excavations in 2008 at Cardal to provide a clearer vision of the architecture and layout of one example of the Manchay culture center. These investigations included excavations on the right and left arms of the U, as well as on the central mound, the central plaza, and sunken circular plazas on the periphery of the three principal mounds. Our findings show that the architecture at Car-

Figure 4.1. Aerial view taken in 1967 of Cardal in the Lurín River Valley, Peru. From Burger (1987, fig. 2).

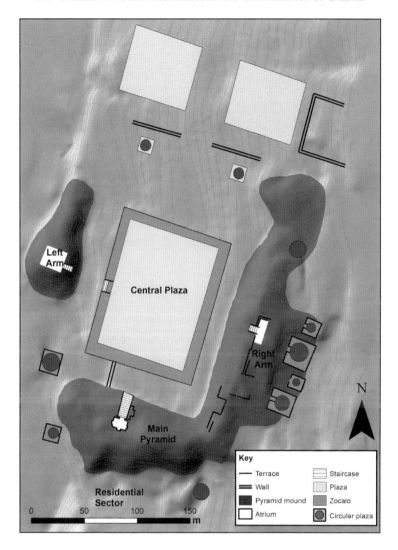

FIGURE 4.2. Architectural layout of Cardal, including structures unearthed in 2008. Drawing by Christopher Milan.

dal is more elaborate than previously appreciated (Figure 4.2). The newly revealed patterns of site design have interesting implications for understanding the social organization and distribution of power during the final centuries of the Initial Period (1200–900 cal BC) along Peru's Central Coast and its transformation over time.

Background

The archaeological site of Cardal is located at 120 masl on the south bank of the Lurín River, roughly 14 km from the Pacific Ocean. It covers roughly 20 ha and includes a core of monumental architecture and an adjacent zone behind the central mound devoted to resi-

FIGURE 4.3. Superimposed staircases leading to the elevated central plaza on the western side of the Cardal site.

dential occupation. Twenty-five ^{14}C measurements have been made on samples taken from the residential and public zones at Cardal and these indicate that the site was occupied for over four centuries, from roughly 1300–850 cal BC (Burger 1987; Burger and Salazar 2009, 2012). Although Cardal is neither the oldest nor the largest U-shaped complex in the Lurín Valley, distinctions belonging instead to Mina Perdida (Burger and Salazar 2009), it is the best preserved of the eight U-shaped centers documented for the valley and is therefore well suited for efforts at achieving a more complete understanding of the layout and the architectural features of U-shaped centers. At the same time, it must be kept in mind that there is considerable variation between these Manchay centers. We anticipate that the findings at Cardal will differ in many details from the situation at other centers, even those such as Manchay Bajo, that are only a few kilometers away.

Results of the 2008 Excavations

Central Open Zone or Central Plaza
The central open area at the Cardal site covers roughly 4 ha and is bordered on three sides by terraced platform mounds. In the middle of this large open space is a raised rectangular environment, measuring 120 by 100 m, that is clearly defined by stone retaining walls. This open area has been assumed to correspond to a public plaza where the members of Cardal's social group and visitors from other centers could join together for religious worship and other community activities such as feasting, exchange, sporting events, and group dances (Scheele 1970; Williams 1985; Burger 1987). This model of plaza activity is influenced by early colonial historical accounts of the activities carried out in massive Inca plazas as well as ethnographic accounts of the way in which plazas are used by traditional Andean and Amazonian peoples (Moore 1996b). Other than our work at Cardal in 1985 (Burger 1987), the interpretation of the central open space in U-shaped centers as a plaza has not been explicitly evaluated by investigations at the centers of the Manchay culture. It was possible that the post-abandonment layer of eroded materials conceivably could have hidden evidence of alternative uses, such as workshop areas, burial grounds, and so forth. One of the goals of the 2008 investigations at Cardal was to test this hypothesis more thoroughly with trenches and other excavations in the central open area.

These investigations in this zone consisted of two sets of excavations. Additional excavations were planned, but could not be carried out because of the lack of cooperation from a local landholder. Fortunately, the excavations that were completed provided valuable evidence about the use of this open environment. The first of these excavations was a 2 m wide transect running for 20 m, located at the midpoint in the "plaza's" western retaining wall and laid out at a right angle to this masonry feature. This trench revealed two sequential episodes of construction and modification. The elevated central plaza featured a hard-packed earthen floor lacking in structures, features, and, with a few minor exceptions, artifacts. From this finding we concluded that initially the central open area was created and used as an undifferentiated open space. Our excavations revealed that the floor was clean and lacked evidence of refuse or production debris except for a few small pottery fragments. In some areas, a layer of fill had been placed beneath the floor to level the surface. Despite this, the prepared floor slopes gently from east to west, reflecting the natural topography of the subsoil.

A thick masonry retaining wall defined the perimeter of the rectangular open space. On the exterior of the midpoint in the western retaining wall we encountered an abutting free-standing staircase that provided access to the elevated packed earth floor from the low zone surrounding the elevated rectangular open area (Figure 4.3). Our excavation in this adjacent zone likewise found no evidence of refuse or structures. In summary, our results

Figure 4.4. A trench excavated in the central plaza revealed a hard-packed floor bordered by a low perimetric bench.

are consistent with the hypothesis that the open central area was designed and used as a formal plaza.

A second episode of construction in the plaza area consisted of the creation of a 10 m wide feature bordering the inner edge of the plaza. This was produced by building a low single-faced retaining wall that runs parallel to the perimetric wall of the plaza. This wall supported a layer of artificial fill covered by a floor, thereby creating a 10 m wide bench running along the west side of the plaza (Figure 4.4). A second lateral staircase was built over the original staircase to reach the plaza's new bench level. The surface of the bench, like the central plaza floor, lacked evidence of any structures or artifacts that suggest permanent features in the carefully constructed central open environment. As noted, these findings are consistent with the traditional interpretation of this open central zone as a plaza for public activities. We hypothesize that the plaza was kept clean because of its ceremonial associations, much like central plaza areas that are usually systematically swept and kept free of refuse in traditional Andean and tropical forest communities (e.g., Urton 1984; see also Burger and Salazar-Burger 1985).

A second focus of investigation was located at the middle of the northern side of the central plaza. The excavations encountered what seem to be the remains of a badly damaged low stone and earthen staircase that provided access to the plaza along the central axis of the site. A narrow trench was laid out perpendicular to the northern retaining wall. Despite the disturbance of the area by modern farmers, we were able to identify the plaza's original packed earth floor and found evidence for the addition of the later perimetric feature. A low 10 m wide bench had been built on top of the plaza's original floor level, very similar to that uncovered in the first plaza trench. The trench excavated parallel to the northern retaining wall once again showed the absence of refuse or other debris either around or on the bench or floor of the central plaza, a pattern consistent with a commitment to ritual cleanliness. The identification of a low bench of the same width in both the northern and western excavation areas is probably not coincidental. This suggests that a low bench probably framed the entire plaza during its final period of use. Judging from the stratigraphy, this bench was not part of the original site design.

The western lateral staircase seems to be have been established at the initial construction of the public architecture and, although it was renovated to provide access to the late elevated bench level, this did not modify the original layout in a significant way. The identification of axial and lateral stairways to the elevated central plaza suggests the presence of an east–west axis as well as the previously defined north–south processional axis of the site (Burger and Salazar-Burger 1991). The east–west axis indicates that there is a functional relationship between the central plaza space and the ritual environments on the summits of the lateral arms of the U. We will return to this point later.

Main Mound

In 1987, our excavations at Cardal focused on the main mound at the apex of the U-shaped layout. These revealed a series of superimposed atria set into the summit of the mound that were accessed using a broad, steep central staircase. The interior atrium environment could not have been seen from the central plaza, but the activities on the staircase and decorated landing would have been highly visible (Burger and Salazar-Burger 1992). In fact, these spaces can be considered elevated stages designed to be seen by those standing in the plaza space below (Figure 4.5). In contrast, the lack of visibility of the ceremonies carried out within the atrium for those standing in the central plaza suggested a degree of exclusivity. This pattern of ritual exclusivity on the main mound was reinforced by our excavations of a free-standing building partially uncovered in 1987 on the eastern extreme of the main mound (L. C. Salazar 2009, figs. 5, 6). Built on a low summit platform with an inset staircase on its eastern end (L. C. Salazar 2009, fig. 4), the multiroom complex included a set of matching dual altars constructed in two of the interior rooms (L. C. Salazar 2009,

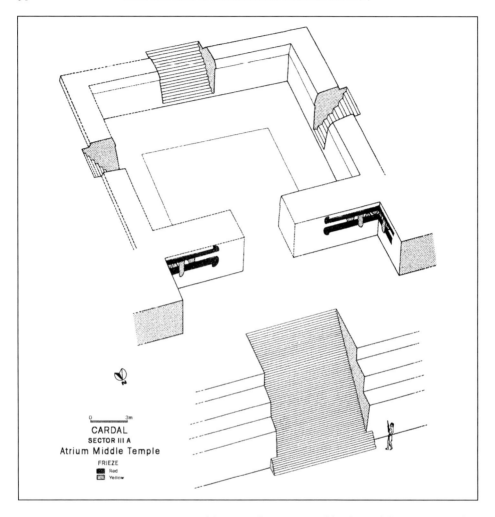

0 3m

CARDAL
SECTOR III A
Atrium Middle Temple
FRIEZE
Red
Yellow

FIGURE 4.5. Isometric reconstruction of the central staircase and landing of the main mound at Cardal. Drawing by Bernadino Ojeda.

fig. 7). These altars would not have been visible from outside the complex. They showed evidence of marine offerings and graffiti with religious themes (L. C. Salazar 2009).

In 2008 we continued our excavations of this ritual complex with additional excavations to the north and west. We found that, although access to the rooms housing the dual altars was restricted, another stepped altar had been erected along the outer face of the building above the central plaza (Figure 4.6). Rituals carried out at this outer altar would have been seen by those in the plaza area below. This outer altar was apparently considered to be essential to the functioning of the summit building, because when the outside altar was covered with fill during the expansion of the building, a similar stepped altar was reproduced along the new outer building wall facing the central plaza. These new finds indicate that the summit building with the dual altars had an important ceremonial function related to the public gathered in the central plaza, as well as for those involved in the more exclusive ceremonies carried out within the summit building's inner rooms. As

Figure 4.6. Altars on the summit of the main mound facing the central plaza at Cardal.

noted, this dual aspect was also present for the atrium area of the main mound with its re-stricted inner sanctum and complementary stage-like central staircase and outer landing

A second focus of our 2008 work at Cardal's main mound was to determine whether there was a rear staircase, similar to the one we had identified at Mina Perdida, that would have provided access to the mound summit without using the steep central staircase. To our surprise, we only found evidence of a short staircase to the east of the site's north–south axis (Figure 4.7). Our interpretation of this short block staircase is that access to the Cardal summit from the rear was by way of a series of small staircases connecting the rear terrace levels located at different points along the back of the pyramid rather than a single staircase running along the site's axis. This architectural pattern at Cardal would have given access to the summit to the occupants living in the residences behind the temple mound, but the connection was de-emphasized by the use of relatively inconspicuous block staircases rather than a visually more impressive linear staircase analogous to the one on the north of the main mound connecting the central plaza to the landing of the summit atrium.

The Lateral Arms

Almost forty years ago, at an earlier International Congress of Americanists, William Is-bell (1976) suggested that the lateral platforms or "arms" (*brazos*) of U-shaped centers such as Garagay expressed the principle of dynamic dualism, a belief central to the cosmology and social organization of its creators (see also Burger and Salazar-Burger 1994). If we ex-tend the logic of this hypothesis further, the lateral arms can be interpreted to correspond to opposing but complementary forces, and perhaps relate to the actual division of the community into two moieties (known in later times as *hanan* and *hurin*). Our decision to investigate the summits of Cardal's right and left arms in 2008 reflected our interest in

FIGURE 4.7. Superimposed block staircases behind the main mound.

testing the dualism hypothesis, as well as getting a better idea of the kind of buildings that had been built on these massive terraced platforms and of the activities that were carried out there.

At all U-shaped Manchay culture centers on the Central Coast, the lateral arms of the complex have differing heights, lengths, and form. In the case of Cardal, the right or eastern arm is longer and more massive. It consists of multiple platform levels, the highest

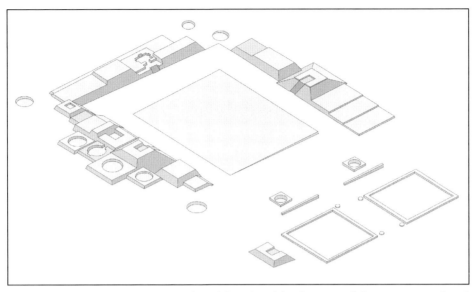

FIGURE 4.8. Isometric representation of Cardal produced for the Museo de la Nación, Lima, based on the 1985 and 1987 excavations. Redrawn by Jacob Welch from a drawing by Carlos Williams.

of which is at the mound's midpoint. In contrast, the left or western arm is significantly shorter, with the highest of the three platform levels at its southern extreme. Notably, however, the highest platform on the left arm is located directly across from the summit on the right arm, suggesting an overall logic in the planning of the complex.

In hypothetical reconstructions of generic U-shaped centers, Williams (1985) depicts free-standing buildings on the summit of the lateral arms that were accessed by way of staircases from the area surrounding the central rectangular plaza. From his visits to Cardal and the results of our excavations there in 1985 and 1987, Williams prepared an isometric drawing of the site for the 1989 opening of the Museo de la Nación in Lima (Figure 4.8). In this hypothetical reconstruction Williams posited a series of inset environments rather than free-standing summit rooms. These central summit chambers were shown opening toward and linked to the central plaza. In many respects they resembled the atrium and central staircase elements on the main mound.

Our work in 2008 on the highest section of Cardal's eastern lateral mound unearthed a steep staircase that rises from the plaza area to the summit of the platform mound, albeit with the use of one or more landings at intermediate points (Figure 4.9). The building on the top of the mound, however, was not inset, but instead was erected on a terraced platform. It was more elaborate than expected. The building entrance made use of engaged painted circular columns and the northern outer walls were decorated with monochrome low relief clay friezes showing repeating wave motifs (Figure 4.10). The interior of the large summit room itself was left clean, but there was evidence of the repeated renovation of floors, often with small subfloor offerings of shellfish. Unlike the constructions on the summit of the main mound, the building on the right arm apparently had a roof that was supported by wooden posts set into the walls; only the holes for these posts were recovered. Adjacent to this large building was a pit of "ceremonial trash" filled with discarded ritual paraphernalia and the head of a decapitated child (Burger and Salazar 2014).

FIGURE 4.9. Central staircase leading up to the summit building on the right (eastern) arm of the complex at Cardal (Sector IIA).

On the other side of the central plaza, our work on the highest platform of Cardal's western lateral mound likewise encountered a steep staircase apparently leading up from the central plaza to a rectangular building on the summit. The entrance to the summit structure lacked the ornamental columns of the right arm, but like the room on the other mound the interior floor of the room had been left free of refuse. This structure on the top of the platform mound was painted red and decorated on its northern outer wall with a polychrome clay frieze. Although badly damaged, the design on the outer wall consisted of a band of repeating canine teeth or fangs shown in relief (Figure 4.11).

As already noted, the summit rooms and their respective staircases are located directly across from each other on opposite sides of the plaza (see Figure 4.2). Although the two buildings seem comparable in function and design, several intentional contrasts can be highlighted: the red color of the outer walls on the western mound and the light monochrome color on the east; the lack of columns on the west compared to the presence of engaged columns on the east; and the use of a frieze with repeating fangs on the west rather than the wave motifs on the east. Finally, on the western lateral arm, access to the adjacent lower middle platform to the north was by way of an abutting staircase running parallel to the outer wall, rather than the more typical perpendicular stairway used on the eastern lateral mound (Figure 4.12). When these contrasting features are considered together, along with the sharp differences in the size and form of the two lateral mounds, it seems reasonable to conclude that there was a desire to intentionally distinguish the architecture on the two lateral mounds from each other, both in terms of construction detail and iconographic symbols. We interpret this patterning as evidence consistent with

Figure 4.10. Monochrome frieze of repeating wave motifs decorating the exterior of the summit building on the right (eastern) arm of the complex at Cardal (Sector IIA).

FIGURE 4.11. Polychrome frieze of fangs from a disembodied mouth decorating the exterior of the summit building on the left (western) arm of the complex at Cardal (Sector VIA).

the long-standing hypothesis that the mounds embody the dual principle that governed the social and religious organization of the U-shaped centers during the Initial Period.

Sunken Circular Plazas

In our 1985 work at Cardal we tentatively identified ten sunken circular plazas ranging from 8 to 14 m in diameter. Seven of these are arrayed along the outer edges of the site's three platform mounds. On the basis of our excavations, we suggested that these public spaces were used for ceremonies by small social groups such as sodalities or lineages (Burger and Salazar 2009). These smaller social units, along with the dual or moiety divisions, were posited as constituting the building blocks of Cardal's social organization. An analogy can be made to the presence of male ceremonial associations among the Pueblo peoples of the southwestern United States and the role that semisubterranean circular or rectangular rooms (*kivas*) play in their ceremonial life (Cordell 1997).

Our earlier investigations showed that each of the sunken circular plazas was distinctive in its details, and that the original height of the surrounding walls would have effectively isolated the activities of each of these environments from the surrounding spaces. Moreover, despite extensive excavations, no direct access between the sunken circular plazas could be found. Each is an individual and independent architectural unit. Unfortunately, the isometric reconstruction by Williams (see Figure 4.8) gives little indication of how these isolated sunken plazas would have been integrated into the rest of the site's activities.

A clue to resolving this problem was recovered in 1987 when an entrance into one of the circular courtyards was located; it faced the back of the eastern lateral arm. Addi-

Figure 4.12. Staircase connecting the upper and middle platform summit environments on the left (western) arm of the complex at Cardal (Sector VIA).

tional excavation revealed a narrow staircase leading up the back of the mound (Burger and Salazar 2009).

During the 2008 excavations, we identified the entryways of two of the other circular plazas along the edge of the eastern lateral mound (see Figure 4.2). In both cases, there was a single entrance facing the back of the mound. We hypothesize that, as in the case of the 1987 example, a series of free-standing staircases exist leading up the platform mound (i.e., the right arm), one corresponding to each of these circular plaza entryways. These stairways would have provided access between the social group carrying out its ritual activities in each circular plaza and a ceremonial environment on the summit. If this is correct, it is possible that yet undiscovered summit buildings are present that face eastward toward the circular plazas rather than westward to the central plaza. Work at another circular plaza located in the area between the main mound and west or left arm also revealed a single entryway, in this case facing the side of the main mound. We hypothesize that a staircase once linked this circular plaza with the adjacent terraced platform mound and summit structures. In future field seasons at Cardal we hope to test our hypothesis that there may have been small summit structures facing in the direction where rituals were carried out in the circular plazas.

Conclusions

We can come to several conclusions on the basis of the 2008 research at Cardal in the Lurín Valley. The investigations provide new evidence for the identification of the central area as a public plaza. The central space, the perimetric bench, and the low zone surrounding the raised plaza were all apparently left free of structures, perhaps to permit activities, such as dancing, sports competitions, banquets, or parades, that required large open spaces. The special ritual character of this large central area is attested to by the extreme cleanliness that was maintained. The perimetric bench could have been used by spectators or by people perambulating around the recessed plaza space.

The 2008 fieldwork further supports our earlier conclusion that the platform mounds were built to support buildings and other environments used for ritual activities. The overwhelming evidence of the religious character of these summit buildings on the main mounds and the lateral mounds would seem to be incontestable, judging from the architectural design, the iconographic evidence, the presence of offerings and altars, and the artifactual associations. Whereas architectural features were continually being modified through rebuilding, the fundamental function of the core complex remained the same over the four centuries of Cardal's occupation. Unlike the situation at Kuntur Wasi and Pacopampa (see Chapters 6 and 8), there is no evidence of a change in access or function that might suggest a major disruption or reorientation in the sociopolitical or cosmological foundations of Cardal.

The findings also support an interpretation of the U-shaped layout as related to a model in which the dual or moiety division of the society is expressed by the two asymmetric lateral arms of the pyramid complex, whereas the community as a whole is represented by the central mound at the apex of the U. Similarly, a material expression of the dual division of the community can be seen in the opposing sunken circular plazas that flank the main north–south axis of the site, whereas the large elevated rectangular central plaza expresses the union of these moieties as a single group with a shared identity, interests, and responsibilities.

In much of the literature on the so-called civic-ceremonial centers of the Initial Period and Early Horizon, emphasis has been put on the increasingly restricted and exclusive environments in which ceremonies were performed out of the sight of the general public. Frequently these ceremonial activities are assumed to be linked to elite religious authorities and the exclusive performances are viewed as reinforcing the power of these individuals. In these studies, exclusivity and inclusivity are seen as alternatives, two different points in the evolutionary trajectory of monumental architecture and the emergence of complex societies.

A somewhat different pattern emerges if one considers the new evidence from Cardal presented here. The built environments on the main mound do have rooms with limited access, but they also have areas intentionally designed to be visually accessible to those in the central plaza below. Moreover, in addition to the north–south axis of the site leading to the main mound, there seems to be an east–west axis marked by the staircases of the central plaza and the staircases leading up the lateral arms of the complex. As discussed previously, an important component of the ceremonial activities at Cardal revolves around the relationship of the people and activities in the central plaza with the rituals being carried out in the summit buildings on top of the lateral platform mounds. We hypothesize that these rituals on the arms of the U would address the concerns of the individual hanan and hurin moieties rather than the community as a whole. The latter would have been carried out on the summit of the central mound. Finally, additional ceremonial activity carried out at Cardal involved even smaller social groups, perhaps secret societies or lineages. The latter rituals may not have been limited to activities within the small semisubterranean circular plazas on the periphery of the public architecture, since the latter were connected by staircases to activities on the summit.

This architectural layout at Cardal suggests a dispersion of power at multiple levels of the society, all of which needed to be incorporated into the U-shaped civic-ceremonial center. Some activities were carried out on the platform summit environments of the main mound and the open plaza in full public view, to guarantee the coherence of the community as a whole, but others on the summits of the arms and the sunken circular courtyards were probably related to smaller social units such as moieties, lineages, and sodalities. In some cases, the construction of sunken circular courtyards were built on top of earlier Initial Period public structures (Burger 1987) and thus were added relatively late in Cardal's history. It would therefore be wrong to think that the heterarchical organization of power implied by this discussion was in the process of being replaced at Cardal by a more hierarchical model of elite power similar to those posited for later Andean polities. On the contrary, the complex and decentralized distribution of power at Cardal seems to have characterized the entire history of the site.

Although the secondary interment of the site's leading families in a cemetery area on the summit of the main mound suggests an effort by this group to increase their power or visibility, or both (Burger and Salazar 2009), this attempt apparently failed or, at the very least, was unable to prolong the viability of the society responsible for the site's continued occupation, renovation, and utilization. Shortly after the burial ground was placed beneath the floor of the central atrium, Cardal was abandoned and it was not reoccupied for over two millennia (Burger and Salazar 2012). These later societies were fundamentally different from the society that built Cardal and the other U-shaped complexes of the Manchay culture.

CHAPTER FIVE

The Problem with Anchucaya

Site Formation Processes at Initial Period and Early Horizon Sites in the Central Andes

Christopher Milan

From the surface, Anchucaya looks like a typical U-shaped temple that would be associated with the Manchay culture (Mesía 2000). The site, located in the middle Lurín Valley (Figure 5.1), is comprised of a series of abandoned agricultural terraces covered with ceramics from several of its occupations, beginning with the Initial Period (1800–800 BC), continuing through the Early Intermediate Period (50 BC–AD 600) and into the Late Horizon (AD 1450–1532). In the middle of the terraces is a U-shaped mound. Such U-shaped monumental architecture is one of the defining characteristics of Initial Period complex society on the Central Coast of Peru (Williams 1980; Burger and Salazar 2008), but the monumental architecture at Anchucaya is not what it seems.

In 2010 and 2011 I excavated at Anchucaya, looking for its Initial Period occupation (Milan 2012). The Initial Period occupation was not to be found in the U-shaped mound, but rather in a small corner of the site. The large mound found at the site was not an example of monumental architecture that dated to the Initial Period. On the contrary, it proved to be an informal refuse deposit that was probably produced during the Late Horizon. The appearance of what seemed to be a U-shaped temple was the result of several taphonomic processes that occurred over the course of three millennia. These same processes can be found at numerous other sites in the central Andes and may affect how we understand Initial Period hamlets.

By looking at three different contexts from Anchucaya, I will discuss not only how the site's taphonomy affected its Initial Period contexts, but also how the often overlooked hamlets reveal a more nuanced pattern of settlement than previously recognized. First, I will focus on the U-shaped mound. As noted above, the site was mistaken for a U-shaped temple by Jane Feltham, Christian Mesía, and several other archaeologists on the basis of surface observations. My excavations found that the mound was probably formed during the Late Horizon and consists of refuse from earlier occupations. In discussing the mound's design, I will highlight some of the aspects that make a U-shaped temple a distinct type of monumental architecture.

Second, I will discuss an undisturbed Initial Period context found in an area of Anchucaya that was not terraced. Terracing is common in the Andes. It is used to create farmland and a stable and level surface for residential architecture (Malpass 1986). It is

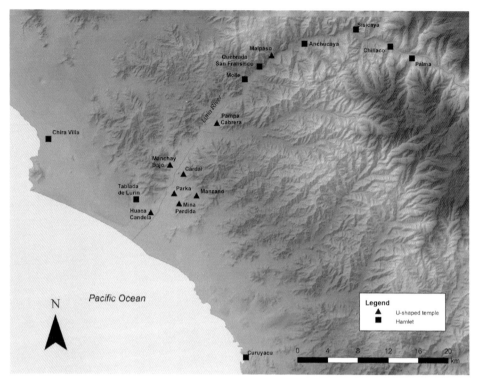

FIGURE 5.1. Map of the Lurín River Valley showing the location of Initial Period sites.

also a destructive practice that affects Initial Period and other prehistoric contexts. This is not a problem unique to Anchucaya and the site formation processes discussed here should be considered by archaeologists working in the Andean highlands and all other terraced sites.

Finally, I will discuss a possible funerary context at Anchucaya. A large quantity of human remains and decorated ceramics were found at the base of a ridge that forms the eastern boundary of the site. The material collected from this context, as well as the rest of the site, provides information on daily life in an Initial Period hamlet as well as on the relationship of the settlement to the nearby monumental U-shaped temple of Malpaso.

Site Description

Anchucaya (Figure 5.2) is situated 37 km inland in the Lurín River Valley and at 750 masl. It is on the eastern side of a dry ravine of the same name. A 2 to 3 m deep dry channel runs along the center of the ravine, and on the opposite side of this channel is a Middle Horizon (AD 600–1000) site referred to as Santa Rosa de Chontay.

The modern gated community of Sierra Morena completely surrounds the site and consists of large country homes for wealthy *limeños* (Lima residents). A modern road within Sierra Morena runs around both Anchucaya and Santa Rosa de Chontay. Although modern construction has affected much of the Lurín Valley and damaged many sites, this

FIGURE 5.2. Aerial view of the Anchucaya site taken in 2013. Google, image © 2019 CNES/Airbus.

road avoids both Santa Rosa de Chontay and Anchucaya and the two sites have suffered little harm as a result of recent construction.

Anchucaya was first identified in 1966 during Thomas Patterson's survey of the Lurín Valley; it was registered as PV48-117. The short account of the site (Patterson, Mc-Carthy, and Dunn 1982) describes it as having an early and a late occupation. Feltham (1983) revisited the site as part of her own survey of Lurín's middle valley area. She discussed the site in greater detail and identified a U-shaped mound that she believed was similar to U-shaped temples in the lower valley. She also claimed that there was evidence for a Lima culture occupation on the ridge to the east of the site.

When Sierra Morena was founded in 1996, Cecilia Jaime Tello and Jorge Silva excavated several test pits to identify the extent of the site for the Instituto Nacional de Cultura. Small pits were placed on the perceived margins of the site. Silva found one sherd from a neckless olla with a comma rim, confirming that the site had an Initial Period or Early Horizon occupation (Silva Sifuentes and Jaime Tello 2000).

The site can be divided into four sectors (Figure 5.3). The first (Sector A) consists of a series of abandoned agricultural terraces that extend from the eastern ridge of the site to the modern road. The terraces average approximately a half a meter in height. They are littered with ceramics from all of Anchucaya's occupations. As noted, the U-shaped mound is located in the middle of the agricultural terraces. It is a small mound, no higher than 2.5 m, and with an area of less than 0.75 ha. On top of the mound there are traces of architecture, including wall foundations. Just south of the U-shaped mound there is a stone-lined sunken quadrangular plaza. On the basis of this architecture, it is likely this plaza dates to the Late Horizon.

Mesía (2000) was the first person to identify the mound as a U-shaped temple associated with the Manchay culture. Feltham had claimed that the material she found on top of the U-shaped mound indicated that it dated to the Initial Period or Early Horizon (Feltham

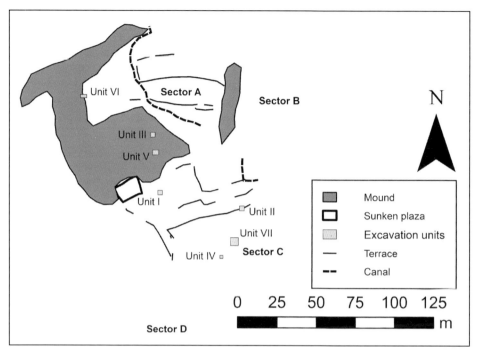

FIGURE 5.3. Excavation units at the Anchucaya site.

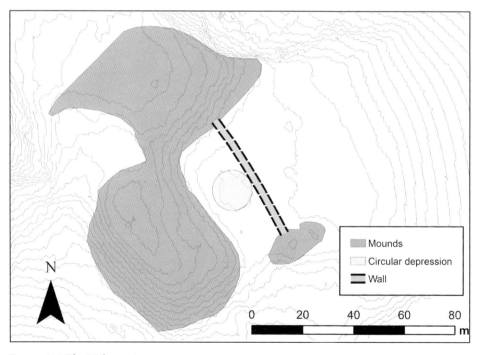

FIGURE 5.4. The Malpaso site.

2010). Because of the layout of the site, Mesía thought it was comparable to other U-shaped temples, and was especially similar to the mid-valley site of Malpaso (Figure 5.4).

To the east of the agriculture terraces and just outside of the ravine there is a narrow mound less than 2 m wide. This mound (Sector B; see Figure 5.3) is different from the U-shaped mound not only in shape, but in construction. It was made using stone and mortar. The construction of the U-shaped mound, which is made of an unconsolidated loose fill, will be discussed in greater detail below. There are several Late Horizon structures to the east of the mound in Sector B.

A natural terrace (Sector C; see Figure 5.3) overlooks the agricultural terraces. The Late Horizon constructions found on this terrace include walls, the foundations of structures, and several multistory buildings. The Late Horizon occupation extends deep into the ravine. On the side of the eastern ridge there are traces of small-scale constructions. Residential terraces on the sides of ridges are fairly common in the middle Lurín Valley, and these may date to the Early Intermediate Period (Milan 2014). Sector D (see Figure 5.3) is a continuation of Sector C farther into the ravine.

Seven excavation units were placed at Anchucaya in 2010 and 2011. Units I, II, and VI were put in the agricultural terraces in Sector A; Unit I was located just 10 m to the south of the U-shaped mound. Unit II was excavated near the eastern ridge and Unit VI was situated in the putative plaza of the U-shaped mound. Units III and V were on the left arm of the U-shaped mound. Units IV and VII were on the natural terrace in Sector C. Unit IV was located in an open area near a Late Horizon wall and Unit VII was placed close to the ridge (see Figure 5.3).

Evaluating the U-shaped Temple Hypothesis

U-shaped temples are a defining characteristic of the Initial Period occupation of the Central Coast of Peru. Many Initial Period and Early Horizon (800–200 BC) monumental sites have U-shaped layouts; however, the term U-shaped temple is used to identify a very specific type of monumental architecture (see for example Burger 1992; Dillehay 2004; Shibata 2008:290; Matsumoto 2010). Discussing U-shaped temples on the Central Coast invokes a specific architectural tradition that represents the exclusive form of monumental architecture in the Chancay, Chillón, Rimac, and Lurín Valleys that is a characteristic of the Manchay culture (Burger and Salazar 2008).

The site of Malpaso provides a good example of the characteristics of a U-shaped temple (see Figure 5.4). Malpaso is located 31 km inland in the middle Lurín Valley, which makes it Anchucaya's nearest neighbor. The two sites, however, are located on opposite sides of the river. Both are situated in the *chaupiyunga,* an arid and narrow climatic zone that serves as a transition from the Pacific coast to the Andean highlands (Fonseca 1972).

The first thing to note about the U-shaped temple at Malpaso is that it has three distinct features: a main mound, a right arm, and a left arm. The layout of these three mounds gives the temple its eponymous shape. The left arm is connected to the main mound (it is common for one arm to connect to the main mound of a U-shaped temple). The temples of Garagay and Manchay Bajo also have left arms connected to the main mound. By contrast, at Cardal and Mina Perdida the right arm is connected to the main mound (see Williams 1980). The one possible exception is Huaca La Florida, where neither arm seems to be connected to the main mound (Patterson 1985).

At Malpaso, the left arm is not only connected to the main mound, but it is also larger than the right arm. At nearly every U-shaped temple one arm is larger than the other, representing the asymmetrical dualism of Andean society (Burger and Salazar-Burger 1994; L. C. Salazar 2009). Excavations on the left arm have uncovered several structures (Milan 2012). The right arm is significantly smaller and is poorly conserved, but according to work at other U-shaped temples, it is likely there were structures there as well (see Chapter 4).

Excavations at multiple U-shaped temples showed signs of constant use and renovation (Burger and Salazar 2008, 2012; Fuentes 2009). The central staircase on the main mound of Mina Perdida was renovated six times (Burger and Salazar-Burger 1998) and at every U-shaped temple excavated there are signs of constant construction (Burger and Salazar 2012). At Malpaso there are indications of three major construction phases on the left arm, with several minor renovations also evident (Milan 2014).

The space between the mounds is the central plaza. Richard Burger and Lucy Salazar discuss the importance of the central plaza and its use at Cardal (see Chapter 4). Briefly, the plaza area is not simply the space between the mounds. Like the mounds, it is a constructed space (Williams 1980; Carrión 1998). Malpaso was built on the alluvial fan of a ravine. Before the construction of the three mounds, the plaza had to be created by leveling the surface.

Malpaso and Cardal are two of the eight U-shaped temples located in the Lurín Valley. The characteristics that define a U-shaped temple have been well documented by research at these two sites as well as at other sites on the Central Coast. When compared to these two sites, Anchucaya's U-shaped mound is an anomaly. Although this mound has a clear U-shaped layout, its similarities to a U-shaped temple end there. It does not conform to the architectural tradition seen at other Central Coast sites. The layout and construction of the mound indicate that it was more likely a Late Horizon structure associated with the terracing of the site.

Anchucaya's U-shaped Feature

As discussed, several components define the U-shaped temple. The layout of three mounds is a key feature. Whereas at every U-shaped temple there are three distinct constructions, Anchucaya is one single mound. The three sections of this mound consist of two "arms" connected by a center section. However, the center section and the left arm are thin and poorly defined. By contrast, the right arm is extremely wide. It is nearly as wide as it is long and has an area that is greater than the left arm, center section, and plaza combined. No other U-shaped complex has any configuration resembling the one at Anchucaya.

The orientation of the two arms also conflicts with the conventional layout for Manchay centers. At every U-shaped temple there is a central axis that runs parallel with the two arms, bisecting the central staircase on the main mound (see Chapter 4). At Anchucaya, the left arm curves to the southwest, changing the axis of the temple. The notion of an axis is important, because it represents an orientation of the ceremonial space (Lathrap 1985). The lack of a central axis at Anchucaya is another testament to the unconventional layout of the site's putative U-shaped mound.

Finally, the plaza at Anchucaya has an abnormal shape for a U-shaped temple. Aside from being significantly smaller than the right arm of the mound, the plaza is not a clearly delimited space. Inside the plaza there are at least two agricultural terraces as well as a terrace that runs between the two arms within the plaza. Moreover, excavations in Unit VI did not find any signs of a plaza floor. The topmost layer consists of agricultural soil superimposed above sterile soil. Unit VI also traversed the center section of the main mound. Significantly, excavations failed to reveal a central staircase.

Even more problematic than the layout of the putative U-shaped mound is its construction fill. Units III and V, placed on the left arm of the mound, reveal several abnormalities in the construction technology of the mound. Unit V was placed near a wall in the hopes of finding signs of structures on the mound. Excavations failed to find a floor or any construction associated with the wall. Likewise, excavations at Unit III did not find any structures that could have been used for ritual practices.

Both units uncovered only a single layer of fill. This is unusual because every U-shaped temple excavated has yielded evidence of multiple construction and remodeling events. The single layer indicates that the mound was built all at once and never remodeled or expanded. The layer of fill is also built directly on top of sterile soil. This would seem to indicate that the mound's construction was associated with the terracing of Anchucaya. The fill itself was made up of refuse. The soil was brown and ashy, containing several cracked and burned stone grinders. A large quantity of broken seashell, primarily crayfish (family Astacidae) and *Mesodesma donacium,* was also recovered from the fill. The ceramics in the construction fill were largely nondiagnostic sherds from bowls and neckless ollas, and many were burned. Most were made from a reddish brown paste tempered with mica or sand. A few sherds were made from a light reddish brown to light red paste tempered with sand. In our investigations of the middle Lurín Valley, this paste is associated with ceramics made during the area's later occupations. One light red sherd from the fill was painted black and white, a design associated with the Lima culture.

The mixture of material is atypical of the constructive fills found in U-shaped temples. At Cardal and Mina Perdida, Burger and Salazar (2012, fig. 14.7) found clean fills constructed of reed bags containing dirt and rock. At Malpaso constructive fills were made from dirt, rock, and broken ceramics, but burned wares and discarded food remains were not part of the fill. Most importantly, constructive fills at U-shaped temples do not include materials from later occupations.

Although the mound at Anchucaya does have a layout that can be described as U-shaped, it is not a temple associated with the Manchay culture. U-shaped temples are made from three distinct components, each a separate construction. While one of the arms can be connected to the main mound, it has its own structure with terraces, a staircase, and rooms for rituals. Burger and Salazar-Burger (1994; see Chapter 4) have argued that the two arms represent the division of society into two, in a form of asymmetrical dualism. The main mound then is represented as the union of these two groups by bringing the two arms together.

A central axis gives a form to the structures and organizes the ritual space (Lathrap 1985). In the Lurín Valley, most U-shaped temples are oriented to the northeast, facing the source of the Lurín River. Burger (2009a) has argued that this is associated with the importance of water and irrigation to agriculture. Anchucaya faces the right direction, but it lacks a central axis, and is thus not organized to be a ritual space.

A third important aspect of the U-shaped temple is the plaza area itself. Although rituals would have been performed on top of the mounds, the plazas represented a public space where people from different settlements could come together for ceremonies. In general, the plazas at U-shaped temples are very large. At Mina Perdida the open plaza zone

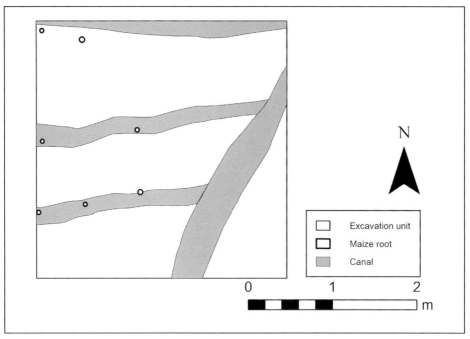

FIGURE 5.5. Profile of Unit II, layer A at the Anchucaya site.

has an area of nearly 10 ha. Even at smaller temples, such as Malpaso or Pucara, the plaza is a delineated space where people can congregate during ceremonies and feasts (Silva and Jaime Tello 2000). At Anchucaya, the putative plaza area is small and does not seem to have been designed for the same set of activities carried out in these spaces at other centers.

In comparing Anchucaya to Malpaso it becomes clear that the former lacks the careful planning seen at the latter. Despite all the variability available within the U-shaped temple architectural tradition (Burger and Salazar 2008), there is a general plan on how such a complex was constructed and maintained. These centers were built as clearly delineated sacred spaces. By contrast Anchucaya's mound is the result of a single construction made from refuse and was not designed for ritual use. Therefore, Anchucaya was not a U-shaped temple.

Initial Period hamlets are not easy to identify from the surface. Monumental sites are much easier to find than small residential sites. In the following section I will show that this problem is especially precarious for Initial Period and Early Horizon sites. Unfortunately, the difficulty in finding residential sites has limited our knowledge of these periods of time.

The Consequences of Terracing

With the exception of Unit II, discussed below, the agricultural terraces associated with the U-shaped mound did not reveal any Initial Period contexts. This is not wholly unexpected. Terracing is a destructive act in which a series of flat surfaces are created on a slope either by digging into the slope or by building long platforms on the slope to provide a

FIGURE 5.6. Painted sherds associated with Unit I, layer A, at the Anchucaya site.

stable and level surface (Sandor 1992; Krahtopoulou and Frederick 2008). Terracing is a common practice in the central Andes and has been documented in several regions (De la Vera Cruz Chávez 1987; Parsons, Hastings, and Matos 2000; Zaro 2007). Large parts of the middle Lurín Valley are terraced and at several sites the terraces are a series of platforms used for residential architecture (Milan 2014).

In the case of Anchucaya, I concluded that the terraces were used for maize (*Zea mays*) agriculture. Units I, II, and VI all show signs of maize agriculture. Just below the surface in each unit, maize roots are found near small abandoned irrigation canals that run in parallel rows (Figure 5.5). The agricultural layer is shallow, never thicker than 0.25 m. Few ceramics are found associated with this layer, but they include pottery from the site's Late Horizon occupation, including strap handles for large vessels and reddish brown sherds decorated with white paint (Figure 5.6). In Units I and VI, the agricultural layer occurs directly on top of sterile soil. This indicates that the terraces were created by digging into the ravine.

Irrigation canals are essential to agriculture in the middle Lurín Valley (Fonseca Martel 1972; Burger 2009a). The water source for Anchucaya is an irrigation canal that begins 1.7 km up valley from the site and runs along the southern margin of the valley. The canal would have directly supplied water to the maize plants found in Unit II. At Unit VI, a canal ran around the U-shaped mound. This is another indication of the link between the U-shaped mound and the terracing of the site.

The creation of the U-shaped mound and its terraces had taphonomic consequences. Any Initial Period contexts located in this part of the site would have been destroyed (Sandor 1992). The evidence from Anchucaya raises the question of to what extent. How many small residential sites have been destroyed by terracing?

TABLE 5.1. Radiocarbon measurements from the Middle Lurín Valley. All accelerator mass spectrometer measurements were taken on carbonized plant remains by DirectAMS Radiocarbon Dating Services, Seattle, Washington, USA.

Lab code	Radiocarbon sample ID	Site	Sample context	Age (uncal BP)	Calibrated date (1-σ range BC)
D-AMS 001928	PAVMEL-1-RBo11	Malpaso	Upper layer of shell midden	3164 ± 27	1493–1313
D-AMS 001929	PAVMEL-1-RBo12	Malpaso	Middle layer of shell midden	3295 ± 21	1608–1437
D-AMS 001930	PAVMEL-1-RBo14	Malpaso	Bottom of shell midden	3343 ± 33	1679–1459
D-AMS 001931	PAVMEL-1-RBo16	Malpaso	Below Unit I, floor 2	3180 ± 27	1446–1271
D-AMS 001932	PAVMEL-1-RBo17	Malpaso	Below Unit I, floor 4	3216 ± 29	1506–1321
D-AMS 002464	PAVMEL-1-RBo60	Malpaso	Unit IV, layer G, below floor 2	3215 ± 30	1510–1321
D-AMS 002465	PAVMEL-1-RBo69	Malpaso	Unit IV, layer I	3162 ± 30	1451–1269
D-AMS 001934	PAVMEL-2-RBo9	Anchucaya	Unit IV, layer C	3172 ± 31	1493–1294
D-AMS 001933	PAVMEL-2-RBo14	Anchucaya	Unit IV, layer D	3280 ± 30	1608–1422
D-AMS 001935	PAVMEL-5-RBo8	Chillaco	Unit VII, layer B	2737 ± 30	904–798

Above It All

Unit IV is located on the natural terrace 2 m above the topmost agricultural terrace. It was placed to the north of the remnant of a wall in an open area on the terrace. The Late Horizon occupation on this natural terrace preserved Initial Period contexts. The two topmost strata in this unit contained a mixture of material from the site's Late Horizon and Initial Period occupations. The third and fourth layers were dark brown and ashy and contained material that exclusively dated to the Initial Period.

The ceramics recovered from the two Initial Period layers were primarily undecorated neckless ollas and bowls. Many of the sherds were burned. The most common type of neckless olla recovered was an olla with a comma-shaped rim (Figure 5.7). Bowl forms varied greatly. Ceramics were made from pastes that were tempered with either sand or mica. Mica temper was found in more than 50% of the ceramics at Anchucaya. The assemblage from Anchucaya resembled material from Malpaso's Rio phase (1600–1300 BC). At both sites comma rims make up over 50% of the olla assemblage and mica is found in the temper of the majority of the sherds present.

The similarities in the ceramics of Anchucaya and Malpaso are supported by two radiocarbon dates (Table 5.1). Carbon samples were collected from both of the Initial

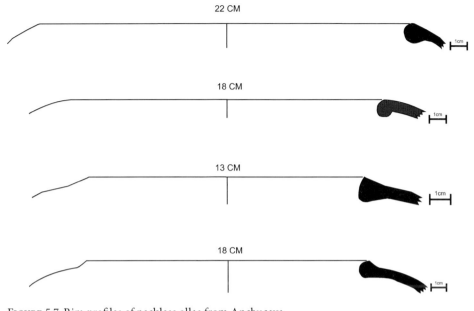

22 CM

18 CM

13 CM

18 CM

FIGURE 5.7. Rim profiles of neckless ollas from Anchucaya.

Period layers. The lower of the two layers was dated to between 1608 and 1422 cal BC. The second Initial Period layer dated to between 1451 and 1269 cal BC. Both dates indicate that the earliest occupation for Anchucaya was contemporaneous with the early occupation of Malpaso (Milan 2014).

Initial Period Conservation

Regardless of where it occurs, terracing is a destructive process. Layers of soil are removed to create a series of flat surfaces on a slope (Krahtopoulou and Frederick 2008). The soil removed invariably contains material from a site's earlier occupation. Although there have been several archaeological studies on the effects of terrace agriculture, no one has really looked at the practice's destructive effect on earlier occupations (Malpass 1986; De la Vera Cruz Chávez 1987; Sandor 1992).

Anchucaya is an example of the problems that Late Horizon terracing can produce for archaeological research. The two contexts discussed here illustrate the effects of terracing on Initial Period sites in the Andean highlands. In the lower part of Anchucaya, terracing completely destroyed earlier cultural contexts. The new agricultural layer was formed on top of sterile soil. In the uppermost agricultural terrace, in Unit II, some Initial Period contexts are disturbed, but a few others are conserved. Only Initial Period contexts in Unit IV, above the agricultural terraces, are protected. This type of horizontal patterning suggests that if an earlier occupation is conserved at a terraced site, then archaeologists would do well to concentrate their efforts on the upper sector (Figure 5.8).

The preservation of an undisturbed Initial Period occupation at Anchucaya sheds light on another issue of site conservation in the Andean highlands. A survey of the middle Lurín Valley found few sites with Initial Period material, and most of these sites

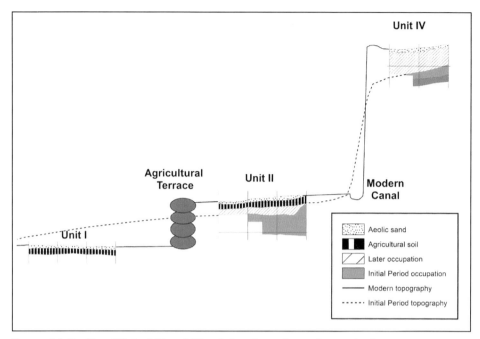

FIGURE 5.8. Profiles of Units I, II, and IV and the effects of terracing on Anchucaya.

also had signs of later occupations. At Anchucaya, Initial Period artifactual material was found on the agricultural terraces where intact Initial Period contexts had been destroyed. Significantly, no Initial Period material was found on the surface of the natural terrace where undisturbed Initial Period contexts were found. This suggests that a larger number of early sites exist than recorded in surveys, but which are buried underneath later occupations that render them invisible to standard surface reconnaissance (Parsons, Hastings, and Matos 2000).

An Initial Period Cemetery

Unit II is on the uppermost agricultural terrace near the ridge that forms the eastern boundary of the ravine where Anchucaya is located. A test pit was placed on the uppermost agricultural terrace to see whether the zone had any Initial Period contexts. As noted, excavations in the lower terraces found soils associated with maize agriculture followed by sterile soil. The topmost layer excavated in Unit II had evidence of four parallel irrigation canals with maize roots. The layer below this seemed to be the foundation of a circular structure. The soil along the western and northern edges of the unit was compact and gray with few artifacts. The yellowish brown soil in the rest of the unit contained a mixture of artifacts from the Initial Period as well as some that may have come from a later occupation. The material from the next layer, layer C, consisted of a loose rocky matrix that was filled with human remains. The other material mixed in this layer included quartz crystals and decorated ceramics that date to the Initial Period. Below this was the final layer, above sterile subsoil.

There are three possible ways that layer C could have been formed. The first is that it was created to raise the height of the terrace. A second possibility is that there was an Initial Period cemetery there and a rockslide disturbed the context. A third is that an Initial Period cemetery was originally located on part of the eastern ridge and the rockslide redeposited the material on the ravine floor.

If layer C had been a construction fill, it would have been found only on the uppermost agricultural terrace. However, excavations on the natural terrace above Unit II revealed a similar layer. Unit VII was located on the natural terrace and relatively close to the eastern ridge, whereas Unit IV was located farther to the west. Unit VII contained a layer of loose rock mixed with archaeological material, Unit IV did not. The presence of similar rocky soil near the same ridge on top of a natural terrace indicates that layer C was not a construction fill, but the result of a rockslide.

In the second scenario, the graveyard was located at the site and the rockslide forcefully deposited a layer of rock and dirt that disturbed the funerary contexts. Although layer C is directly on top of sterile soil, artifacts associated with funerary contexts (human bone, ceramics, quartz crystals) were found throughout the layer. If the rockslide had disrupted a cemetery, then one would expect the human remains to be concentrated near the lower part of the layer. This was not the case. Bones were evenly distributed throughout the layer.

This suggests that the undisturbed funerary contexts were originally located on the nearby ridge. Aside from the problems with the other two hypotheses, the concentration of archaeological material would also suggest that the cemetery was located on the ridge. A later excursion up the ridge found material suggesting that there had been an archaeological site above Anchucaya. In other parts of the middle Lurín Valley disturbed funerary contexts (disarticulated and fragmentary human remains) are regularly found on hillsides, and burying the deceased on hillsides seems to have been a long tradition.

The material recovered from layer C consisted of human remains, broken and disarticulated bones, ceramics that date to the Initial Period, and quartz crystals. None of the material seemed to come from one of the site's later occupations. Unlike the layer above, there were no diagnostically late ceramic fragments such as strap handles, vessels decorated with paint, or ceramics made with light red pastes.

The human remains recovered from layer C at Anchucaya represent a minimum of nine individuals. There was at least one infant, two children, one adolescent between the ages of 13 and 18, and five adults. These numbers roughly correspond to the demographics of other early agricultural Andean communities, where infant and child mortality was relatively common (Benfer 1990; Vradenberg 2009). Because of the fragmentary nature of the human remains, it is not possible to gather more information about the health and mortality of the population at Anchucaya.

The ceramics from this layer are similar to those found in Unit IV. The majority of the fragments came from undecorated neckless ollas and bowls, and the most common vessel form is the neckless olla with a comma-shaped rim. Bowl forms varied. The tempers used to make pastes primarily consists of sand or mica, a pattern that once again is similar to the Rio Phase assemblage from Malpaso.

Most of the decorated Initial Period sherds recovered from Anchucaya came from this context. Decorative styles differed slightly at Anchucaya and Malpaso. At Malpaso ceramics were adorned with a variety of techniques, including incisions, zoned punctuation, and rocker stamping. At Anchucaya the majority of decorated sherds are decorated

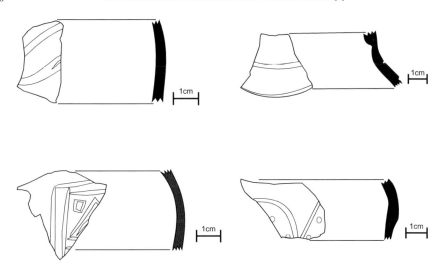

FIGURE 5.9. Decorated sherds from Anchucaya.

with incisions (Figure 5.9), some forming simple geometric designs. There are only three instances of zoned punctation at Anchucaya. Although this is rare at Anchucaya, it is common at Malpaso throughout its occupation. Other decorative techniques found at the U-shaped temple, such as rocker stamping, were not found at the hamlet.

An abundance of quartz crystals was recovered from layer C. Quartz crystals are associated with ritual practices during the Initial Period; crystals have been recovered from ritual sites, including Kotosh, Chavin de Huántar, and Huaricoto (Burger 1992). Quartz crystals were also found on the left arm of Malpaso. However, the association of quartz crystals with human remains is unusual for the Lurín Valley. Graves found at Cardal did not have quartz crystals associated with them (Burger and Salazar-Burger 1991). The ritual practices at Anchucaya could be distinct from those at Malpaso.

Life in Anchucaya

On the basis of these three contexts, it is possible to reach some basic conclusions about Anchucaya's Initial Period occupation. First of all, it was a small hamlet without monumental architecture. The hamlet was likely occupied for several centuries, perhaps between 1550 and 1300 BC. The people that lived there most likely buried their dead on the nearby ridge.

Beyond understanding the nature of Anchucaya's occupation, the artifacts collected from the site show where the settlement fits into the larger Initial Period occupation of the Lurín Valley. It is very similar to what is found at the U-shaped temple of Malpaso. This is not especially surprising given that Malpaso is not only the closest temple to Anchucaya, but it is the closest Initial Period site in general. Both settlements produced and decorated their ceramics in similar ways. At the very least there was regular contact between the two settlements and this is reflected in a similar material culture.

Despite a close relationship with Malpaso, evidence for local ritual practices at Anchucaya shows that it was not a completely subordinate settlement. It was an autonomous community. Although similar, the ceramic assemblages from the two sites have their differences. In particular, the designs found on ceramics at Anchucaya represent a local production of decorated wares.

The practice of funerary rituals at the site also indicates that Anchucaya was an independent settlement. The population of Anchucaya probably went to Malpaso for religious ceremonies, but there were also localized practices. The findings from Anchucaya should raise questions about the relationships between Initial Period civic-ceremonial centers and nearby hamlets. The bulk of literature on the Initial Period focuses on monumental sites and presupposes that residential sites were simply subordinate to the nearest center (Silva 1998). Seen from the hamlet's perspective, the relationship between Anchucaya and Malpaso was complicated. Hamlets were not only defined by their affiliations to temples, judging from the material culture found at the site.

Conclusions

In this chapter I have focused on the taphonomy of Anchucaya and the challenges it presented. A cursory look at the site seemed to indicate that it was a U-shaped temple related to other such temples of the Manchay culture on the Central Coast of Peru. However, excavations showed that it was a hamlet with a relationship to the nearby U-shaped temple of Malpaso.

I focused on the taphonomic processes affecting three particular contexts to show how they affected the way archaeologists had understood Anchucaya. But Anchucaya is not a unique site. It is likely that many other Initial Period hamlets have been similarly affected by later terracing and landslides. Initial Period villages and hamlets are underrepresented in the archaeological record, because they have been hidden by later occupations and post-dispositional processes such as alluviation and landslides.

The data collected from Anchucaya suggests how research at hamlets would change the way scholars look at the emergence of complex society in the Andes. Society was not based solely on civic-ceremonial centers. There were also a number of villages and hamlets with ties to those centers. In the case of Anchucaya we can see that it had close ties to the temple of Malpaso, but should not be considered simply a subordinate settlement. Whereas ceramics from all the Initial Period sites in the middle Lurín Valley were distinct, the similarities between the assemblages show that all of the sites shared an affiliation. At the same time, ritual practices were not the exclusive domain of the temple. There is not only evidence for ritual practices at Anchucaya, but they were different from those found at Malpaso. As archaeologists look for similar villages in the Andes, a more complex relationship between centers and villages will come to light.

Acknowledgments. This chapter could not have been written without Richard Burger and Lucy Salazar, who were kind enough to invite me to participate. I would also like to thank the Whitney and Betty MacMillan Center for International and Area Studies at Yale University and the Josef Albers Traveling Fellowship for funding excavations at Anchucaya and other sites in the middle Lurín Valley. Excavations at Anchucaya could not have been done without the hard work of José Luis Fuentes, Gabriela Oré, Josue Ancalle, and Hugo and Javier Rojas. Jane Baxter, Sarah Baitzel, and Ana Cecilia Mauricio all looked at drafts of an earlier manuscript that served as the foundation for this chapter, and Ronald Faulseit gave me a forum to work out the final parts of this chapter.

CHAPTER SIX

SOCIOECONOMIC TRANSFORMATIONS AT THE CEREMONIAL CENTER OF KUNTUR WASI

Raw Materials, Craft Production, and Leadership

Kinya Inokuchi and Isabelle C. Druc

This chapter discusses several socioeconomic processes at Kuntur Wasi, a ceremonial center used during the Formative Period in the northern Peruvian Andes. Our discussion is based on the results of the petrographic (mineral) analysis of the ceramics of this center triangulated with stylistic, architectural, and other archaeological data.

Clarifying issues related to the procurement of raw materials, production, distribution, and consumption of products, as well as labor for building and maintaining the ceremonial centers, is crucial to begin to understand the socioeconomic processes of the Formative Period of the Central Andes. To this end, we can expect that the analysis of the raw materials used to produce the ceramics found at Kuntur Wasi will shed some light on these processes, considering that ceramics are abundant in all archaeological phases of this site. The ceramic data testifies to the development of Kuntur Wasi, with differences observed across archaeological phases in technological and stylistic traditions or in the way ceramics were produced. These changes are interpreted within a socioeconomic perspective to reach a broader understanding of leadership and control for this area of the Andes during this period.

The archaeological site of Kuntur Wasi is located on a hill called La Copa at 2,300 masl in the province of San Pablo, Cajamarca (Figure 6.1). The Japanese Kuntur Wasi Archaeological Project excavated at the site for twelve field seasons, from 1988 to 2002. From this research four basic phases were established: the Idolo (ID) Phase (950–800 cal BC), the Kuntur Wasi (KW) Phase (800–550 cal BC), the Copa (CP) Phase (550–250 cal BC), and the Sotera (ST) Phase (250–50 cal BC). These correspond to nine architectural subphases (ID-1, ID-2, KW-1, KW-2, CP-1, CP-2, CP-3, ST-1, and ST-2) (Onuki, Kato, and Inokuchi 1995; Onuki and Inokuchi 2011).

At the start of the Kuntur Wasi Phase a new large-scale architectural complex was built, individuals were buried in special tombs, stone monoliths were raised, and a canal system was established (Onuki, Kato, and Inokuchi 1995; Inokuchi 2008). This information, and the archaeological and stylistic data, suggest the intrusion of a group from the North Coast at the beginning of the Kuntur Wasi Phase. First, there are very few continuities of the cultural tradition of architecture and ceramic styles between the Idolo and Kuntur Wasi Phases. Major innovations in temple architecture during the Kuntur Wasi

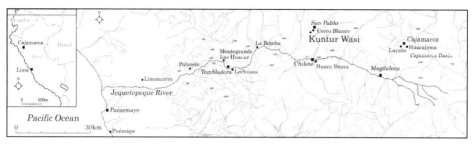

FIGURE 6.1. Jequetepeque Valley and archaeological sites in the Formative Period.

Phase are observed. A new basic temple plan was designed: an 8.7 m high three-tiered wall surrounding the principal platform, a U-shaped arrangement of platforms around the sunken plaza, and an underground canal system. None of the previous Idolo Phase constructions were reused (Inokuchi 2008). Also, ceramic characteristics changed abruptly in the Kuntur Wasi Phase, in that a new production type and similarities with the ceramic style of the North Coast appeared, while the local traditional way of producing pottery continued in parallel. In some other centers in the northern highlands, such as Huacaloma, the same ceramic tradition of the northern highlands was maintained for the same period. Second, the four special graves, which contained gold objects, were installed during the construction of the new central platform (Onuki, Kato, and Inokcuhi 1995; Onuki and Inokuchi 2011). Some of the ceramic vessels and gold artifacts of the graves display the characteristics of the cultural tradition of the North Coast of Peru, Cupisinique. We suppose that those graves were secondary burials in a ceremonial process that destroyed the previous platform, interring individuals and offerings transported from their original tombs on the North Coast, and constructing a new platform above that (Onuki, Kato, and Inokuchi 1995). Third, considering radiocarbon dates, some ceremonial centers on the coast seem to be abandoned around 800 to 700 BC, which coincides with the beginning of the Kuntur Wasi Phase (Onuki 1994; Onuki, Kato, and Inokuchi 1995).

Construction activity was intense during the Copa Phase. In addition to two major modifications of the ceremonial center, the floors were renewed several times, and new platforms, plazas, and rooms were erected (Figure 6.2). Considerable labor was needed for the construction. During the second subphase of the Copa Phase many rooms were built around the plazas. There are more space divisions, which suggests that the temple in the Copa Phase saw a multiplication of its functions, possibly linked to goods production, because both finished and unfinished artifacts were found in the ceremonial area. In particular, in the Copa Phase, excavation in the North Plaza and its surroundings revealed a concentration of clay spindle whorls and objects made from agate (a variety of chalcedony) and shell of the bivalve mollusk *Spondylus*; the latter were found mostly in the form of flakes and fragmented objects (Figure 6.3). Importantly, this area of the site did not serve only for production or as a workshop. In fact, it had many of the most important symbolic representations dating to the Copa Phase, such as three carved stone monoliths and a high relief depicting a jaguar–serpent. In this area archaeologists also found new connections to the canal system that were created for ceremonial use. The products made in this area must have been linked to the temple activity during the Copa Phase, and as such may have acquired higher value.

In addition to stones, bones, and shell artifacts, much ceramic material was found

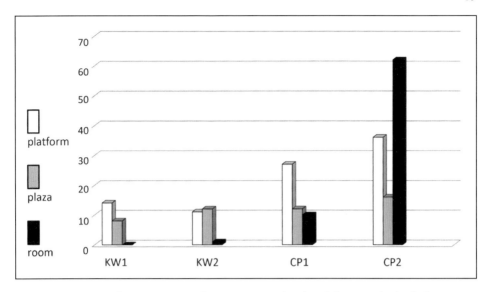

FIGURE 6.2. Degree of construction in the Kuntur Wasi (KW) and the Copa (CP) subphases.

in Kuntur Wasi. However, no evidence of ceramic workshops in the temple precinct has been discovered so far. Ceramic analysis provided interesting results that can be examined in the light of the architectural, stylistic, and socioeconomic changes observed at Kuntur Wasi, particularly during the Kuntur Wasi and Copa Phases. These results are detailed in the following sections, after a brief presentation of the corpus of study and analysis methodology.

Ceramic Data and Raw Materials: Production Issues

A program of paste analysis that included petrography, X-ray diffraction, and LA-ICP MS (laser ablation inductively coupled mass spectrometry) was initiated in 2010, with comparative samples and more archaeological ceramics added over the following years. The petrographic study, in particular, allowed us to address questions of technology, production, and provenience. The results of this study are presented after a review of the main stylistic ceramic types of each phase (the sixty-one stylistic types identified on the site are presented elsewhere; Inokuchi [2008]; see Druc, Inokuchi, and Shen [2013] for a discussion of the X-ray diffraction results and Druc, Inokuchi, and Dussubieux [2017] for the LA-ICP MS results).

The Idolo Phase ceramics are of local tradition with influences from the northern highlands such as the Cajamarca Basin (e.g., Huacaloma) and the Pacopampa area. A few rare exceptions relate to finely decorated ceramics of coastal and other influences or proveniences. In the Kuntur Wasi Phase, two broad category types were recognized: Kuntur Wasi (KW–KW) and the Sangal Complex (KW–SG). Most of KW–KW ceramics display strong coastal stylistic influences. The main stylistic types of KW–KW fine ceramics with influences from the coast are: KW–Negro Fino, KW–Rojo Fino, KW–Marrón Fino, and KW–Gris Fino, all with highly polished surfaces and very compact paste; and KW–Negro

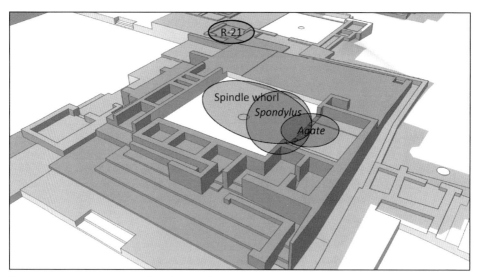

FIGURE 6.3. Concentrations of artifacts in the area surrounding the North Plaza of the Copa Phase. In the central section, excavation recovered 86 clay spindle whorls, 808 agate objects, and 134 fragments of *Spondylus* shell. Section R-21 contained 12 *Spondylus* fragments, 26 stone flakes and tools, 10 bone artifacts, and 8 clay artifacts.

Grafitado and KW–Rojo Grafitado painted with graphite. (The mineral composition of many ceramics within these groups, and in particular the grafitado ceramics, display nonlocal characteristics as well. Others imitate the style, but use local materials, which still indicates a foreign influence or a demand to supply foreign taste by local potters [Druc et al., in press].)

For stirrup-spout bottles, there are similarities in form and decoration between KW–KW ceramics and the Cupisnique ceramics of the later phase. The Sangal Complex appeared sometime during the Kuntur Wasi Phase and is distinguished by local stylistic and paste characteristics. During the following Copa Phase, ceramics are of local style with standardized forms and decorations. In the last phase, the Sotera Phase, ceramics are again influenced by the Cajamarca Basin (e.g., at the Layzón site). These stylistic influences point to broader-scale influences or relationships, which could account for the socioeconomic changes observed at Kuntur Wasi. The results of the ceramic paste analysis will be examined with this perspective in mind.

The petrographic corpus of analysis totals 110 archaeological ceramic fragments; 69 comparative samples were subjected to petrographicor X-ray diffraction, or both. A macropaste analysis of more than 330 additional fragments was also performed, looking at paste composition and texture with a digital handheld microscope. LA-ICP MS was also used to analyze the clay composition of ceramics and comparative samples (Druc, Inokuchi, and Dussubieux 2017).

The petrographic corpus consists of 19 samples from the Idolo Phase, 33 KW–KW samples from the Kuntur Wasi Phase, 11 KW–SG samples of the Kuntur Wasi Phase, 34 samples from the Copa Phase, and 13 samples from the Sotera Phase. Note that a mineral composition group does not necessarily correspond to a stylistic type, but can reflect characteristics linked to a production site, workshop, technical tradition, or ware form. As a starting point, we decided to select the samples by stylistic type. We chose more than one sample per type to acknowledge variability in decoration and shape, and we checked that the ceramics chosen would have a representative paste, determined through macroscopic analysis.

Petrographic Analysis

There are three questions that we can address using the data generated by the petrographic analysis of the Kuntur Wasi ceramics: (1) What trends can be seen in the raw materials of the ceramics found in Kuntur Wasi, and how do these trends change across archaeological phases? (2) When considering the mineral composition of the ceramic raw materials and the geological data around the site, what trends can be seen related to the presumed source areas of these materials? Most importantly, were these materials gathered locally or were they nonlocal? (3) What are the characteristics of the techniques used in the production of ceramics for each archaeological phase?

The petrographic analysis was conducted through the study of thin sections: a small section of the ceramic fragment (ideally 0.5 cm by 3 cm) is cut from its profile, glued on a glass slide, and thinned to a thickness of 30 μm. This kind of analysis is minimally destructive. The thin sections are examined with a transmitted-light microscope. As the light shines through, it is possible to identify the minerals present, as well as other paste characteristics such as texture, color, nature, shape, size and distribution of the inclusions, among others. Only inclusions larger than the clay minerals can be studied, because of the limits of the resolution of the petrographic microscope. Consequently, the information retrieved concerns the minerals and other inclusions of silt and sand-size range that characterize the materials used by the potter, as well as the technology of manufacture. This allows us to reach conclusions about technological traditions and the possible origin(s) of the raw materials, in particular the material(s) added to the clay base to make it less plastic or coarser if needed (which we call temper).

The first step of the petrographic analysis was to group the ceramic thin sections according to the mineral composition of the sand-size crystals and rock fragments present in the paste, regardless of style attribution. Within each petrogroup (compositional category) finer subdivisions can be made. One of the premises of compositional analysis is the idea that a mineral or chemical signature points to a geological area and can suggest possible proveniences or technological traditions that use specific raw materials or paste recipes.

In the sample from Kuntur Wasi, initial petrographic analysis revealed the presence of four main petrogroups with the following distinguishing characteristics: Petrogroup A (PGA) has a volcanic paste of acid composition and pumice; Petrogroup B (PGB) with intrusive rock fragments of acid to intermediate composition; Petrogroup C (PGC) with weathered tuff and volcanic material of intermediate composition; and Petrogroup D (PGD) of mix compositions. Internal variability in Petrogroup B and the discovery in 2013 of a local source with intrusive-subvolcanic lithic fragments similar to those seen in many Copa Phase ceramics in Petrogroup B led us to create a new petrogroup, Petrogroup E (PGE). This last category regroups ceramics made with a sediment rich in plagioclase and intrusive-subvolcanic lithoclasts, whereas Petrogroup B ceramics are characterized by an intrusive composition of granitic to granodioritic character. According to comparative samples and geological data, the ceramics in Petrogroup E are probably local productions,

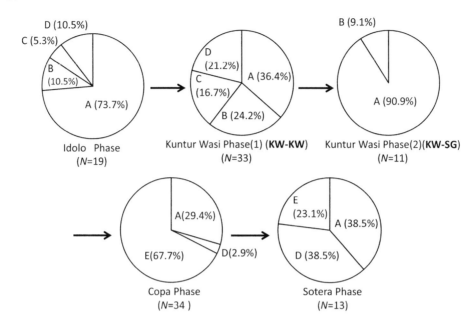

FIGURE 6.4. Frequency of Petrogroups A, B, C, D, and E by archaeological phase.

whereas ceramics in Petrogroup B are nonlocal. These provenience attributions will be discussed further below. The main local groups are Petrogroups A and E, with Petrogroup A continuing throughout all archaeological phases. Most of Petrogroup C displays compositions that are atypical or nonlocal, and Petrogroup D regroups mixed ceramics with sedimentary-volcanic material of either local or nonlocal provenience. The new group attributions modify the ware percentages per compositional groups originally presented in 2012. Also, the temper source rich in subvolcanic material less than 6 km from the archaeological site discovered in 2013 could account for the production of two-thirds of the Copa Phase ceramics.

Data Interpretation

The percentages of samples for each petrogroup reveal that almost half of the Kuntur Wasi ceramics have acid volcanic paste (Petrogroup A, 46.36%). The rest is divided into Petrogroup B (10%) with intrusive granitic to granodioritic material, Petrogroup C (6.36%) with intermediate volcanic material, Petrogroup D (13.64%) with sedimentary-volcanic inclusions, and Petrogroup E with intrusive-subvolcanic clasts and plagioclase crystals (23.64%) (Table 6.1).

   If we examine the petrogroups for each archaeological phase, several observations can be made (Figure 6.4). In the Idolo Phase most fragments have a dark to black core, noncompact, volcanic paste grouped within Petrogroup A (73.7%) with a subdivision into a large, local PGA1 (68%) group with rhyolitic characteristics (many quartz and pyroclastic fragments), and a small PGA2 group with plagioclase, quartz, and pyroclastic of possible nonlocal provenience. In the Kuntur Wasi Phase, the KW–KW ceramics display more

TABLE 6.1. Distribution by phase of ceramic fragments analyzed with petrography in petrogroup (PG) subdivisions (A–E).

		Petrogroup								
		PGA		PGB		PGC		PGD		PGE
Phase	Total sample size	n	%	n	%	n	%	n	%	n	%
Kuntur Wasi (all phases)		51	46.36	11	10	7	6.36	15	13.64	26	23.64
Idolo	N = 19	14	73.7	2	10.5	1	5.3	2	10.5	0	0
Kuntur Wasi	N = 33	12	36.4	8	24.2	6	16.7	7	21.2	0	0
Sangal Complex (Kuntur Wasi Phase)	N = 11	10	90.9	1	9.1	0	0	0	0	0	0
Copa	N = 34	10	29.4	0	0	0	0	1	2.9	23	67.7
Sotera	N = 13	5	38.5	0	0	0	0	5	38.5	3	23.1
Total all samples	N = 110										

paste varieties in relation to stylistic variability, and 24.2% show an intrusive, nonlocal composition, characteristic of Petrogroup B. Point-counting analysis of ceramic thin sections in Petrogroup B shows higher compositional variability than in other petrogroups and these results suggest multiple points of production for the ceramics in this group.

In contrast, the KW–SG ceramics present very little paste variability, and all samples but one fall within PGA1 with its characteristic volcanic composition. In the Copa Phase, the use of intrusive-subvolcanic temper (Petrogroup E) becomes the most common production strategy (67.7%), even though the tradition of using volcanic temper persisted.

Let us now examine the trend of the raw materials used in ceramic production. Because of the variation in ceramic types, some found in great quantity yet others very rare, the figures must be slightly corrected. From the frequency data of stylistic types in the Kuntur Wasi and Copa Phase layers, and according to the amount of rim fragments (Onuki, Kato, and Inokuchi 1995), we calculated petrogroup frequencies for these two phases. For this calculation, we have defined a tentative "petrogroup point" as stylistic types that have ceramics belonging to different petrogroups. For example, of the three samples of CP-Marrón (CP-Brown) ware selected, one grouped with Petrogroup A ceramics, the other two with Petrogroup E. To reflect this, 33.3% of fragments of CP-Brown ware will be counted as pertaining to Petrogroup A and 66.6% to Petrogroup E. According to the calculation, there is very little difference between the two frequencies both in the Kuntur Wasi Phase and the Copa Phase (Figures 6.5, 6.6).

Several special tombs with gold ornaments and other prestige items and ceramic vessels were also found in Kuntur Wasi. Thirteen vessels belong to the Kuntur Wasi Phase, and eight to the Copa Phase. Because of the value of these ceramics, no thin sections were

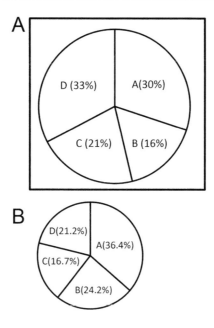

FIGURE 6.5. Frequency of Petrogroups A, B, C, and D in the Kuntur Wasi Phase (KW–KW). **A.** Sector B4, 12ᵃ (286 rims). **B.** Frequency by samples (33 samples). Stratigraphic data from Onuki, Kato, and Inokuchi (1995).

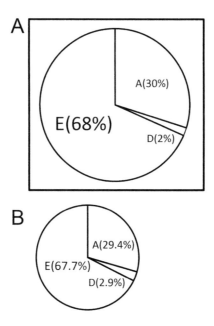

FIGURE 6.6. Frequency of Petrogroups A, D, and E in the Copa Phase. **A.** Sector B4, 5ᵃ (820 rims). **B.** Frequency by samples (34 samples). Stratigraphic data from Onuki, Kato, and Inokuchi (1995).

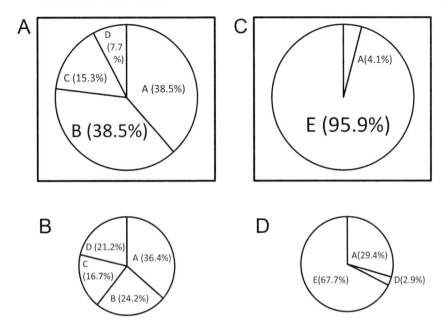

FIGURE 6.7. Frequency of Petrogroups A, B, C, D, and E for the special tombs ceramics. *Left,* the Kuntur Wasi Phase (KW–KW); *right,* the Copa Phase. **A.** Percentages for 13 ceramics from 6 tombs. **B.** Frequency of petrogroups (33 samples). **C.** Percentages for 8 ceramics from 2 tombs. **D.** Frequency of petrogroups (34 samples).

made for analysis, but a tentative petrogroup point can be calculated as mentioned above. We can thus estimate that Petrogroup B should be better represented in the ceramics of the special tombs of the Kuntur Wasi Phase than the other petrogroups. On the other hand, in the Copa Phase, the Petrogroup E should be more prominent than the others in the ceramics of the special tombs (Figure 6.7).

Considering these results, we approach the question of proveniences and uses of a special paste type, as characterized by the presence of intrusive material (Petrogroup B) and by the presence of intrusive-subvolcanic material (Petrogroup E). Interestingly, the stylistic types found in Petrogroup B are not well represented in the Idolo Phase. During the Kuntur Wasi Phase, fine ceremonial wares are made with both intrusive (Petrogroup B) and volcanic pastes (Petrogroup A). In the Copa Phase, the fine ceremonial wares represent the majority of Petrogroup E ceramics (i.e., bowls with geometric motifs, red bowls, and stirrup spout bottles).

Sourcing Ceramics and Raw Materials

To determine provenience from mineralogical data, we have to consider the local and regional geology and examine comparative materials. The geology around Kuntur Wasi is characterized by volcanic sediments, with small metamorphic and sedimentary deposits in Sangal, and alluvial deposits in San Pablo. A geological survey of the site and its surroundings conducted by Shinsuke Yomoda (2002) highlighted the presence of volcanic

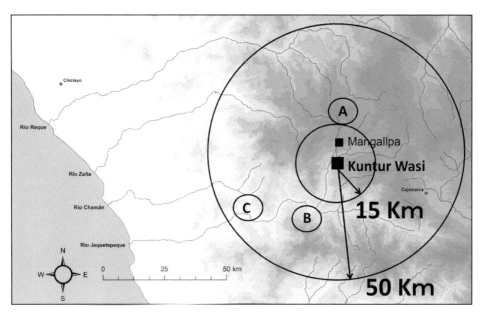

FIGURE 6.8. Three large intrusive rock outcrops within a radius of 50 km of Kuntur Wasi. **A.** San Miguel de Pallaques. **B.** Contumaza. **C.** Tembladera.

material and clay deposits that could have allowed ceramic production nearby. Notably, the volcanic material in the ceramics from Kuntur Wasi is similar to that used for local ceramic production in Mangallpa, a modern ceramic production center located about 8 km north of Kuntur Wasi. In addition to the prominent volcanic character of the local geology, pyroclastic deposits can contain fragments of crystals and rocks torn away from the subsurface or deeper during volcanic eruptions. In the area of Kuntur Wasi, subvolcanic fragments were found in a pyroclastic ash flow just north of San Pablo, in Cerro El Montón. A subvolcanic rock forms at lower depth than other intrusives. It is porphyritic and presents intermediate grain sizes. The crystals and lithoclasts are also often broken. The comparative material (sample number 15F-03) collected in 2013 displays these characteristics. It is very rich in plagioclase and lithoclasts of intermediate composition. The similarity of this sediment to the aplastics seen in many of the Copa Phase ceramics (Petrogroup E) is striking, suggesting that this or a similar source could have been used, and implying local production for the Copa Phase ceramics with this composition.

As for the provenience of the intrusive temper seen in the paste of the ceramics of Petrogroup B, a local origin is excluded, as no granitic or granodioritic intrusive rock outcrops exist in the immediate vicinity of the ceremonial center. At the regional level, there are three large intrusive bodies that crop out within a radius of 50 km: (1) north of Kuntur Wasi in the area of San Miguel de Pallaques; (2) south of the Jequetepeque River Valley in the Contumaza area; and (3) in the Tembladera area (Figure 6.8). In 2011 we collected and analyzed outcrop samples from these areas and expanded our search in 2012 to include material eroded from these outcrops found in riverbeds, ravines, and valley bottoms. According to the analysis of the comparative material, few rock samples present mineral compositions similar to that of the Kuntur Wasi ceramics. Rather, our observations point more to the use of eroded or derived intrusive material, such as sands and consolidated

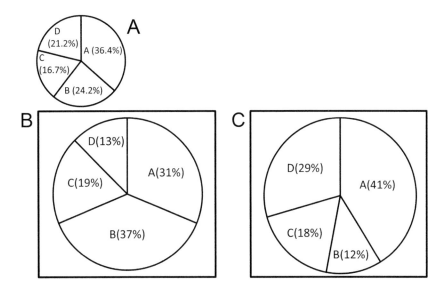

FIGURE 6.9. Petrogroups A, B, C, and D of two categories of ceramics of the Kuntur Wasi Phase. **A.** Frequency by samples (33 samples). **B.** Types of ceramics from the coast (16 samples). **C.** The other types of ceramics (17 samples).

sedimentary-intrusive materials (Druc et al. 2017). Also, the use for ceramic production of the very small granodiorite–diorite outcrop between Mangallpa and San Miguel de Pallaques, some 12 to 14 km north of the ceremonial center, was ruled out in view of its composition and lack of accessibility (based on field survey and unpublished geological map of the Kuntur Wasi–Tembladera area by Pedro Navarro Colque, 2012, Instituto Geológico, Minero y Metalúrgico, Lima). Thus, ceramics tempered with sediments derived from intrusive bodies probably came from the middle Jequetepeque Valley or nearby area, where this type of sediment is found.

Compositional Diversity

As we have seen, petrographic results suggest that during the Kuntur Wasi and Copa Phases, several sources of raw materials were used. Of the two major stylistic categories of KW–KW ceramic in the Kuntur Wasi Phase, one may have been introduced from (or influenced by) the coast and the other was more local (Figure 6.9). In addition, most of the stylistically "coastal" ceramics are found in Petrogroup B with intrusive material.

In the Copa Phase, the majority of the ceramics are standardized in form and decoration, and stylistically local. They also display a finer and more standardized paste preparation than in other phases, using probably sieved material of a particular granulometry. The amount of ceramics produced and the observed standardization suggest that there were many potters and a consensus on how to create a product in high demand in the Kuntur Wasi temple. In addition, the use of subvolcanic material of local origin, available less than 6 km from the center, suggests a concentration of workshops using the same source. This situation is different from the Idolo Phase and the Sangal Complex that also have ceramics of local or regional styles, but produced with a different volcanic paste that corresponds to pyroclastic outcrops 8 km away. These outcrops, and the same production style, have been in use even in the later phases, when the subvolcanic material and intensive Copa Phase production were in full operation. This leads us to think that at least two communities of practice or communities of potters were active concurrently at (or for) Kuntur Wasi.

For the provenience of the wares with intrusive temper, the most probable area of production is the Jequetepeque Valley, which in different places has sandy materials with intrusive fragments similar to some of the temper seen in the Petrogroup B ceramics. Several Formative sites are also known in this area. In that case, we can speak of long-distance ware distribution. The hypothesis of on-site production by itinerant potters with nonlocal material, or production by local potters obtaining their material from afar, cannot be discarded, as this seems to have been a production mode with a long tradition in this region (Isabelle C. Druc, unpublished report, "Análisis Petrográfico de la Cerámica de Kuntur Wasi 2010–2011," University of Wisconsin-Madison, Department of Anthropology; Ramón 2011).

Conclusions

The results of the petrographic analysis of the ceramic raw materials can be interpreted in several ways and different production scenarios could be proposed. The reason for this is that there are several production and distribution patterns that we can envision due to how potters usually work (according to ethnographic studies), where the materials came from, and where the workshops could have been located.

Such patterns might include the following possibilities.
—*Nonlocal production.* The source(s) of the raw materials and the ceramic workshop(s) were located far from the temple, and the finished products were brought to the temple.
—*Local production.* Potters located close to the temple using nearby raw materials crafted ceramics in local workshop(s) and brought them to the temple.
—*Local production with foreign material.* The raw materials (clay, temper, or both) were collected far from the temple and brought by potters to the area surrounding the temple, where their workshops were, to later bring the finished product to the temple.
—*Local production with foreign material.* Itinerant potters who traveled seasonally made ceramics near the temple with their material.

These scenarios are not mutually exclusive and could co-occur. Additionally, for each of these patterns the organization of production could vary as to who would control the work, resources, or type of products to be produced. The work could have been under the supervision of temple leaders or the potters could have operated as independent suppliers, and different degrees of relationship could have existed between the temple and the craftspeople. To reach a conclusion these options must be considered along with the archaeological data, type of raw materials, production of nonceramic artifacts, and workforce used for the temple construction or its remodeling.

Looking at the archaeological and stylistic data, we see that the influence of the coastal area during the Kuntur Wasi Phase was important, but temporary. The new temple constructions served to ascertain the power of the ceremonial center and of its leaders, and as the center developed the people took advantage of the great religious authority of the temple. The ceramic data reinforces this image for this period, with a diversity of ceramic styles and paste compositions suggestive of long-distance distribution networks. In the Copa Phase we see more frequent construction activities and craft production than in the Kuntur Wasi Phase and a shift in ceramic production with heavy emphasis on local production. We can assume that the Copa leadership, probably well integrated within the local society and in connection with the temple, became more assertive.

The leaders of the Copa Phase must have controlled or had power over more people than in the earlier phase, supervising their labor for the renovations of the temple and the production of different goods, possibly including ceramics. The goods produced on temple grounds probably represented upscale commodities or more prestigious items, for which precious or ordinary raw materials were needed. The traces of agate and *Spondylus* shell production and the architectural divisions observed in the temple area suggest some control of production activity by the Copa leaders.

As for the ceramics, we have no evidence of on-site production as yet. The potters were not necessarily under direct control of the Kuntur Wasi temple leaders, but could have operated as independent producers, however probably responding to a stylistic and formal standardization demanded by the ceremonial center or the local elite. The workshops could have been located in the site's surroundings, such as in Sangal or close to the actual town of San Pablo at the foot of Cerro El Montón. In a way, this can be considered a disguised form of power exercised by the religious and economic center of Kuntur Wasi at that time, imposing decorative and formal canons displaying a specific ideology.

The two options of direct or indirect control are important and characteristic of leadership power during the Formative Period in the Central Andes. The first interpretation relates more to a socioeconomic power exercising a certain control over the local workforce and the products crafted in the temple area. The second interpretation taps into the idea of ideology as power to harness the will of the people. A third option combines both kinds of power. More research, exploring the bone, lithic, and shell industries found at the site, as well as comparative analysis of the ceramics and their different production contexts at the local and regional levels should help provide a more definitive vision of power at the Kuntur Wasi temple.

CHAPTER SEVEN

A Shift in the Use of Animals in the Northern Highlands Formative Period

Climate Change or Social Adaptations?

Kazuhiro Uzawa

Animal domestication began in the early Holocene in multiple regions throughout the Afro-Eurasian world. Herding systems for a variety of species dispersed throughout the surrounding areas during the late Holocene. In South America, the domestication of camelids began in the Central Andes and possibly in the south-central Andes in the Middle Holocene. After the emergence of domesticated camelids at certain places, there was a gradual shift from hunting to herding in the surrounding areas (e.g., Wheeler Pires-Ferreira, Pires-Ferreira, and Kaulike 1977; Mengoni Goñalons and Yacobaccio 2006). It is clear that animal domestication and herding activities developed independently across the continent. It can be, therefore, that there were common factors acting simultaneously over a wide range of regions affecting the shift in animal use from hunting to herding. Why did prehistoric people reduce their hunting practices and begin herding during the Holocene? Are there any common factors that generated subsistence changes over multiple regions at more or less the same time?

The classical framework claims that animal domestication was prompted by technical improvements in animal handling, climatic changes, or the need to expand food production subsequent to population growth, or possibly for all these reasons (e.g., Peak and Fleure 1927; Childe 1951; Boserup 1965; Binford 1968). Although these hypotheses were proposed on the basis of archaeological evidence mainly from the Middle East, they have yet to be tested in the Americas. Also, these models focus on the origin of domestication and do not provide explanations for the dispersal process of the domesticated animals into peripheral areas. In the Andes, the dispersal of domesticated camelids has been regarded by archaeologists as a natural process of technological innovation and does not seem to have attracted their attention.

Our previous studies, however, have revealed that domesticated camelids had dispersed to the northern highland area of Peru during the Late Formative Period (Uzawa 2008). This was at least about a thousand years after the estimated emergence of the domesticated form in the Central Andes. A rough estimate of the speed of dispersal would be about 1 km per year. Considering the use of the llama as a pack animal over a wide area in the Andes, this estimated speed is surprisingly slow. The technological innovation hypothesis does not seem to be very persuasive in explaining this sluggish pace of adaptation.

Considering the biological and cultural process of domestication, the following explanations are suggested: (1) technological improvement for breeding domesticated camelids could have taken considerable time because the camelids had adapted to the high altitude of the high grasslands (*puna*); (2) the Northern Highlands could have been blessed with a stable environment that enabled a traditional subsistence way of life that was based on hunting to be sustained; (3) camelid herding was of importance for local subsistence in higher altitude regions such as the puna, where people needed to acquire agricultural products from lower altitudes. (The adoption of herding by the societies located at lower altitudes was probably generated by social requirements of some kind.) The second and third models are not exclusive and may affect each other.

The growing importance of camelids at the Formative sites is indicated by increasing composition ratios of the taxa in the archaeological bone assemblages. This reflects not only the success of herding, but also the diminution of the hunting of other animals, most notably deer. In other words, camelid herding and deer hunting are recognized as compensating activities when considering zooarchaeological data. This phenomenon can be seen from different points of view. Keeping camelids made it possible to dispense with deer hunting. On the other hand, a decrease in hunting made necessary a new source of animal meat, such as camelids.

To evaluate the validity of these interpretations, it is important to study deer hunting more closely in conjunction with the introduction of camelids. At first, it may be more efficient to determine whether the availability of deer resources altered before and after the introduction of camelids near the site. Then, the social factors including the purpose and the method of hunting should be considered as a reason for the shift in the utilization of animals.

The zooarchaeological data presented here concern the shift from hunting to herding and place special emphasis on the reduction of deer hunting in the Northern Highlands of Peru. This data will then be compared to equivalent data from Japan. Although paleoenvironmental information connecting these two circumpacific areas is not available, both regions do share common characteristics relating to animal use patterns. Neither area was the center of animal domestication, but rather were peripheral zones that accepted domesticated animals such as llamas and pigs. Hunting activities seem to have diminished at the same time in the Holocene.

In the Japanese case, the climate cooled after 2000 BC (Yasuda 1989). This climate change has been suggested as the cause of a terrestrial resource depression and population decrease at the end of the Middle Jomon Period, particularly in eastern Japan (Koyama 1978, 1984; Imamura 1996). Moreover, this environmental degradation probably generated pressure on the hunting of the deer population. This biosupposition is supported by an exhaustive mortality profile of deer derived from faunal remains in the Late Jomon archaeological assemblages (Koike and Ohtaishi 1985; Koike 1992). Therefore, in the case of Japan, it is possible to argue that environmental degradation could have stimulated the socioeconomic change from Jomon, a hunting and gathering society, to Yayoi, a farming society.

The stability of the population of hunted animals is usually assessed by its age profile. Mortality profiles of sika deer from Japanese archaeological sites are used as a comparative base for discussion here. However, a mortality profile of an animal species is biased by the hunting method used, as well as the environment in which the species lives. This discussion presents alternative models of the social context for animal use.

South American Camelids

There are four species of camelids in South America. The guanaco (*Lama guanicoe*) and vicuña (*Vicugna vicugna*) are wild, and the other two species, the llama (*Lama glama*) and alpaca (*Vicugna pacos*), are domesticated. Since the nineteenth century there have been many discussions of the phylogenetic relationship among these species, but recent biomolecular studies have shown that llamas are descended from guanacos, and alpacas were domesticated from vicuñas (Kadwell et al. 2001). Among Andean pastoralists, past and present, both llamas and alpacas have been used as a source of food, hides, and fiber. Additionally, llamas have provided labor as pack animals.

Wheeler's studies in the 1980s showed that the domestication of South American camelids occurred between 4000 and 4500 BC (Wheeler 1984, 1995). This took place in the puna ecosystem of the Central Andes, more specifically in the Junin highlands. Recently, archaeological evidence from the south-central Andes, northern Chile, and northwestern Argentina has become available. It has been argued that these regions also could be good candidates for domestication centers (Mengoni Goñalons and Yacobaccio 2006). At any rate, it is accepted that domesticated camelids had been dispersed throughout the southern and central highlands by 2000 BC.

Nonetheless, previous studies argued that the chronological time frame for the radiation of domesticated camelids to the Northern Highlands was still ambiguous (Shimada and Shimada 1985; Miller and Burger 1995; Uzawa 2008). This is partly because it is difficult to discriminate between domesticated forms and wild species that were hunted, such as guanaco and vicuña, from fragmentary bone samples. To clarify the introduction process of the domesticated camelids we have chosen a study area outside of their natural habitat distribution.

Materials and Methods

Kuntur Wasi Site

In this study I focus on Kuntar Wasi, a Formative Period site in northern Peru. The site is situated at an altitude of 2,300 m near the upper reaches of the Jequetepeque River, which flows down the western slopes of the Andes. Kuntur Wasi is one of the largest ceremonial sites in Peru's Department of Cajamarca (Figure 7.1). Kuntur Wasi was first studied by Tello and his colleagues in 1946 and was investigated in greater depth by a research team from the University of Tokyo from 1988 to 2004 (Onuki 1995). This long-term program of large-scale excavations yielded rich archaeological finds, including elaborate burial goods made of gold and other exotic materials.

The construction of the temple consists of four phases: the Idolo Phase (950–800 BC), the Kuntur Wasi Phase (800–550 BC), the Copa Phase (550–250 BC), and the Sotera Phase (250–50 BC) (see Chapter 6). Bone samples were collected from all these periods. According to the definition of Pulgar Vidal (1981), the site is near the boundary of *yunga* and *quechua* zones and has a relatively arid and moderate climate. Kuntur Wasi is situated outside of the natural distribution of wild camelids and modern residents of the area do not breed llamas nor alpacas on the surrounding land. Therefore, wild camelids such as guanaco and vicuña were unlikely to have been included in the bone assemblages from the site.

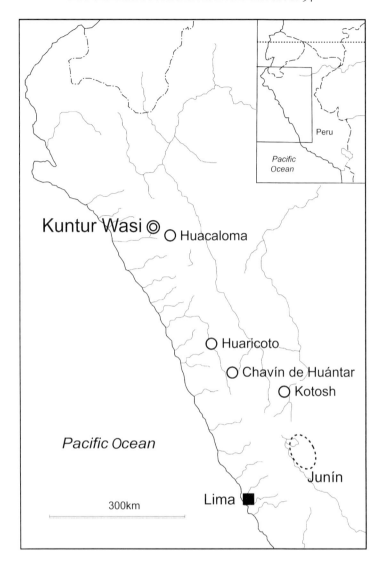

Figure 7.1. Map of the Kuntur Wasi study area. These sites distribute in a relatively straight line from the Junín highlands. Some are located at much higher altitudes compared to Kuntur Wasi.

Mortality Pattern of Deer

As mentioned earlier, the stability of animal resources is reflected in the mortality profile of the bone assemblages (e.g., Caughley 1966, 1977). The analyses of mortality patterns in deer samples used three age classes, according to the Stiner system (Stiner 1991): Juvenile, Prime Adult, and Old Adult. The Juvenile category consists of individuals from birth to approximately three years, at the time the fourth premolar is shed. Separation of the Juvenile and Prime age groups in this study best corresponds to the female's entry into the reproductive phase. The Prime Adult and Old Adult boundary is determined by how much of the tooth is left relative to the complete form and by the appearance of the occlusal surface. The Old Adult stage begins at roughly 60% of the maximum potential lifetime. The probability that old animals will build up nutritional stores is also correspondingly lower than in prime adults.

To estimate the age group of the individuals, the lower fourth deciduous premolar (dp4) and the lower fourth premolar (P4) were examined. Because the dp4 is replaced with P4 when the deer enter the Prime Adult stage, the relative frequency of these teeth represents the age composition between juvenile and adult. Prime Adult and Old Adult were determined by the wear status of P4. The mortality profile of sika deer (*Cervus nippon*) in the Japanese cases that was used for comparison was taken from the study by Koike (1992).

Results

Introduction of Domesticated Camelids to Kuntur Wasi

From the Kuntur Wasi sample, about 4,000 specimens were identified as either skeletal elements or species level. Although thirteen taxa were recognized, cervid and camelids were the dominant species, totaling over 80% of the bone specimens. Our previous studies indicated that the taxonomic composition was changing through time (Uzawa 2008; see results summarized in Figure 7.2 with other Formative Period assemblages studied by different authors). The relative proportions of camelids and cervids were calculated using the number of identified specimens of these taxa. We can see that during the Idolo Phase there are few camelids at the site, implying that the wild camelids were not distributed near the site during that phase. The camelids found after this period were most likely domesticated. Camelids start to appear at the site during the Kuntur Wasi Phase, but only in low proportions. The proportion of camelids increases from this point forward through time. This suggests that they gradually became more important for subsistence at Kuntur Wasi. The proportion of camelids and cervids was almost equal by the end of the Sotera Phase (50 cal BC).

According to osteometry, most of the camelid individuals correspond to the size of llamas, and those to the size of alpacas are few. Considering the lack of incisors in the tooth collection that show the diagnostic morphology of the alpaca, most small individuals were probably young llamas.

In comparing the chronological change of the camelids frequency with the equivalent data from other sites located in different areas, more southern sites show a high proportion of camelids even in the early phases of the Formative Period (e.g., Miller and Burger 1995). As Miller and Burger argue, this is most likely because these samples probably contain wild camelids such as guanaco and vicuña that had been hunted. In any case, camelid proportions increase over time at all sites. The overall tendency suggests that domesticated camelid dispersal occurred in the Late Formative Period. At the same time, these curves show not only the introduction of animal herding, but also a diminishing emphasis on hunting.

Deer Hunting at the Kuntur Wasi Site

There are several species of cervid in the Andes, including white-tailed deer (*Odocoileus virginianus*), taruca (*Hippocamelus antisensis*), mazama (*Mazama americana*), and pudu (*Pudu mephistophiles*). The inhabitants of Kuntur Wasi hunted only white-tailed deer. This

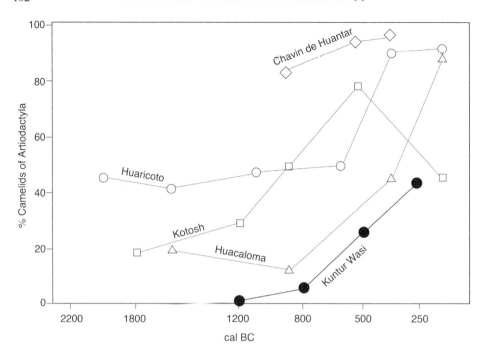

FIGURE 7.2. Chronological change in the proportion of camelids at Kuntur Wasi. Data for other sites: Chavín de Huántar (Miller and Burger 1995); Huacaloma (Shimada 1982); Kotosh (Wing 1972); Huaricoto (Sawyer 1985). After Miller and Burger (1995:430, fig. 5).

species is found in relatively arid and warm places (Nowak 1999). In the Peruvian Andes, the yunga environment provides these conditions and the Kuntur Wasi site is located on the yunga's upper edge.

The deer bones found at Kuntur Wasi were not in their the correct anatomical positions, but rather were scattered about in the archaeological deposits. Most of the bones were fractured and about 10% had cut marks. Some showed modification related to tool production. It has been suggested that deer were hunted as a source of food and materials.

Deer Mortality Patterns Before and After Camelid Herding

Although deer hunting was maintained throughout the first millennium BC, the question is whether the mortality profile of deer changed before or after the introduction of domesticated camelids in the Late Formative Period. A total of 72 specimens of dp4 and P4 teeth were collected from Middle to Late Formative Period sediments and assessed for their age group. In the Idolo Phase sample, there was no dp4 (Juvenile) tooth, but nine P4 teeth were found. Eight were estimated to be Prime Adult and one to be an Old Adult individual. The Kuntur Wasi Phase assemblage contained 17 Juvenile, 21 Prime Adult, and 2 Old Adult individuals. In the Copa Phase, 13 Juvenile, 10 Prime Adult, and 5 Old Adult individuals were estimated. The mortality pattern of white-tailed deer from the Idolo Phase, the Middle Formative Period, showed a bias for Prime Adult animals, and in the later periods the number of Juvenile animals increased. These changes in mortality patterns indicate a chronological shift from a living structure to a U-shaped pattern during the Middle to the Late Formative (Figure 7.3).

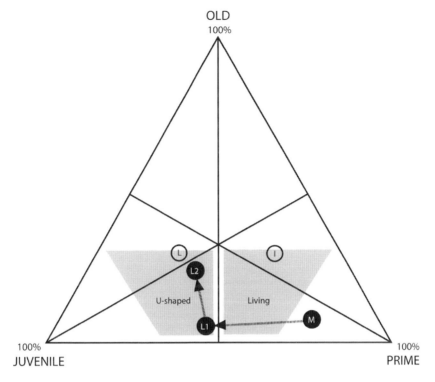

FIGURE 7.3. Three age groups (Old Adult, Juvenile, and Prime Adult) converted to percentages and plotted according to Stiner's classification system (Stiner 1991). The distribution of the two most common mortality patterns, attritional (U-shaped) and living structure, are shown as gray areas. The chronological shifts in the mortality profiles from the Peruvian and Japanese cases generally showed a similar pattern. Deer hunting by the Late to Final Formative populations seems to have been conducted under high hunting pressure. *Abbreviations:* I, Initial Jomon site (ca. 7,000 BP); L, Late Jomon site (ca. 3,000 BP); L1, earlier phase of Late Formative Period at Kuntur Wasi; L2, later phase of Late Formative Period at Kuntur Wasi; M, Middle Formative Period at Kuntur Wasi.

Deer Hunting during the Late Jomon Period in Japan

To better understand the results of mortality shift at Kuntur Wasi, Japanese cases of prehistoric deer hunting were compared (Figure 7.3). Two published age profiles of deer remains were used. Ishiyama and Fuyuki shell midden sites provided Initial and Late Jomon samples, respectively (Koike 1992). Ishiyama, an Initial Jomon Period (ca. 5000 BC) sample, falls into the living structure zone with relatively high proportions of Prime Adult animals. Whereas Fuyuki, a Late Jomon Period (ca. 2000 BC) sample, falls within the U-shaped, or attritional, zone with a low percentage of Prime Adult individuals and a relatively high proportion of Juvenile deer.

As noted, the mortality shift from the Middle to Late Formative Period in the Andean sample indicates a pattern similar to those of the Initial to Late Jomon Period in the Japanese case. The mortality pattern of white-tailed deer from the Idolo Phase of the Middle Formative Period at Kuntur Wasi likewise showed a bias for Prime Adult animals. On the other hand, the mortality pattern of the later Formative showed a more U-shaped profile with Juvenile and Old Adult individuals dominating.

Discussion

The chronological shifts in the mortality profiles from the Peruvian and Japanese cases generally showed a similar pattern. Deer hunting by the Copa Phase people at Kuntur Wasi seems to have been conducted under conditions of high hunting pressure.

Many Japanese scholars have suggested that the cooling climate around 2000 BC resulted in a significant population decline as well as a decrease of large settlements at the end of the Middle Jomon Period (Koyama 1978, 1984; Yasuda 1989). In the Final Jomon Period, the average temperature was lower than it is today. It is believed that the climate change in the Late to Final Jomon was the cause of a depression of wild food resources. This was perhaps the cause of the subsistence change that included animal herding, which occurred in the Yayoi Period. It may be possible to credit this change of mortality patterns in the Peruvian assemblage to environmental degradation as in the case of Jomon. If so, camelid herding would have provided an attractive alternative source of animal meat for the population.

Direct evidence of environmental change between the Middle and Formative Periods in the northern Peruvian highlands is not available, and therefore the model remains speculative. However, archaeological data suggests a dynamic population flow caused by environmental change in the northern coastal region. Onuki (1994) claimed that temples were discarded in the northern and central coasts of Peru after 800 BC. He referred to this phenomenon as "coastal vacancy." Seki and his colleagues referred to the possibility that the coastal vacancy could have been caused by El Niño, the periodic warming of ocean currents in the eastern Pacific (Seki and Sakai 1998). El Niño is known to cause heavy rains followed by large-scale flooding in coastal regions and drought in the highlands (Shimada et al. 1991). If the coastal vacancy was caused by a climate event such as El Niño, it would have also affected the highlands.

There is another possible reason for the mortality shift in deer hunting activities in the Late Formative Period at the Kuntur Wasi site. The second model focuses on the overall subsistence change caused by the acceptance of camelid herding. It is asserted that complex society developed in the Late Formative rather than in the Middle Formative (see Chapter 8). In the Northern Highlands and elsewhere, deposits from the Middle Formative Period contain artifacts that were transported to the site through long-distance trade (Burger 1992). Exotic materials brought long distances by trade also have been recognized from the Late Formative Period. At the Kuntur Wasi site, for example, rich archaeological remains, including artifacts made of gold, tropical shell, precious stones, and obsidian, were found in burial and other contexts of the Kuntur Wasi and Copa Phases.

Seki (2006) considered the appearance of these exotic artifacts in the Late Formative to indicate the development of an elite class that controlled long-distance trade. Additionally, he claimed that these elites used these luxury items to form the base of their political power. If this is the case, establishing secure trade routes would have been of considerable significance to them. According to this model, domesticated camelids, more precisely llamas, would have contributed noticeably in transporting materials between widely separated societies (see also Burger 1992).

This explanation that the introduction of domesticated camelids to the site was undertaken in connection with the development of a complex society seems to be consistent with the fact that deer hunting was carried out until the end of the Sotera Phase, the last phase of the Formative Period. Following this line of reasoning, one can consider that the introduction of domesticated camelids was not necessarily intended to resolve the need for meat, but rather because it fulfilled a social function.

In modern Andean pastoralist society, especially the puna region of the southern highlands, llamas are used to transport agricultural products from lower altitudes to residences at higher elevations, regardless of whether the products were produced by the people themselves or whether they were supplied by farmers (Murra 1972; Flores Ochoa 1979; Nielsen 2009). This classic vertical control model may not be as relevant for the Northern Highlands, where the altitude is lower than in the south and the cropland is closer to the residential sites. It is suggested that the use of domesticated camelids as pack animals would not have been a vital tool for the Kuntur Wasi people who lived near the boundaries of the yunga and quechua zones. Additionally, the warm and semi-arid environment near the site could have provided consistent hunting resources even in times of climate distress.

If this is the case, the mortality profile showing high hunting pressure on the deer population may reflect hunting selectivity caused by the implication of ritual use of camelids. Llama and alpaca were frequently sacrificed at the ceremonial center, and the age of these individuals are premature in many cases. Although the skeletal remains of deer at Kuntur Wasi site were not from clear sacrificial contexts, young deer may have been purposefully selected for ritual use in a way analogous to camelids.

Another explanation could be from a change in hunting methods. An example of this would be switching from individual hunting to communal drives or trap-hunting. It is predictable that independent or small-group hunters would target Prime Adult animals. This type of procurement activity would provide nutritious game with less damage to the deer population than hunting Juvenile individuals. Large-scale communal drives and trap-hunting, on the other hand, are recognized as methods that capture a substantial number of Juvenile animals (Frison 1991).

Conclusions

This study has explored the interactions between the development of animal herding and the decrease in the importance of hunting during the Late Formative Period at Kuntur Wasi, a site in the Northern Highlands of Peru. Whether the introduction of domesticated camelids was caused by environmental degradation or prompted by social developments such as trade between remote societies, domesticated camelids became a trigger to change the whole subsistence system during the Late Formative in northern Peru.

There is a need for additional research to get a better understanding of this matter. Other than providing more statistically robust data on deer mortality profiles, future research might address detailed studies of deer hunting practices, including the method and season required. Determining the season of death for deer from the annual rings of teeth would supply useful information on the organization of hunting activities. There is also a need to explore whether any trace of environmental change is found on archaeological fauna during the Middle to Late Formative Period. In particular, information relating to microfaunal remains that are sensitive to climate change should provide valuable data relating to the paleoenvironment in the Northern Highlands.

CHAPTER EIGHT

EMERGENCE OF POWER DURING THE
FORMATIVE PERIOD AT THE PACOPAMPA SITE

Yuji Seki, Diana Alemán Paredes,
Mauro Ordoñez Livia, and Daniel Morales Chocano

The main objective here is to offer an interpretation of the social complexity and the emergence of power during the Formative Period in the Central Andes through the analysis of architecture and materials recovered at the archaeological site of Pacopampa in Peru (Figure 8.1).

Recent Andean archaeological studies have clarified that relatively egalitarian societies of the Early and Middle Formative Period transformed into societies in which social differences were tangible in the Late Formative Period.

Richard Burger and Lucy Salazar have reported that Early Formative Period corporate architectural structures in the Lurín Valley of the Central Coast were enlarged by repeated renovation, a situation that could not occur through hierarchical disposition based on strong leadership (Burger and Salazar 2014). By analyzing the pottery and architecture, they concluded that each corporate structure carried its own identity according to the group residing there.

We find a similar phenomenon at the Huacaloma archaeological site in the Northern Highlands where a large corporate structure increased in size through repetitive renovation activities (Terada and Onuki 1982, 1985). This Middle and Late Formative ceremonial center has neither storehouses for surplus products nor evidence of differences in burial treatment (Figure 8.2), and therefore it is assumed that its society was egalitarian (Seki 2014). As several corporate structures can be found nearby in Huacaloma, it seems that each ceremonial center was supported voluntarily by its own group.

On the other hand, we have much evidence of social differentiation in the Late Formative Period. For instance, the well-known archaeological site Chavín de Huántar has been referred to as the capital of the pristine state until the last century. Today few archaeologists insist on this scenario, but it is no exaggeration to say that the Chavín society had characteristics of social complexity. A residential area belonging to the elite group was found around the site (Rick 2005; see also Burger 1984a; Miller and Burger 1995). The complex iconography that formerly served as the basis of chronology and cosmological studies can now be interpreted as a representation or the medium of the political authority of leaders.

At the Kuntur Wasi archaeological site in the Northern Highlands the architecture

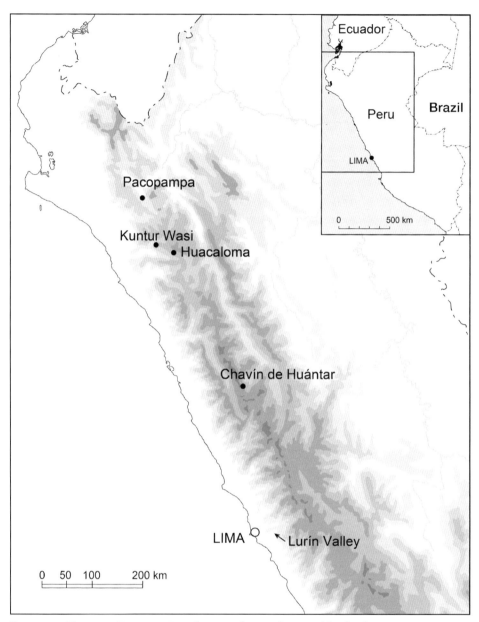

FIGURE 8.1. The major Formative Period sites in the Northern Highlands of Peru.

was developed in the Kuntur Wasi Phase (800–550 cal BC), and the main structure was aligned symmetrically to a main axis (Figure 8.2). Four special tombs associated with several offerings were unearthed at the main platform (Onuki 1995). These tombs were uniquely shaped in a form resembling a woman's long boot. Cranial deformation was only found for the individuals buried in these tombs, indicating the beginning of social differentiation (Seki 2014). Precious offerings—like *Strombus* and *Spondylus* shell artifacts from the Ecuadorian coast and stone ornaments made of sodalite from Bolivia—indicate the

cal BC	Period		Pacopampa	Kuntur Wasi	Huacaloma
		Final		Sotera	Layzón
250	Formative				
		Late	Pacopampa II	Copa	EL
500				Kuntur Wasi	
800					Late Huacaloma
1000		Middle	Pacopampa I	Idolo	
1200					Early Huacaloma
1500		Early	Pandanche		
1800					

FIGURE 8.2. Chronology of the Formative Period sites in the Northern Highlands.

importance of extensive interactions such as long-distance trade, as well as being evidence of the power exercised by leaders who controlled these materials.

Cultural remains, such as the pottery from the Kuntur Wasi Phase, strongly suggest a relationship with the North Coast and the Cupisnique style, and radiocarbon dates from the special tombs are older than the beginning of the Kuntur Wasi Phase. This evidence suggests that the individuals in the tombs were removed from the North Coast, probably as mummies (Kato 2014). The prosperity of Kuntur Wasi Phase, then, began as a result of natural disasters at the coast (Onuki 2011).

In this context, we introduce the archaeological data recovered from the Pacopampa archaeological site as new evidence to evaluate the dynamic change from the Middle to Late Formative Period, which also can be observed in this site. In addition, we will discuss the process and elements of social differentiation in the archaeological context. Although the social change in the Late Formative Period has always considered Chavín de Huántar as its axis, we will emphasize regional diversity in the formation of power from a perspective of the larger Northern Highlands. We will also focus on how emerging leaders can acquire and maintain power, taking as a reference the use of space, patterns of access, and architectural components related to the construction of social memory.

Architectural Developments at the Pacopampa Archaeological Site

The site of Pacopampa is situated on the eastern slopes of the Andean mountain range in the Northern Highlands of Peru, next to the village of Pacopampa in the Querocoto District, Chota Province, Department of Cajamarca (Figure 8.3). The site is at 2,500 masl, on the left bank of the Chotano River, one of the tributaries of the Marañon River.

FIGURE 8.3. General view of the Pacopampa site.

The Pacopampa site is composed of three large platforms (Figure 8.4). The main masonry constructions are located on the third (or upper) platform. The site has been investigated by several archaeologists (Rosas La Noire and Shady Solis 1970; Fung Pineda 1975; Morales 1980), but these efforts were limited in scale and duration. This chapter uses primarily the results of the Pacopampa Archaeological Project, organized through an agreement between the Universidad Nacional Mayor de San Marcos and the National Museum of Ethnology of Japan. This project has investigated the site since 2005. From stratigraphic data recovered from these excavations, our project has established the existence of two sequential phases: Pacopampa I and Pacopampa II (Seki et al. 2008). Recently we reconsidered the calibrated age ranges as follows: Pacopampa I (1200 cal BC–700 cal BC) and Pacopampa II (700 cal BC–400 cal BC) (see Figure 8.2). Each of these phases is subdivided into two subphases: IA and IB, and IIA and IIB, respectively.

Before proceeding, we will briefly summarize the architectural sequence. The architecture from phase Pacopampa I, subphase IA, can only be observed now at the western portion of the Third Platform. A stepped platform dating to this subphase was identified, and in the north portion there is a staircase. During subphase IA several platforms and small patios were built in front of that platform. Nevertheless, we have no clear evidence of how access was organized or controlled in the total architectural disposition.

During subphase IB the architectural plan of the site was drastically changed. Radiocarbon dating reveals that this event took place at approximately 900 cal BC or a little later. Recent studies show that the large-scale retaining walls of the First, Second, and Third Platforms, along with staircases between the platforms, may have been built at that time.

At the western portion of the Third Platform, the previous constructions of subphase IA were sealed and the new platform (Western Platform) was built. On the Western

FIGURE 8.4. Major architectural features and the topography of the Pacopampa site.

Platform, the Circular Building was constructed along with a lower square platform at the eastern front of the building (Figure 8.5). The Circular Building is 28.5 m in diameter and 1.4 m in height. The access to the top of the structure is unknown. However, on the low square platform attached to the Circular Building three benches covered by fine clay plaster were found and, in front of them, hearths with evidence of burning were unearthed (Figure 8.6).

Around the same time, Main Platform-I was built on the southwest portion of the Third Platform. On top of this we unearthed Main Building-I with its five rooms. Access to these rooms was along the main axis of the Main Building-I, with the exception of a room located at the extreme west that has two symmetric entrances (Figure 8.7). Although only the foundation of a wall between the entrances was preserved, we identified red and green pigments, possibly the traces of mural painting. It is likely that visitors to the Main Building-I could see the multicolored painted wall through the entrance.

In the first room on the east side, hearths with evidence of burning were found dug into the floor and later covered by a gray plaster. The floor was modified at least four times. After the first and second floors were used, several small pits were dug and filled with soil before the next floor was made. The sizes and the locations of the holes are inconsistent with an interpretation as post holes, particularly because their location would have obstructed access. Therefore, we suggest that these holes were related to a religious activity linked to the abandonment of each floor. In one hole we found a bead made of chrysocolla and in another an obsidian projectile point. Interestingly, the floor associated with the second renovation features a large pit (10PC-C-Hoyo-11) with a diameter of nearly 1 m and a depth of 1 m (Figure 8.8). Most of the pit was destroyed by the digging of another pit belonging to the next phase (IIA), which contained the tomb of the "Lady of Pacopampa" (Entierro 09-02, discussed below). In the fill of the earlier pit we recovered two lithic ves-

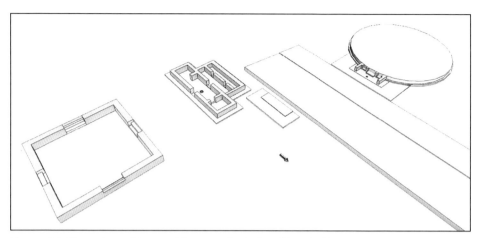

FIGURE 8.5. The major architectural features of subphase IB at the Pacopampa site.

sels, one made of anthracite. These unusual artifacts and the form of the pit suggest that the early pit could have been a tomb.

The Sunken Squared Court measuring 30 m on a side and 1.20 m in depth is located in front of the Main Building-I (Figure 8.9). It has four axial stairs, one in the middle of each wall. The axis of the Main Building also passes through the center of the stairs at the Sunken Plaza, and the centers of the staircases between the First, Second, and Third Platforms. Because the axis also passes the middle of another sunken court on the Second Platform, which we have not investigated intensively, we suppose that the court may also have been constructed during this subphase. In consequence, almost all structures of this subphase were in an orderly arrangement along the axis.

This axis crosses the Pacopampa site and passes through the middle of Montículo Laguna, another mound where we discovered an access to the uppermost platform. This axis also leads to the mountain Cerro Tarros through the Laguna Negra, although the lake is not visible from Pacopampa. It has been suggested that this axis was also arranged in re-lation to the rising of the Pleiades constellation (Sakai et al. 2007). Considering the impor-tance of the Pleiades to the Andean agricultural calendar (indicating the beginning of the planting period) and the meaning of water for agriculture in general, the location of the ceremonial center at Pacopampa was interpreted as chosen by the leaders to control and carry out a ritual related to fertility and other aspects of cosmology. However, additional architectural data recovered from recent excavations have forced us to reconsider this idea. As Sakai and his colleagues show (see Chapter 9), the direction of the rising of the Pleiades is related to the architecture of the early subphase IA, but not to the architecture of the sub-phase IB. The new axis created during the Pacopampa IB subphase was parallel to another axis, that of the Circular Building–La Capilla, introduced by a new leadership. Although the new axis cannot be directly related to the Pleiades, it is consistent with the concept of human control of the landscape.

Subphase IIA is defined by the modification through covering or reuse of the ar-chitectural components of the previous subphase, while preserving certain elements and aspects of the earlier architectural organization (Figure 8.10). An access to the east façade of the Circular Building was added, although the rectangular platform attached to the building was covered with a thick fill. Also, the retaining wall was made higher. We found

FIGURE 8.6. Three benches close to the Circular Building (subphase IB) at the Pacopampa site.

a clear use of the space on the top of the building for the first time, because new architectural components were constructed there.

The Main Platform-I was sealed with construction fill during subphase IB and then used as the base of another platform, Main Platform-II. This latter platform supported Main Building-II with its eight square rooms. The access and entrances to these rooms maintained the same axis as the previous IB subphase, with the exception of the last room located at the extreme west. The route to reach this last room was indirect and followed a zigzag path, suggesting a degree of control and the importance of access to it. Notably, the Sunken Squared Court was reused during this subphase.

In 2009, a tomb (designated 09-02) located along the main axis of the Main Building-II was found. It had been built after the abandonment of the Main Building-I and before the constructions of subphase IIA. The tomb has a cylindrical shape, with an oval opening ranging from 0.8 to 1 m in diameter and reaching a depth of 2 m (Figure 8.11). At a depth of 1.5 m, plain slabs of andesite rock were found piled one over the other within the tomb shaft. On removing them we found five ceramic vessels. There was a small bottle in the northern part of the tomb and three vessels were unearthed in the southern part of the tomb (Figure 8.12). A small bowl with concave walls and a flat base was found covering a pedestal dish (*compotera*). There were signs of burning on the bottom of the compotera, and this suggests a funerary ritual carried out with the burial. Between the two groups of ceramics the tomb diameter was reduced. A large slab was left leaning against the wall of the tomb. After removing this slab and excavating 0.50 m below the ceramic vessels, skeletal remains of an individual were found at the bottom of the tomb (Figure 8.13).

A series of offerings accompanied the skeleton, including a pair of gold earrings measuring 6 cm in diameter, with a weight of 17 to 19 g, a pair of gold earrings with dimensions of 25 by 11 cm and weighing 48 to 50 g (Figure 8.14), and objects made with

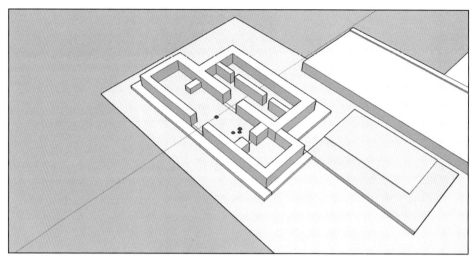

FIGURE 8.7. The Main Building (subphase IB) at the Pacopampa site.

marine shells identified as Pteriidae (Víctor F. Vásquez Sánchez and Teresa E. Rosales Tham, 2010 unpublished report, "Análisis e identificación taxonómica de muestras de moluscos de Pacopampa," Centro de Investigaciones Arqueobiológicas y Paleoecológicas Andinas ARQUEOBIOS, Trujillo). A radiocarbon measurement of 2330 ± 40 BP (Beta-265642; δ13C = −19.4‰) was taken from a bone of the buried individual.

The individual was an adult female between 20 and 39 years old with a height of 1.62 m (Nagaoka et al. 2012). Data obtained at the Kuntur Wasi site (in the northern mountains of Peru) shows that the average height for men and women in this period was 1.50 m and 1.40 m, respectively. Therefore, the woman buried in the elaborate tomb at Pacopampa was taller than most of the men and women of her time. Her skeleton also shows signs of cranial deformation and was adorned with red (cinnabar) and blue (azurite) pigments.

Social Complexity at Pacopampa

Researchers often use the analysis of access control to examine social complexity. Freidel and Schele (1988) studied the emergence of royal authority using evidence from Cerros, a Preclassic Maya site in Belize. The change in access to the top of the temple and visibility of the ritual are key to understanding the process of reinforcement of power. The importance of space in the visibility of ritual for Andean audiences has recently been emphasized as related to authority (Moore 1996a; Rick 2005; Burger and Salazar 2012).

In the case of Pacopampa, in subphase IB we have evidence of access control in the series of the structures along the main axis. The Sunken Squared Court on the Second Platform has a dimension of 50 by 50 m. This large open space was suitable for accommodating many visitors in the ceremonial center (Figure 8.15). On reaching the upper platform (Third Platform), the other sunken court can be seen. However, it is smaller in scale and would have fit fewer visitors. Moreover, there is no direct access that allows a visitor to ascend from the Second Platform to the Third Platform.

FIGURE 8.8. Small pits dug in a floor associated with a second renovation during subphase IB. The large pit at right is probably a tomb.

Access control is also noticeable at Central Platform-I, which is on the west side of the Sunken Court of the Third Platform. As mentioned previously, we can observe that the farther a person moves from the main entrance, the stronger the access control becomes. Even from the front space activities in the back room could not be observed, because the room did not have its entrance in the axis. In any case, the evidence suggests that access to this building was for a very limited group of people.

However, evidence of access control in subphase IB is slightly weak, because there would have been better visibility of the ritual from the Circular Building. This can be interpreted as the intention to make the ritual visible to a large audience. In this sense, access control is not strong here.

In the following subphase IIA, an increase in access control is more noticeable. At the Main Building-II, there are more rooms and it is more difficult than in the previous subphase to arrive at the last room, which has only one entrance. As stated, the last room was especially important because of increased control over its access. The construction of a staircase and a space on top of the Circular Building in subphase IIA also shows the intensification of access control. It is probable that a small group of the society could step onto the upper space, so that their visibility to the audience below standing around the building was assured, because there is no architectural evidence that the space at the summit of the Circular Building was closed by any structures.

Note, however, that access control does not necessarily represent the establishment of social differentiation. Complex arrangements or designs of corporate structures were reported from several sites from the Early and Middle Formative Period, and this characteristic does not necessarily indicate the existence of strong authority (Burger and Salazar 2014).

The difference between Pacopampa and other early sites can be found at the tomb buried in an important building. Although no traces of bone were unearthed there, it is probable that a large hole at the Main Building-I is a tomb, judging from its size, location

FIGURE 8.9. The Sunken Squared Court with a staircase of the Third Platform.

in Main Building-I, and association with unusual lithic objects. How does this evidence connect with social differentiation?

Clearly the evidence from subphase IB is not enough to answer this question, but data from Tomb 09-02 (Lady of Pacopampa) belonging to the next subphase IIA gives us some clues. The tomb was located at the first room of the Main Building-II along the main axis. This axis was very important and most of the constructions were arranged to it. Considering the ritual characteristic of the site, the main axis could be equal to the center of the cosmology. In this sense, the tomb would have had an important role in this cosmology. Moreover, the stratigraphic position of the tomb indicates that it was prepared before the completion of the Main Building-II. The lack of traces of sacrifice on the skeletal remains leads us to the hypothesis that a female individual died of natural causes and was brought from another place to implant her important presence into this space. This situation is very similar to the case from the Kuntur Wasi site. During the construction of the new ceremonial center in the Kuntur Wasi Phase (contemporaneous with the Pacopampa II Phase) at least four individuals were brought from other places, probably from the North Coast, and were buried in the main platform before the building was finished. Then what kind of symbolic or social meaning can we read from the tomb?

The cranial deformation of the Tomb 09-02 individual recovered from required active modification measures while the person was still an infant. This deformation suggests that the female from this tomb was destined in childhood to become a leader (Nagaoka et al. 2012). In other words, the buried female lived in a society where social differentiation was established. This interpretation reinforces the idea mentioned above, that the individual was brought from another place, because we know the immature state of social differentiation in the previous subphase IB.

The establishment of leadership, power, and social differentiation in subphase IIA at the Pacopampa site can be seen in other archaeological data from the same tomb. The

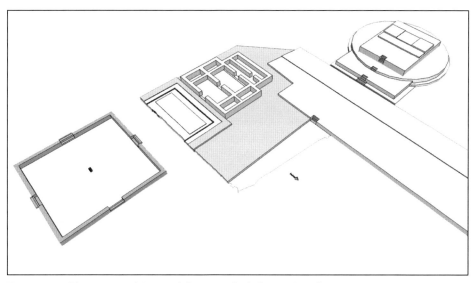

FIGURE 8.10. The major architectural features of subphase IIA at the Pacopampa site.

depth and unusual form of the tomb has not been found anywhere else in this site, suggesting a special funerary treatment for the individual and the exceptional labor invested. A ritual that used fire during the funerary process was only found at this tomb in the site. The associated offerings also indicate that this woman had a particular position in society. The gold and marine shell objects (Vásquez and Tham, 2010 unpublished report), as well as cinnabar, came from distant places (Burger, Lane, and Cooke 2016). Again, a similar situation can be observed at Kuntur Wasi where several tombs belonging to the Kuntur Wasi Phase contained gold offerings, seashells, pottery, and cinnabar (Onuki 1995).

In summary, not only access control for the architectural disposition, but also placing a particular tomb associated with unusual offerings in the main building, show us the emergence of leadership, power, and social differentiation at Pacopampa. This phenomenon first appeared in subphase Pacopampa IB and intensified in the next subphase IIA.

The Characteristics of Power at Pacopampa

Can we absolutely find the emergence or establishment of power, leadership, and social differentiation in the Northern Highlands of the Central Andes? The answer is "no." Previous comparative studies (Seki 2014) between Kuntur Wasi and Huacaloma indicate that the emergence of social differentiation could not be confirmed at Huacaloma. As mentioned, since monumental architecture can be found at Huacaloma, it could be assumed that leadership related to architectural and religious activities already existed. However, there is no evidence of social differentiation, such as burials, associated with special offerings, or architectural differentiation between leaders and nonleaders. Thus it would be better to suppose that the monumental structures at Huacaloma were built, modified, or renewed by the cooperative labor of a community associated with a weak form of leadership.

At Kuntur Wasi there is evidence for social differentiation. Moreover, we can clearly identify the differences in ceramic and architecture at both sites. Neither present a hierar-

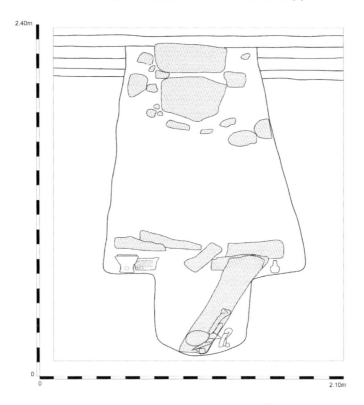

FIGURE 8.11. North-south cross section of the "Lady of Pacopampa" (Tomb 09-02).

FIGURE 8.12. Pottery offerings in Tomb 09-02.

chical relationship between them. It is possible to say, then, that a heterarchical situation can be observed in the societies of the Northern Highlands.

What is the main contrast in social differentiation between Kuntur Wasi and Huacaloma? The intensity of exchange and specialized production of artifacts were key elements in increasing the complexity of society (Seki 2014). The control of the acquisition of exotic or unusual goods was a clue to how a leader at Kuntur Wasi might gain power. Similar aspects from the Pacopampa IIA subphase, like the particular tomb associated with gold objects, marine shell, and cinnabar, suggest that the source of power for leaders originated from the control of exotic goods. However, recent studies at Pacopampa suggest an alternative interpretation.

The Pacopampa site yielded many copper objects like needles, pins (*tupus*), and other ornaments. The quantity of these objects is greater than at Kuntur Wasi. Other than these objects, several instruments, such as a copper chisel and a ceramic crucible or mold, were unearthed, along with slag (Figure 8.16). This evidence indicates that copper objects were produced at Pacopampa. This interpretation is reinforced by X-ray fluorescent analysis of the surface of some molds, where gold and copper were detected (Julio Fabián, personal communication). In addition, a geological survey around Pacopampa discovered a mine of secondary copper minerals such as chrysocolla, malachite, and azurite (Shimizu et al. 2012). At Pacopampa, these raw materials were recovered from the layers belonging to the IIA subphase. Although some of these minerals were used to make lithic ornaments like beads, the malachite and azurite probably were also used as a copper-bearing source. The experiments carried out at the laboratory in Japan showed that, under certain conditions, a copper nugget can be smelted from malachite and azurite dug from the mine near Pacopampa (Shimizu et al. 2012). Because of this, we suggest that the power of the leader or leaders of Pacopampa was formed not only by controlling the exchange of exotic goods, but also by the production of copper objects. The azurite pigment covering the skull of the individual from Tomb 09-02 (Lady of Pacopampa) had its own symbolic meaning, but it would also be possibly connected with the control of copper production. This aspect constitutes a particular characteristic of Pacopampa that cannot be found at other sites, such as Kuntur Wasi.

The difference in the source of power between Pacopampa and Kuntur Wasi is related to how architecture was used in the previous phase. Whereas platforms and courts in the former Idolo Phase were totally covered with new constructions from the Kuntur Wasi Phase at Kuntur Wasi, in Pacopampa's architectural sequence there is a continuous use of the same axis in the structures. The Circular Building and the sunken squared courts at Pacopampa had been reused in the subphase IIA, by modifying them or adding architectural elements. It is certain that the Main Building-I belonging to subphase IB was covered with fill, but above it new buildings (the Main Building-II) in the next subphase IIA were constructed along the previous axis. The important tomb in the subphase IIA was prepared at the nearly same place where the previous tomb was located. Reusing the same axis, structures, and burial place would indicate continuity in the control of landscape and cosmology, especially if the axis is connected to the location of another mound around Pacopampa and a mountain, as mentioned before.

We do not know precisely the reason why continuity was favored rather than a negation of past practices, such as with the Kuntur Wasi case. However, we suppose that the leader at Pacopampa intentionally drew on the previous authority or power for the support of the people.

The material culture, such as the pottery of subphase IIA, is thoroughly different

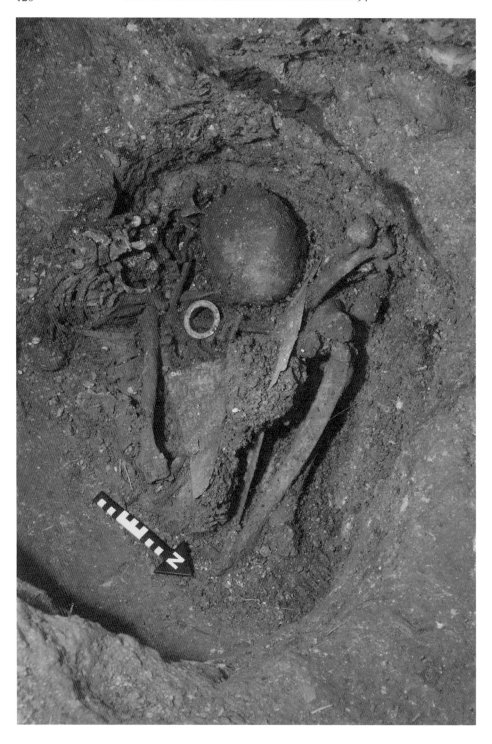

Figure 8.13. The Lady of Pacopampa female burial in Tomb 09-02.

than in the former subphase IB. The new style of pottery is greatly influenced by the North Coast Cupisnique style. The hypothesis mentioned above, that the individual of the tomb could have been brought from another place, indicates that a new leader or other authorities could also be newcomers, but other members of the society would have been the same at Pacopampa since the previous phase. If society was formed by a negotiation between leaders and common people, the new leader at Pacopampa may have chosen a traditional way to control the ideology instead of drastically changing it.

The continuity or succession from subphase IB to IIA allows us to observe another aspect of the architecture at Pacopampa. During our excavations we recorded several ditches in subphase IB where stone walls should have been located. When these walls were dismantled, they left these traces. Considering that large fine-cut stones were used in the architecture in subphase IIA, some stones from the previous phase were very likely to be removed and reused for the new building (Figure 8.17). In general, the quality of the stone in the latter phase is much worse than the earlier phase. The stone in subphase IB is hard and has a smoothed face, whereas the stone from the later phase is easily broken and has impurities such as fossils. It seems that the people in subphase IIA reused the stone blocks because they wanted better materials for the new building, but another interpretation could be that people in subphase IIA reused stones not for practical reasons, but for a ritual or political intention.

Social Memories and the Power

At Classic Maya sites it is common to see the continued use of older building elements incorporated into new architectural design, perhaps in a way similar to the case of Pacopampa. Rosemary Joyce suggests that the persistence of visible reused stones was not an accident, but an intentional way to create a long-term social memory (Joyce 2003:112). She said that a monumental building set with older components, such as significant Maya stone stelae and altars associated with the inscriptions, could provide information about the person, date, and events to privileged visitors.

Recent memory studies also offer new archaeological perspectives. According to these studies, social memory is generally defined as a collective notion, not an individual one, about "the way things were in the past" (Van Dyke and Alcock 2003:2). Construction of social memory will frequently be connected with ancestor worship, mythological antiquity, and legitimation of authority (Alcock 2002). The last of these is relevant here.

It is important to emphasize that the creation of social memory is an ongoing process, because memory will be recalled or thrown away as the present occasion may demand (Van Dyke and Alcock 2003:3). The construction of social memory is achieved through a variety of practices that can be divided in two categories, according to Rowlands (1993). One category is inscribed memory practices, like the construction of commemorative monuments that are visible materially. The other is incorporated memory practices, like ritual behavior, narratives, representations, and objects. Naturally, it is easy for the archaeologist to access the first category. However, some ritual behavior, like mortuary practices and feasting, also leaves visible traces about the creation of social memory. Representations like mural painting and stone statues, and bone or stone objects, can also be occasionally identified as important media for commemorative functions. Along with these elements, the "place" is also an unforgettable element for the creation of social mem-

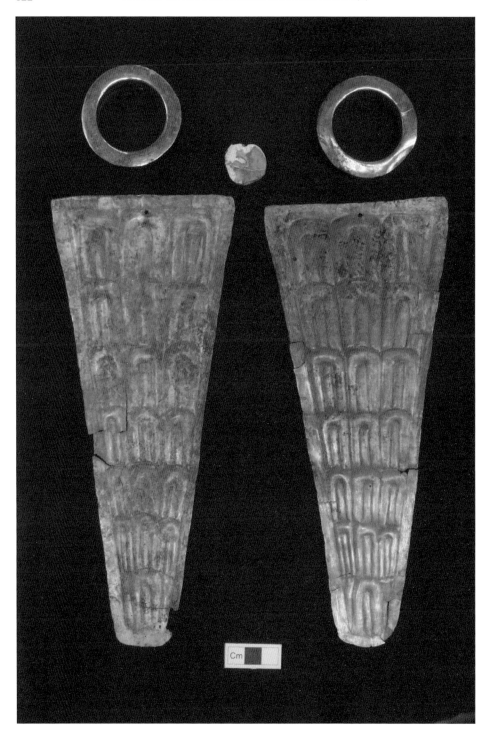

FIGURE 8.14. Triangular gold earrings, gold circular earplugs, and a lithic object made of chryso-colla associated with Tomb 09-02.

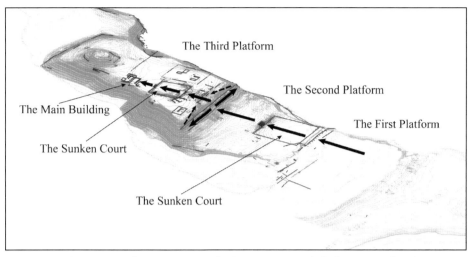

FIGURE 8.15. Access control in structures at the Pacopampa site (subphases IB and IIA).

ory. A particular "place" was inscribed with special meaning if some past event was held there (Van Dyke and Alcock 2003:5–6).

In the Pacopampa case, the reuse of the main axis and architectural components can be classified as inscribed memory practices. Moreover, if we accept the idea presented by Joyce, architectural activities that incorporate older stones in new construction at Pacopampa can be interpreted as a way to create or maintain social memory. Visitors can remember some ritual events held there in previous phases by observing architectural components of previous phases incorporated in the new building. The mixture of older fine-cut stone and brittle stone in the new phase at the same wall looks unattractive, but it may have its own important meaning related to the construction of social memory. But why did the leaders of Pacopampa choose to preserve social memory by reusing older architectural components?

The key could be the evidence that this occurred at the same time as the emergence of new power. This aspect indicates that the creation of social memory at Pacopampa could be related to the formation of power or the legitimation of authority. As mentioned above, the leader at Pacopampa chose to make use of previous architecture, tradition, and cosmology, since he or she needed to construct social memory in a way that common people could easily follow.

Joyce points out other important aspects about the creation of social memory in the Maya case: regulation through space. Social memory is created and strengthened by repetitive and frequent movement through the space in a Maya site (Joyce 2003:112). Daily regulation and regular circulation related to a ritual event in a space urge the creation and recreation of social memory. The stone sculpture and roadway will conduct visitors to move to a regular route. In this sense, succession and reusing previous architecture at Pacopampa would contribute to securing a continuous regulation of the site for a long period. Visitors participate in the creation of social memory by following the regular route through staircases, courts, and small rooms. By tracing the route, visitors can recognize the ease and difficulty of access to particular areas. This recognition is connected with the legitimation of the power of the leaders, and social differentiation.

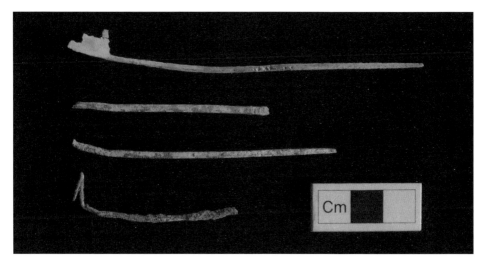

FIGURE 8.16. Copper pin (*tupu*) and chisel recovered from a subphase IIB cavity (Hoyo 09-05).

Social Memory of the Female Founder of the Society

Even if the previous architectural axis and components were reused at Pacopampa, new architectural designs, space, or landscape were also born. One of the most significant features is a tomb. As Van Dyke and Alcock (2003:4) indicate, mortuary practices or commemoration of the dead are the principal ritual behaviors used to construct social memory. In Andean archaeology, Peter Kaulicke (2014) also pointed out that through mortuary practices the "invisible past" is transformed to a "visible past" and repetitive ritual activities help to preserve and recreate memories. In the case of Pacopampa, the Main Building-II, which has an unusual tomb with several offerings, must be considered a commemorative space of the dead. The ritual activities held here recalled the dead (see the discussion below).

Consider also the archaeological evidence dating to the latter part of Pacopampa II Phase (subphase IIB), when Main Building-II was modified. An open canal belonging to subphase IIA located in front of the Main Building-II was filled with soil. We found many shallow pits in the fill that contained burned organic materials such as animal bone and copper objects. These pits seemed to constitute a ritual activity dedicated to the Main Building-II. The interesting thing is that such ritual activities seem to be related to the dead. The artifacts recovered are bone palettes, copper needles or pins (tupus), and a bone tube. The needles and pins found in these offerings are usually related to female dress and weaving, and they are associated with the female tombs at Pacopampa. Therefore, the ritual activities may have served to perpetuate the social memory associated with the Lady of Pacopampa through an extended use of the space in or near the Main Building-II. But, are periodical or occasional ritual activities the only way to maintain or reconstruct social memory? We suppose it is difficult to construct social memory only through ritual behavior, because the tomb and the individual are invisible after the burial. Another possible way to achieve it is through the production and display of a monolith.

There is a possible clue in the design on a monolith that was extracted by Rafael

FIGURE 8.17. A retaining wall of the Third Platform built with two types of limestone.

Larco Hoyle (*La Crónica,* October 1, 1939) from the Pacopampa site and now exhibited at the Museo Larco Herrera in Lima (Figure 8.18). The image depicts a frontal figure with a feline face and a human body carved using a bas-relief technique. Two wings that extend out from both sides of the lower body have a triangular shape oriented downward and both resemble the form of the gold earrings of the Lady of Pacopampa. The feather designs on the earrings were done using an embossing technique on these gold objects (see Figure 8.14). Another iconographic detail that reinforces our interpretation is the distinctive triangular shape of the earrings, which is reminiscent of the wing of a bird.

Another interesting aspect of the monolith is that the sexual organ of the figure is represented as a mouth with fangs. This convention has been referred to as the vagina dentata. The iconography of the jagged vagina can be found on several monoliths and prehispanic objects in the Central Andes and is interpreted as a feminine characteristic (Lyon 1978). This coincides with the sex identified for the individual buried in the tomb of the Lady of Pacopampa. Unfortunately, the stratigraphic or chronological position of the monolith cannot be confirmed, because of the lack of excavation data or provenience information recorded by Larco Hoyle (*La Crónica,* October 1, 1939). However, because of the similarity between the iconography of the monolith and the earrings, there is a high probability that the monolith also belongs to Pacopampa II and was located near the Main Building-II. If so, the monolith would have served to construct and reconstruct social memory related to the dead.

A monolith has great significance for commemoration. Stone as a material has an extended permanency in comparison with other materials like clay, and can be used to form objects that are relatively large in comparison with other permanent materials such as metal. In this sense, a monolith is well suited to transmit permanently a fixed message

FIGURE 8.18. Monolith with bas-relief figure from the Pacopampa site. Photograph courtesy of the Museo Larco Herrera, Lima. Illustration from Roe (1974:54, fig. 24).

to the audience and visitors (Kato 2014). The appearance of the monolith coincides with the emergence of social differentiation at Late Formative Period sites like Chavín de Huántar, Kuntur Wasi, and Pacopampa (Burger 1992).

From the monoliths of Chavín de Huántar, Rick (2005). deciphers something important, that social or religious leaders adopted or took advantage of cultural resources or elements that existed previously in the Andes—like the iconographic representations of animals and hallucinogens—to take control of power or authority. Moreover, the leaders at Chavín de Huántar not only used these elements, but also added human representation to them to indicate that only the societal representatives (such as the leaders) could manage the ideological sector. A monolith is, then, a good means to transmit permanently such a message.

A process similar to the one at Chavín de Huántar can be seen at Pacopampa. The iconography of the Pacompapa I Phase is dominated principally by attributes of animals such as the head and body; these are generally presented on the surface of the ceramics. Monoliths with anthropomorphic representations were recently unearthed near the staircase between the First and Second Platform belonging to Pacompapa II. In this sense the establishment of the power and authority is connected to the embellishment of the monolith with anthropomorphic representations. In other words, the emergent leaders probably used the monolith to construct social memory, and ultimately for the establishment of power and authority.

Conclusions

The data from Pacopampa almost corresponds to that from Kuntur Wasi: the relatively egalitarian societies of the Early and Middle Formative Period were transformed into societies of the Late Formative Period, when social differences were tangible. However, at Pacopampa the change began to appear a little earlier, from the latter part of the Middle Formative Period (subphase IB). At both sites, the emergence of social differentiation is associated with orderly architectural design and tombs buried at the main construction. In Pacopampa, there is control of access to constructions along the axis.

At the same time, we can identify differences in the sources of power used by leaders of the two sites: the leaders at Kuntur Wasi focused on long-distance trade of precious goods and rejected previous architectural structures (and probably the earlier ideology as well). The leaders at Pacopampa focused on the production of copper objects as well as long-distance trade, and they chose partly to respect the traditional ideology. Reusing the axis and some architectural components indicate the incorporation of the landscape and its related ideology or cosmology in the new social arena. What is particularly ingenious is the installation of the main tomb: where an important person—perhaps a founder of the society—was buried at the main construction along the axis, and at the same time the person to be commemorated was replaced by installing a new tomb (the Lady of Pacopampa). To reuse older architectural materials for the new architectural space also may carry a meaning similar to that mentioned above. The leaders from Pacopampa seemed to operate and to control in a traditional way to establish power and authority, so that ordinary people or visitors would accept the new social circumstances and participate in the construction of a common social memory.

This chapter has discussed the variety of ways leaders came to have power, and how this can be inferred by interpreting architectural aspects of these sites. The analysis of cultural remains from Pacopampa is ongoing. Zooarchaeological studies seem to show that animals were used not only as a source of food for ordinary life and ritual feasting, but also as a means of transportation for trade goods. Human bone analysis is indicating not only dietary aspects, but also migration and blood relationships. This data will later be related to the transformation of ideology, social memory, and ultimately the entire society. We must further examine the ideas presented here by considering this new data.

CHAPTER NINE

MONUMENTAL ARCHITECTURE, STARS, AND MOUNDS AT THE TEMPLE OF PACOPAMPA

The Rising Azimuth of the Pleiades and Changing Concepts of Landscape

Masato Sakai, Shinpei Shibata, Toshihiro Takasaki, Juan Pablo Villanueva, and Yuji Seki

Our earlier work (Sakai et al. 2007) on the relationship between cultural landscape and construction activity at the Formative Period temple of Pacopampa in Peru's District of Querocoto, Province of Chota, Department of Cajamarca (Figures 9.1, 9.2) discussed the main axis that passes through the center of the eastern and western stairs at the sunken plaza of the site's Third Platform. We observed that this axis corresponded to the azimuth of Pleiades rise in 500 BC (Sakai et al. 2007:63), but because of limited excavation data a few problems remained to be explored.

Nonetheless, the Pacopampa Archaeological Project has since continued investigations at this site every year and new data from recent excavations have changed our understanding of the monumental architecture and its chronology at Pacopampa (Seki et al. 2008; Seki 2014; Figures 9.3, 9.4). The two phases—the Pacopampa I Phase (1200 cal–800 cal BC) and the Pacopampa II Phase (800 cal–500 cal BC)—established at the site are now each subdivided in two subphases: IA and IB, and IIA and IIB (Seki 2014). It is now clear that the architecture of Pacopampa subphase IA had a very different axis from that of Pacopampa IB, IIA, and IIB. The Circular Building, whose chronological position was not known in 2007, has been shown to date to Pacopampa subphase IB. The sunken plaza of the Third Platform, which we considered to belong to Pacopampa II, turns out to have been constructed during subphase IB and ceased to be used as a plaza at the end of Pacopampa subphase IIB (500 BC).

The research for this chapter was conducted as a part of the Pacopampa Archaeological Project and the archaeological data used here are derived from its published works (Seki et al. 2006, 2008; Seki 2014). Reconsidering the architectural and astronomical data available for the site, we realized that there are three problems that need to be examined thoroughly. The first is that it must be made clear why the architectural axis at the site corresponded to the rising azimuth of the Pleiades, a star cluster in the constellation Taurus, in the year 500 BC, when construction activity ceased at the site. The second is whether the secular change (slow changes in the motion of stars) of the rising azimuth of the Pleiades was recognized at the site or not. If recognized, how was this celestial event related to the beliefs of the society? The final problem is methodological. What is the most appropriate way to conduct the study of astronomical archaeology in relation to archaeological excavations?

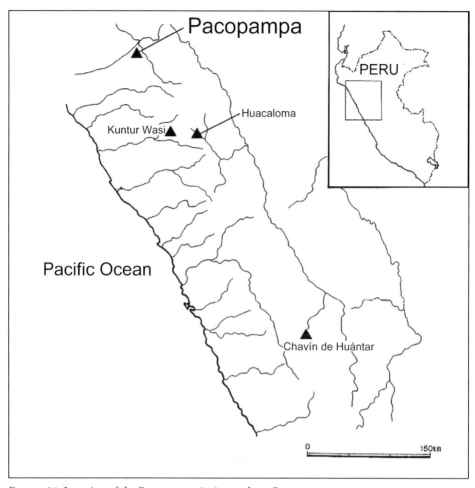

FIGURE 9.1. Location of the Pacopampa site in northern Peru.

Here we discuss the construction activities at Pacopampa in light of recent work in astronomical archaeology and landscape archaeology. Archaeoastronomy can be a productive field of research because it deals with how people in the past recognized and reacted to astronomical phenomena. However, archaeoastronomy sometimes falls victim to ethnocentrism, because it analyzes ancient architecture from the perspective of modern astronomy. Some astronomers decide what is meaningful and what is not in ancient architecture without sufficient consideration of the worldview of people in the past or the distinctive nature of archaeological sampling. As Pauketat (2013:60) described, it is necessary to conduct "analyses of robust fine-grained and large-scale datasets where object biographies, depositional histories, and genealogies of cultural practices might be traced." To approach the problems derived from the nature of archaeological fieldwork, astronomical archaeology needs to be treated as part of archaeology rather than be approached as archaeoastronomy, which pertains to astronomy.

The changing landscape at Pacopampa is one of the key issues presented here. Landscape is a concept closely related to "place" and "space," which are differentiated from

FIGURE 9.2. View of the Pacopampa site looking toward Cerro Pozo Negro.

each other by Tilley (1994) in his influential work on the phenomenological approach. According to Tilley, "places are always far more than points or locations, because they have distinctive meanings and values for persons. Personal and cultural identity is bound up with place" (Tilley 1994:15), while "space can only exist as a set of relations between things or places. Space is created by social relations, natural and cultural objects. It is a production, an achievement, rather than an autonomous reality in which things or people are located" (Tilley 1994:17). He then defines the relationships between architecture and space in the following way:

> Architecture is the deliberate creation of space made tangible, visible and sensible. This is why buildings play a fundamental role in the creation and recreation, production and re-production of existential space and have profound structuring effects on perceptual space. (Tilley 1994:17)

Using these concepts, we will attempt to understand the changes in the landscape at Pacopampa.

Astronomical Archaeology: Problems with Sampling Procedures

Two sources of uncertainty must be noted in the practice of astronomical archaeology. One is uncertainty in dating, especially of construction activities. The other is uncertainty in archaeologically determining the direction or orientation of architecture.

In the case of dating, radiocarbon samples can be obtained from several contexts, such as the inside of a hearth, on the floor, and from architectural fill. In general, however,

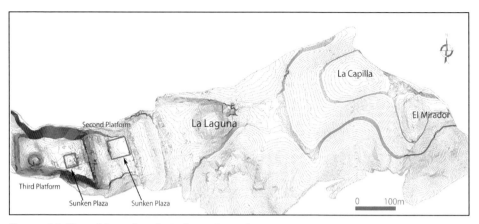

FIGURE 9.3. Plan of the archaeological complex at Pacopampa.

we do not date all the samples gathered, but rather tend to choose those most appropriate for defining the chronological position of architecture. The contextual information of samples is important because it guarantees the reliability of the dates used to interpret architecture. Therefore, it is necessary to collect as many appropriate samples as possible to define the proper chronological position of the architecture.

However, this is possible only in an ideal case. In reality, several obstacles prevent collection of good samples during archaeological fieldwork, such as the scale of excavation, the state of site preservation, and other environmental factors. In these cases, generating proper chronological estimates becomes difficult. In addition, although radiocarbon dating can produce absolute dates, these dates inevitably include a range of uncertainty. Moreover, it is necessary to date several good samples rather than a single sample to properly estimate dates for architecture. It is therefore impossible to determine a specific year for the chronological position of a given example of architecture. Defining the beginning and ending dates for when a structure was used is likewise difficult and also inevitably contains error.

Astronomical archaeology attempts to understand how people in the past recognized celestial bodies and astronomical phenomena. To do this it calculates the movements of the celestial bodies in the past. This type of calculation can produce specific dates that are quite precise. Absolute dates from radiocarbon dating show error ranges of several dozens of years, but the errors in astronomical calculation are minimal. However, there are several problems to be considered before carrying out these calculations.

Determining the direction of walls is crucial for this type of research. Where walls are made of stones and mud mortar, it is sometimes obvious that they are not exactly straight and the direction of a construction inevitably has its own variations. The direction of architectural elements also differs depending on the method of measurement applied in the field. For example, different measurement points in a wall can produce different wall directions. Sometimes small excavation units make it impossible to evaluate architectural direction properly. Several other factors, such as land subsidence, the downward pressure in stratigraphy, and later destruction derived from site formation processes can lead to misunderstandings of the original position of architectural elements. Therefore, it is important to conduct a thorough evaluation to select appropriate architectural elements that show original direction. As is the case with radiocarbon samples, contextual information

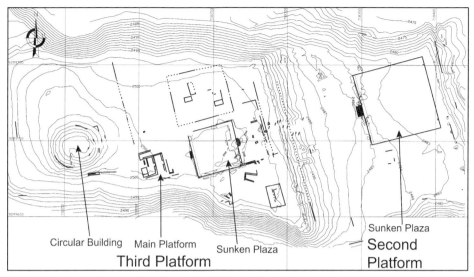

FIGURE 9.4. Plan of the third and second platform at the Pacopampa site.

needs to be presented for these evaluations. That is, one should explain why a construction was selected for analysis and others not. To define dates properly through astronomical calculations, it is necessary to collect a large amount of appropriate data on architectural direction.

Chronology is a crucial issue for the practice of astronomical archaeology. However, because of the nature of radiocarbon dating, the beginning and ending dates of a construction inevitably contain error ranges. Measurements of wall direction used for astronomical calculations can also differ depending on methods of excavation and measurement, and on site formation processes. In practicing astronomical archaeology these factors need to be considered and explained.

The Rising Azimuth of the Pleiades

Astronomical Consideration

The azimuth (location on the horizon) of a star at sunrise gradually changes over time according to Earth's precession. We obtained the rising azimuths of the Pleiades since 2000 BC (Figure 9.5, axis A measured clockwise from true north), at the Pacopampa site (06°20′7.12″S, 79°01′47.34″W) at an altitude of 2,498 masl using StellaNavigator v. 8 (AstroArts 2006). The Pleiades have a spatial extent of about one degree, so we took one of its bright stars, 20 Tauri (Maia), to represent the cluster. We therefore obtained azimuths of 80.06 degrees and 76.28 degrees in 1200 BC and 500 BC, respectively.

There are several factors that affect astronomical calculations, including atmospheric refraction, horizon altitude, atmospheric absorption, dip, and so on. The uncertainties extend even to a culture's definition of "rising." By knowing the path of stars, it is not difficult to correct the measured values of the apparent rise to calculate the rise at the ideal horizon. Whether people might make this correction depends on their cultural background. However, the rate of change in the rising azimuth for a given observatory

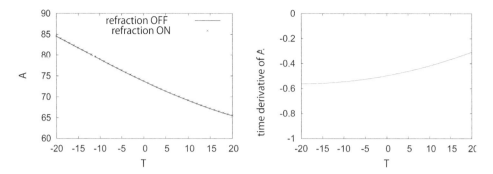

Figure 9.5. The rising azimuth of the Pleiades at the Pacopampa site, showing (*left*) the rate of secular change (A) as a function of the number of centuries (T), measured positively after AD 1. The solid line indicates the case that ignores atmospheric refraction, whereas the crosses indicate that the atmospheric refraction is included. On the right is the rate of change in units of degrees per century.

would be universal and probably not affected by the above factors. We think that in the case of the Temple of Pacopampa the uncertainty of the rising azimuth of the Pleiades is approximately 0.5 degree and no more than one degree.

Method of Calculation

Our astronomical calculations were determined as follows. We calculated the time derivative as:

$$\dot{A} = \frac{dA}{dT}$$
$$= -0.5449 + 0.00327(T+10) + 0.00015(T+10)^2$$

where A is the rising azimuth of the Pleiades, T is the century, and $\dot{A}$ is in degrees per century. We find that the value of $\dot{A}$ was quite stable during the centuries we considered (Figure 9.5); it measured -0.545 ± 0.02 degree per century between 1500 and 500 BC.

    With this value, we see during an interval of seven hundred years a change of A is $-0.545 \times 7 = 3.82 \pm 0.14$ degrees. As mentioned, this result is firm and not affected by any natural factors; thus, this value should be constant over the centuries. This may not be the case if there is a change in how the measurement is made, which defines the star's rise.

    Let us now consider uncertainties in the measurement of A in more detail. The azimuth at the time of a star's rise is defined by the intersection of the path of the rising star and the horizon (R in Figure 9.6). The atmospheric refraction moves a star's apparent position upward so that the rising azimuth is changed. The difference caused by this refraction effect (see Figure 9.5) is very small: $\Delta A = +0.086$ degree from 2000 to 500 BC (plus indicates a southward drift).

    The apparent rising point (P) would be different from R (see Figure 9.6) if, for example, the measurement is made with a certain elevation angle (altitude from the horizon) given by the ridge line. The elevation of Δh and the difference in the azimuth ΔA are related by

$$\Delta A \approx \Delta h \tan x \qquad\qquad \textit{Equation 1}$$

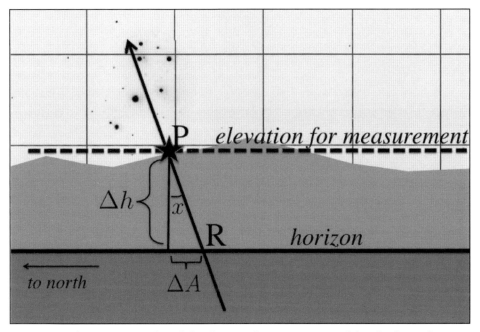

FIGURE 9.6. The rising azimuth and the elevation for measurement of the Pleiades at the Paco-pampa site. The rising azimuth depends on the elevation angle used. The grid shows one degree intervals; A, azimuth of the rising star; h, elevation; P, apparent rising point; R, intersection of the path of the rising star with the horizon; x, inclination of the path of the rising star from the verti-cal; ΔA is a difference of A.

where x is the inclination of the rising path of the star from a vertical line. This approxima-tion can be applied when Δh is small. If the measurement is made in southern latitudes, the path of a star inclines to the north (see Figure 9.6) and the azimuth is displaced to the north. Here for the Pleiades x is 14.9 degrees in 1200 BC and 17.5 degrees in 500 BC.

The elevation measurement is also affected by atmospheric absorption. Because of the atmospheric absorption, the Pleiades observed at 0 masl look dim very near the hori-zon, but are clearly seen at an elevation higher than $\Delta h = 5$ degrees, where they are three magnitudes brighter (Allen 1973). Note that the absorption is so small at the Pacopampa site, at 2,498 m, that we do not need to consider the effect of atmospheric absorption.

At the Pacopampa site the atmospheric absorption is so slight that we used the ho-rizon as the elevation for this measurement. On the horizon, or at $\Delta h = 1.9$ degrees, the rising of the Pleiades is postulated as observable at the site from 1200 to 500 BC. From this relationship (see Equation 1), if we use $\Delta h = 1.9$ degrees as the elevation measurement, then ΔA is −0.540 degree in 1200 BC and −0.599 degree in 500 BC.

$$\Delta h = - \sqrt{\frac{H}{1\,\text{km}}} \text{ degrees}$$

The dip (downward angle blow the horizon) is also known to affect the measure-ment where H is the height above sea level. This would be important when an observation is made on a mountaintop. At Pacopampa, however, observations were made on a hill surrounded by mountains, so that this would not be a factor in the observation of the rising azimuth. The Pleiades star cluster itself has an apparent size of about one degree in

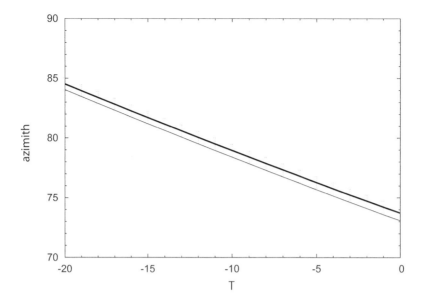

FIGURE 9.7. The rising azimuth and the finite extent of the Pleiades at the Pacopampa site. The rising azimuth (thick line) at the horizon and that measured at the elevation of 1.9 degrees (thin line), nearly the angles at which the Pleiades had risen at the Pacopampa site from 1200 to 500 BC. The dashed vertical bars indicate the finite extent of ±0.4 degree of the Pleiades.

the horizontal direction (see Figure 9.6). Therefore, we expect uncertainties of about ±0.4 degree in the measurement of the position of the Pleiades.

From this discussion we see that the ideal rising azimuth (Figure 9.7, thick line) is measured at the elevation angle of 1.9 degrees, and the effect of the finite size is ±0.4 degree (Figure 9.7, dashed vertical bars at each point). Thus, the most important factors that cause uncertainties in determining the rising azimuth are (1) the elevation angle that is used to determine the azimuth at star rise (the ridge line, the atmospheric absorption, and others), and (2) the apparent size of the Pleiades cluster itself. We think that the uncertainty of the rising azimuth of the Pleiades is approximately 0.5 degree, but no more than one degree.

Construction Activities at the Pacopampa Site

Pacopampa IA and Location Selection

The temple of Pacopampa, or the Pacopampa site, is surrounded by mountains. Generally, those with pointed summits are locally called *picchu* and regarded as sacred places to be worshipped. Among the mountains around Pacopampa, Cerro Pozo Negro (see Figure 9.2) can be included in this category. Located 20 km to the southwest of Pacopampa, the mountain can be seen from the site. The lakes on the mountaintop are the source of the Leche and Reque Rivers, whose waters run to the Pacific Ocean. Cerro Pozo Negro can therefore be considered to be sacred and intimately related with water.

To the northeast of the temple of Pacopampa there are three mounds, El Mirador, La Capilla, and La Laguna; the distance from them to Pacopampa is about 800 m, 700 m, and 300 m, respectively (see Figure 9.3). In considering the landscape around Pacopampa, it is notable that these three archaeological sites are located on natural hilltops. Past research has confirmed the presence of Pacopampa I and II Phase pottery at El Mirador and La Capilla (Flores 1975; Morales 1980, 1998) and Pacopampa I at La Laguna. El Mirador is believed to be the location of the quarry that provided construction materials for the monumental architecture at Pacopampa (Masaaki Shimizu and Marina Shimizu, personal communication). In other words, El Mirador can be considered as the source of the monumental architecture at Pacopampa.

Pacopampa is located exactly on the straight line joining Cerro Pozo Negro and El Mirador. This geographic relationship is not a coincidence, but intentionally connects the site with the two sacred and origin places.

ARCHITECTURAL DIRECTIONS
Construction of monumental architecture began as early as the Pacopampa IA subphase. Five architectural stages (1–5) are identified that represent continuous renovations carried out in subphase IA.

The measurement of wall directions in each stage is influenced by both the size of a wall itself and the size of the excavation unit. Only the wall at stage 4 can be used for an astronomical archaeological analysis, because the walls of the stages 1, 2, and 5 are 0.1 m, 0.3 m, and 0.75 m in length, respectively, and thus are too short to be used to measure direction. Although the stage 3 wall is 5.1 m in length, it is low and made of small stones, too unreliable for this analysis because the fragility of the construction material could permit a shift from its original location. Only the stage 4 wall is appropriate for study, since it is made of two layers of large stones and thus probably maintains its original position, necessary for this analysis (Figure 9.8).

MONUMENTAL ARCHITECTURE AND THE PLEIADES
In this section, we will evaluate the possibility that the architectural axes of the Pacopampa IA subphase constructions were placed in accordance with the rising azimuth of the Pleiades. The architecture of subphase IA was constructed from 1200 to 1000 BC. The rising azimuth of the Pleiades during this period was 80.057 to 79.863 degrees (clockwise from true north). The direction of the stage 4 wall is 10.415 to 9.873 degrees (counterclockwise from true north). If the wall was part of a rectangular structure, the east–west axis is 79.585 to 80.127 degrees (clockwise from true north), which is very close to the rising azimuth of the Pleiades in the year 1200 cal BC (the difference is 0.070 to 0.472 degree). With this analysis, it seems reasonable to assume that construction activities of this subphase were carried out using the rising azimuth of the Pleiades (Figure 9.9).

Monumental Architecture in Pacopampa IB
The architectural plan of the Pacopampa site radically changed in Pacopampa subphase IB, ca. 1000 cal BC or slightly later (Seki 2014:185). The constructions of the previous subphase IA were sealed. The large retaining walls of the Third Platform were probably built at the same time. In the southeast section of the Third Platform, the Main Platform-I and a 30 by 30 m sunken plaza were constructed. In the western section of this platform a Circular Building of 28 to 29 m in diameter was built with a low square platform at the eastern foot of the building (Figures 9.10, 9.11, 9.12). On this square platform three benches were constructed. The central bench measures 2.30 to 2.40 m in length, 90 cm to 1 m in width, and 24 cm in height. The central bench faces La Capilla (Figure 9.13). We believe that the

FIGURE 9.8. Walls from subphase IA at the Pacopampa site. At left is a stage 4 long wall.

architectural axis of the Circular Building in subphase IB was defined using the direction to La Capilla observed from the central bench. The other constructions of subphase IB (the Main Platform-I, a sunken plaza, and the constructions around them) are arranged parallel to the direction mentioned above.

Whereas the Main Platform-I and a sunken plaza were placed on the Third Platform, which corresponds to the highest location in the temple of Pacopampa, another sunken plaza was constructed on the lower terrace, the Second Platform. The sizes of these two sunken plazas are quite different; the plaza on the Second Platform is far larger than the one on the Third Platform. These three constructions share the central axis, which was arranged to pass through the top of La Laguna. Since the center point of the Circular Building is true west of this point of the sunken plaza, the arrangement of the sunken plaza and the Circular Building seems to have been carefully planned with precise measurements.

Construction Activities in Pacopampa II

PACOPAMPA IIA
The previous constructions of Pacopampa subphase IB were reused during subphase IIA. The Circular Building was continually used during this period. A new access consisting of three staircases to the top of the Circular Building was added to the east façade (Figure 9.14). When these staircases were constructed, the central bench was buried under them. Because the axis of the staircases corresponds to the direction to La Capilla, it is probable that the top of the Circular Building was set as the new observatory in the Pacopampa IIA subphase.

The tomb of the "Lady of Pacopampa" (see Chapter 8) was built after the abandon-

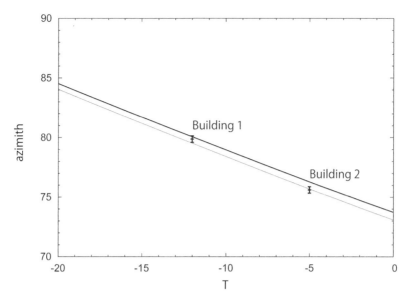

FIGURE 9.9. Rising azimuth of the Pleiades in relation to construction activities at the Pacopampa site. The directions of Buildings 1 and 2 are indicated with error bars on the astronomical calculation. Building 1 is dated to 1200 BC and Building 2 to 500 BC. The rising azimuth (thick line) is at the ideal horizon and the measurement at the elevation of 1.9 degrees is also plotted (thin line). Within errors in measurement of direction and astronomical uncertainties of about 0.5 degree, the orientations of the buildings are consistent with the rising azimuth of the Pleiades.

ment of the Main Platform-I and before the construction activities of subphase IIA. This important burial was placed on the central axis of the Main Platform.

DENIAL OF THE CENTRAL AXIS IN SUBPHASE IIB

The central axis of the sunken plaza on the Third Platform matches not only that of the Main Platform-II, but also the central axis of the sunken plaza on the Second Platform. As discussed earlier, this axis was created in the Pacopampa IB subphase based on the direction to La Capilla from the observatory of the Circular Building, and was inherited by the Pacopampa IIA constructions.

However, the north and south stairs of the sunken plaza on the Third Platform were closed in subphase IIB and it is probable that the west and east stairs were closed as well. This change suggests a rejection of the axis that functioned during subphases IB and IIA. Although the central axis was rejected, the plaza itself continued to be used in subphase IIB with the new accesses on the northwest and southeast corners.

MONUMENTAL ARCHITECTURE AND THE PLEIADES AT THE END OF SUBPHASE IIB

The end of the Pacopampa IIB subphase (500 BC) corresponds to the time the architectural axis matched the rising azimuth of the Pleiades (see Figure 9.9). The construction of monumental architecture ceased at the same time.

For example, the north wall of the sunken plaza is oriented about 75.879 degrees (clockwise from true north) and the south wall about 75.336 degrees. Since the rising azimuth of the Pleiades in 500 BC was 76.280 degrees, the difference from the north wall was about 0.401 degree and that from the south wall was about 0.944 degree. However, in

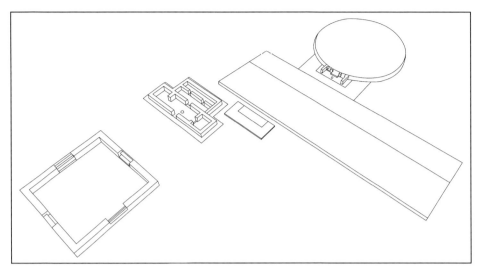

FIGURE 9.10. The Circular Building and the Main Platform-I from subphase IB at the Pacopampa site. Courtesy of the Pacopampa Archaeological Project.

400 BC the rising azimuth of the Pleiades became 75.757 degrees and thus the orientations of the north and south walls of the sunken plaza almost match with it. At approximately this time, large-scale construction activities at Pacopampa ended. Given the astronomical calculations presented above, it is probably safe to say that the alignment of the rising azimuth of the Pleiades with the main architectural axis at Pacopampa could be observed from 500 to 400 BC. In this case, 500 BC can be interpreted as when this alignment began to be recognized.

Discussion

The Pleiades and Subsistence Economy
Why was the rising azimuth of the Pleiades an important criterion for setting the central axis of the monumental architecture at Pacopampa? Modern ethnographic data helps us to deal with this question. The farmers in the Peruvian south-central highlands still observe the Pleiades in relation to their agricultural activities, as do farmers in other regions of the world. Orlove and his colleagues provide the following important ethnographic account that sheds light on this issue:

> Across the Andes in Peru and Bolivia, Indian farmers gather in small groups in the middle of the night in late June. They climb high ridges and often ascend to the peaks of mountains. … The farmers huddle together in eager expectancy. They are waiting for the moment when they can see the Pleiades, a star cluster in the constellation Taurus. At this time of year, the Pleiades become visible low in the northeast sky only as dawn nears. The farmers believe that they can use the particular appearance of the Pleiades to forecast the timing and quantity of precipitation that will fall in the rainy season, months later. (Orlove, Chiang, and Cane 2002:428)

As Orlove and his colleagues note, in late June, farmers go to the mountaintops at night to observe the rising of the Pleiades. This activity is believed to be useful for

FIGURE 9.11. The East Stair of a sunken plaza at the Third Platform at Pacopampa.

forecasting the beginning of the rainy season and how much rain will fall. In their narratives, when the Pleiades rise large and bright, farmers will have a good harvest; when they rise small and dim, the harvest will be poor. Ethnographic studies have reported that this type of Pleiades observation is also used to forecast El Niño events and thus to estimate the amount of rainfall in the coming rainy season (Orlove, Chiang, and Cane 2000, 2002).

Observation of the Pleiades goes back to prehispanic periods (Avila 1966; Aveni 1981; Urton 1981; Urton and Aveni 1983). Some scholars suggest the possibility that the monumental architecture of Chavín de Huántar was used for this purpose in the Formative Period (Urton and Aveni 1983:229; Burger 1992:132). On the other hand, Rick (2008:12–13) recently has argued that the monumental architecture of Chavín de Huántar was related to solstice alignment rather than to the Pleiades.

Considering that the observation of the Pleiades is useful in forecasting rainfall and that the architectural alignment at Pacopampa accords with the rising azimuth of the Pleiades, it is difficult to deny that observation of the Pleiades was probably conducted at the temple of Pacopampa. As we have described, the temple of Pacopampa is located on the top of a mountain and its architectural alignment matches the rising azimuth of the Pleiades in the Pacopampa IA subphase. This suggests that monumental architecture at Pacopampa was used as an observatory for the Pleiades. It is likely that people gathered there to observe the rising azimuth of the Pleiades and discussed the appropriate time for planting according to what they saw. Probably the gathering of community members for this astronomical observation played an important role in integrating Pacopampa society. The temple of Pacopampa would have functioned as an astronomical observatory in this social context.

FIGURE 9.12. The Circular Building on the Third Platform at Pacopampa.

The Pleiades and Power

If the Pleiades were regarded as a useful indicator for forecasting rainfall, people could have been observing it for a long time. Even after setting up the architectural axis in accordance with the rising azimuth of the Pleiades during Pacopampa IA, people continued to make astronomical observations and in the later phases the site was probably regarded as appropriate for observing the Pleiades.

During Pacopampa IB there were large-scale renovations of the monumental architecture, and a sunken rectangular plaza and platform were constructed on the Third Platform, which occupies the hilltop. Another sunken plaza was placed on the Second Platform, located below the hilltop. It was much larger than the one on the hilltop and thus could accommodate far more people (Figure 9.15). Recent excavations showed that at the beginning of subphase IIA an important burial with gold artifacts (the Lady of Pacopampa tomb) was placed in the Main Platform-I. These data suggest that a change occurred in the manipulation of power in the Pacopampa society (Seki 2014). Apparently this change is reflected in the architectural design (see Chapter 8).

In the Pacopampa II Phase, there was no access to the hilltop, where architecture was concentrated, so it is evident that such access was restricted. Only a small group was allowed to observe the Pleiades from the hilltop, while most of the population viewed it from the plaza at the Second Platform. Probably the people who had access to the top of the temple monopolized the knowledge and the procedures to interpret the astronomical phenomenon as a source of power. By predicting the timing and amount of rain, they could estimate the best time for planting, an ability that would have helped them to display and justify their authority in the society.

FIGURE 9.13. View of La Capilla and El Mirador from the Circular Building.

Recognition of the Secular Change of the Rising Azimuth of the Pleiades

PACOPAMPA IA

The rising azimuth of the Pleiades gradually changes through time. In a hundred years it moves to the north approximately 0.5 degree. If the monumental architecture of Pacopampa was constructed in relation to the rising azimuth of the Pleiades around 1200 BC (Pacopampa subphase IA), after two hundred years (i.e., 1000 BC) the architectural orientation became one degree off from the rising azimuth, a discrepancy that can be visually recognized on the ground.

The excavation data reveal that the Pacopampa IA hilltop architecture was renovated at least five times. Although the available architectural data are limited for this subphase, it is likely that the monumental construction activities during these renovations followed the direction of original walls constructed around 1200 BC without adjusting for the changing azimuth of the Pleiades. However, two hundred years later, around 1000 BC, the gap between the architectural axis and the rising azimuth would have been noticeable, and led to the recognition that the azimuth of the rising Pleiades had moved to the north.

PACOPAMPA IB

The recognition of this "gap" between the architectural axis and the rising azimuth of the Pleiades is reflected in the large-scale renovations of monumental architecture around 1000 BC. The architectural axis was not adjusted in relation to the rising azimuth. Instead, the designers of the temple adopted a new axis using orientation toward the top of La Ca-

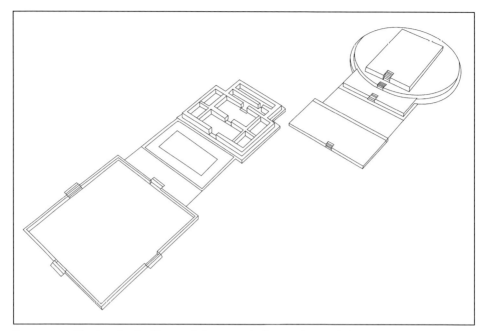

Figure 9.14. The Circular Building and the Main Platform-II from subphase IIA at the Pacopampa site. Courtesy of the Pacopampa Archaeological Project.

pilla from the central bench at the eastern foot of the Circular Building. Because the view from this bench was open, it was an appropriate setting for an astronomical observatory. During this subphase, a new platform and sunken plazas were constructed parallel to the line from the observatory to the top of La Capilla. Specifically, the direction to La Capilla seen from the observatory was 75.642 degrees and the central axis of the sunken plaza was 75.913 degrees, a difference of less than 0.3 degree.

Since the rising azimuth of the Pleiades was 78.963 degrees in 1000 BC, a difference of 3.321 degrees existed with the new axis. According to our calculations, the Pleiades rose from La Capilla at approximately 400 BC. It is possible that people might have anticipated that the Pleiades would rise from La Capilla in the future, but it is impossible to know to what extent they had calculated this with any precision.

Changing Recognition to Landscape

As we have shown, during Pacopampa IA the monumental architecture was built using the rising azimuth of the Pleiades to orient the main axis, and access to the hilltop constructions was not restricted. However, beginning in subphase IB, the direction to the top of La Capilla was used to define the main axis and access to the hilltop architecture of Pacopampa was restricted. At this point it is worth considering who carried out the construction activities and how they were organized. The unrestricted access in subphase IA suggests that the building activities were carried out through corporate labor by local community members. On the other hand, the restricted access of the later subphases and phases seems to imply the presence of an elite class of leaders who designed the architecture and directed the public constructions. This point is supported by the osteological analysis of the Lady of Pacopampa burial, which dates to the very beginning of subphase

Figure 9.15. The central staircase between the First Platform and the Second Platform. There is no access to the Third Platform.

IIA and was associated with gold artifacts (see Chapter 8). The cranial deformation of this individual implies that the social status of the elite class in Pacopampa was inherited (Seki et al. 2008; Nagaoka et al. 2012).

During Pacopampa IA, community members constructed their landscape in a way related to the conventional view of associating the Pleiades with agricultural activities. By observing the Pleiades, they could forecast the rainfall, predict the harvest, and decide the time of planting. These were routine agricultural activities included in daily life, and the temple of Pacopampa was the preferred place to practice these activities.

However, from subphase IB onward, the emerging elite class produced an architectural space for themselves. The subphase IA constructions built by corporate labor were buried, and a new space was produced on the hilltop by constructing another platform to support another sunken plaza. This architectural space was intimately linked to nearby mounds. As mentioned above, the axis of subphase IB constructions was defined by a line parallel to that from the observatory to La Capilla. In addition, the central axis of the platform (Main Platform-I) and sunken plaza was arranged to pass through the top of La Laguna.

This change in the architectural axis corresponds to the production of a new spatial order in the monumental architecture of Pacopampa. The emerging elite class adopted orientation with the mounds as the basis for the main axis of the monumental architecture rather than the rising azimuth of the Pleiades, which moved through time. Probably, mounds played an important role in justifying the elite authority and new religious system associated with them.

In addition, the elite class at Pacopampa seems to have accelerated interregional interactions, beginning in subphase IB. The U-shaped arrangement of monumental architecture seen in contemporary sites such as Chavín de Huántar in the central highlands and Kuntur Wasi in the Northern Highlands appears at Pacopampa and the presence of exotic objects of gold, cinnabar, and sea shells also suggests interactions beyond a regional level.

In considering the creation of this new landscape in subphase IB, the concept of "landscape on move" is useful (Bender 2001:5–13). The emerging elites who had knowledge of the world outside of the region moved the landscape and produced a new spatial order in the monumental architecture. That is, the elite class took the lead in the monumental construction projects of subphase IB, which contrast with that of the former phase.

During subphase IIA at Pacopampa, the astronomical observatory was moved from the foot to the top of the Circular Building, thereby providing a finer view. It is reasonable to say that the landscape of subphase IB was inherited by those of subphase IIA. However, this situation radically changed at the beginning of subphase IIB. Probably people became aware of the secular change of the rising azimuth of the Pleiades and realized that the Pleiades would rise from the top of La Capilla in the near future. This threatened the authority of the spatial order produced by the elite class. The space would be tied to the stars rather than the mounds, because the wall directions would match the rising azimuth of the Pleiades. This was not an acceptable situation for the elite class, because they had produced a spatial order and an associated religious systems focusing on mounds. The closure of the main stairs of the sunken plaza in subphase IIB can be interpreted as the reaction by the elites to this situation. It suggests that the landscape produced by the elite class was being undermined.

The End of Monumental Construction and the Collapse of Interregional Networks

At the end of the Pacopampa IIB subphase around 500 BC, Pacopampa ceased to function as a center of interregional importance. This period corresponds to a time of radical changes in contemporary ceremonial centers, such as the end of the Kuntur Wasi Phase at Kuntur Wasi and the Late Huacaloma Phase at Huacaloma. In accordance with this change, the network of interregional interactions collapsed and the local elites were unable to obtain exotic goods used to establish and reinforce their authority.

As discussed above, the elite class produced a landscape and spatial order in relation to mounds and used them as a source of power and authority. However, as a result of the secular change of the rising azimuth of the Pleiades, the landscape and the spatial order of the elite class in relation to mounds were threatened. It became impossible to maintain the superiority of their landscape and spatial order. Therefore, the elite class lost important sources of their power and authority and probably became incapable of continuing monumental construction projects.

The cases of Kuntur Wasi and Huacaloma are relevant to considering the case of Pacopampa. Although no longer part of an interregional network, these centers continued to function by transforming into regional centers. These examples contrast with the case of Pacopampa, a site that did not become a regional center and simply ended its history as a large ceremonial center.

Through the long-term observation of the Pleiades, people could have known that in the ancient times the star cluster had risen from the top of El Mirador, a mound located to the south of La Capilla, and that the rising azimuth was gradually moving to the north. Around 500 BC they finally recognized that the secular movement of the rising azimuth had reached La Capilla. This phenomenon might have been interpreted as the end of a big block of time, perhaps the end of their history, and this could explain the end of monumental construction activities at Pacopampa.

Conclusions

In the Pacopampa IA subphase, observation of the Pleiades was a part of communal agricultural activities at the temple of Pacopampa. In this subphase, the architectural axis of the monumental architecture aligned with the rising azimuth of the Pleiades. Construction activities were carried out through corporate labor in the community, and monumental architecture functioned not only as a symbol of social integration, but as a place to observe the rise of the Pleiades. Probably the temple was open to all the community members and was used as a place for gatherings to decide the issues of agricultural activities, such as the timing for planting and harvesting. These issues could have been evaluated by the community members through the empirical knowledge about the correlation between the Pleiades and rainfall. By the end of Pacopampa IA, the gap between the site's architectural axis and the rising azimuth of the Pleiades became visually notable, and this enabled people to recognize the secular change of the rising azimuth of the stars.

In the Pacopampa IB subphase, the main axis of the monumental architecture was moved to match the direction of a mound. This change is important because people had recognized the secular change of the rising azimuth of stars and probably thus changed the axis to orient with a fixed and unmoving criterion, mounds. The mounds selected to define the axis were regarded as sacred places and were actively used to justify the authority of the emerging elite class and their religious ideology.

In this subphase, large-scale renovations of the monumental architecture were carried out at Pacopampa, which adopted a U-shaped layout similar to that seen in the several contemporary sites in northern Peru. An important burial at the conclusion of this subphase, or the beginning of the next subphase, was associated with exotic artifacts of gold, cinnabar, and shell. These goods were not available locally and thus clearly were brought to Pacopampa from outside through interregional interactions. The new spatial order and landscape in this subphase were produced by the emerging elite class that had contact with the societies outside of the region. In this new spatial order, the access to the monument at the hilltop was restricted to a small number of people, probably elites, and the others, or commoners, gathered in the sunken plaza placed on a lower terrace that has no access to the upper part of the monument.

The spatial order of subphase IB was inherited in the Pacopampa IIA subphase despite the modifications in architecture. Although the axis was maintained, the observatory was moved from the foot of the Circular Building to its top, probably for the purpose of obtaining a better view.

In subphase IIB, people began to recognize that the Pleiades would rise from the top of La Capilla in the near future and that at that time all the architectural orientations would be aligned with the rising azimuth of the Pleiades. This astronomical phenomenon made the relationship between the temple and the stars more explicit than that between the temple and mounds. This threatened the authority of the elite class, whose spatial order and associated religious systems focused on the mounds. In subphase IIB, the main stairs of the sunken plaza were closed, probably as a reaction by the elites to this phenomenon, which implies that the landscape produced by the elite class was becoming unstable. At the same time, contemporary centers ceased to function as centers of interregional importance, which also influenced Pacopampa society. As a result, monumental construction activities at Pacopampa ended around 500 BC.

This study clarifies problems raised in an earlier article (Sakai et al. 2007), yet the following two issues remain to be evaluated by future research:

1. Although five architectural stages are recognized in the Pacopampa IA subphase, we assume that the architecture at each stage followed the orientation of the older walls rather than being modified based on actual observations of the rising azimuth of the Pleiades. Because the excavations were limited, we do not have enough data to evaluate this hypothesis and thus data on the orientation of the architecture of subphase IA still need to be collected.

2. The preceding studies document the presence of the Pacopampa subphase IA pottery at El Mirador and La Capilla (Flores 1975; Morales 1980, 1998). However, it is difficult to identify from pottery styles whether use of the sites began in subphase IA or subphase IB. For a better understanding of the spatial order and social organization of Pacopampa, it seems necessary to excavate at these two other mounds.

CHAPTER TEN

DIACHRONIC CHANGES IN SOCIOPOLITICAL DEVELOPMENTS AND INTERREGIONAL INTERACTION IN THE EARLY HORIZON EASTERN MONTANE FOREST

Ryan Clasby

Scholars have long suspected that the peoples of the eastern slopes were significantly involved in the historical processes that led to the development of sociopolitical complexity in the Central Andes, beginning with Julio Tello and his explanation for the tropical forest influence in Chavín iconography (Tello 1922, opp. 10, 1940:635–636; Willey 1951:105; see also Burger 2009b:74). Donald Lathrap (1970) later expanded on this idea in his seminal publication *The Upper Amazon,* which synthesized the archaeology of the eastern slopes. Lathrap's work provided detailed descriptions of the material culture from this zone, and showed that this culture shared stylistic affinities with contemporary materials from the Andean coast and highlands. From these similarities, Lathrap argued that the communities of the eastern slopes were deeply integrated into exchange networks with the Andes during the Initial Period and Early Horizon and developed unique cultural identities that were reflective of these long-distance relationships.

Unfortunately, a lack of archaeological investigation made it difficult for Lathrap to describe eastern slope societies in any significant detail. This problem persisted as few sustained, large scale investigations were carried out in the ensuing decades. Despite significant advances in studies concerning the origins of sociopolitical complexity in the Central Andes, the eastern slopes remain little understood from the perspective of settlement patterns, sociopolitical developments, and economy.

In recent years, however, there has been a surge of interest in the eastern slopes, particularly within the Jaén region of the northeastern Peruvian Andes, culminating in several archaeological investigations (Olivera 1998, 2013, 2014; Valdez 2007, 2008, 2011, 2013a, 2013b; Yamamoto 2007, 2008, 2011, 2013; Clasby and Meneses Bartra 2013; Clasby 2014a, 2014b). These investigations are beginning to reveal the type of societies that existed within the eastern slopes and provide a rich data set from which to understand long-term sociopolitical change at both site- and region-based scales. In addition, it is becoming possible to contextualize these developments within a larger prehistorical narrative concerning the rise of sociopolitical complexity in the Central Andes.

Here I use new data from the site of Huayurco in the Jaén region to explore diachronic changes in sociopolitical complexity in the eastern slope societies during the Early Horizon and the effect that interregional interaction had on these developments. I

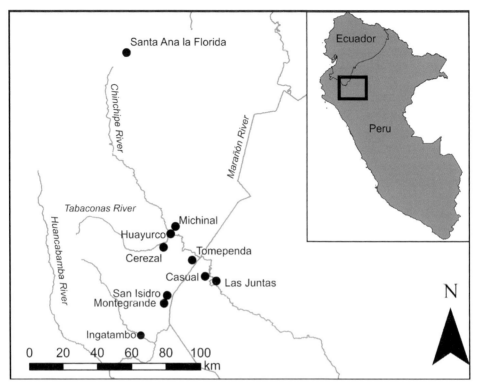

FIGURE 10.1. The major river valleys and sites within the Jaén region of Peru.

then examine Huayurco in relation to other investigated sites in the Jaén region to form a broader understanding of the cultural patterns that existed there during the Early Horizon, the results of which will be contextualized within the larger historical processes in the development of complex societies in the Central Andes.

The Jaén Region

The Jaén region, located along the Peruvian–Ecuadorian frontier (Figure 10.1), is particularly well suited for understanding sociopolitical developments in the eastern slope societies and their relationship to the Andean highlands and coast. The Jaén region is situated in the eastern half of the Huancabamba Depression, a relatively low and narrow section of the Andes. The Huancabamba Depression is a series of low-lying ridges and basins resulting from a physical interruption of the Central and Eastern Cordilleras by the Chamaya River drainage system (Raymond 1988; Young and Reynel 1997; Duellman and Pramuk 1999; Wiegend 2002; Koch, Venegas, and Böhme 2006). Coupled with the low elevations of the Western Cordillera (rarely exceeding 3,500 masl), this break results in a westward extension of the eastern montane forest that blurs the division of coast, highland, and tropical forest that characterizes much of the Central Andes.

The Chamaya drainage that causes this interruption encompasses several river systems originating in the Peruvian and Ecuadorian highlands. These rivers, including the

Huancabamba, Tabaconas, Chamaya, Chinchipe, and Utcubamba, converge in the Jaén region, joining the Marañón River as it turns east (see Figure 10.1). Together these valleys create a series of natural corridors that connect the tropical forest to the Andean highlands and Pacific coast, which would have promoted movement and exchange between these different environmental zones.

Although the Jaén region is broadly characterized by montane forest, variation in altitude and rainfall has significant effects on the local climate, leading to micro-environments such as high altitude grasslands or *páramo* (generally found above 3,200 masl), montane cloud forest (1,700–3,300 masl), and dry forest (300–1,700 masl) (Young and Reynel 1997). Much of the region, especially along the lower river valleys, corresponds to dry forest and is characterized by hot, humid temperatures and xerophytic vegetation, its aridity the result of rain shadows (see Neill [2007a], [2007b]). In addition to acting as a geographical bridge between coastal, highland, and tropical forest environments, the Jaén region also forms part of a cultural frontier between different archaeological culture areas. Indeed, many scholars treat the Huancabamba Depression as a transitional zone between the Northern and Central Andes (Guffroy 2008; see also Burger 1984b, 2003b).

Archaeological Research in the Jaén Region

The Jaén region's archaeological potential was first borne out with the discovery of the Huayurco site along the Chinchipe–Tabaconas confluence in 1961 by Pedro Rojas (1961, 1985; Lathrap 1970). Rojas, in an attempt to evaluate Tello's hypothesis that the Chavín culture had its roots in the Marañón River system, located Huayurco during a three-year expedition to the northeastern Peruvian Andes. Through test excavations Rojas identified a burial with several offerings that were suggestive of both local and nonlocal origins. These included a brownware bottle, worked marine shell items, and many finely carved stone bowls (14 complete vessels and 130 fragments; see Clasby 2014b). The ceramic bottle form and the stone bowl iconography shared stylistic traits with early traditions found in coastal, highland, and tropical lowland sites, leading Lathrap (1970:108–109) to suggest that Huayurco, through the production of stone bowls for export, was involved in early interregional exchange networks connecting the Andean highlands to the Amazon rainforest.

Subsequent investigations by Ruth Shady (1973, 1987, 1999; Shady and Rosas 1979) in Bagua and Jaime Miasta (1979) in the lower Chinchipe and Tabaconas Valleys provided further insight into the material culture of the Jaén region. Shady's Bagua investigations were important in outlining a relative ceramic sequence for the late Initial Period and Early Horizon.

More recently, the Jaén region has hosted several large scale investigations (Valdez 2007, 2008, 2011, 2013a, 2013b; Yamamoto 2007, 2008, 2011, 2013; Olivera 2013, 2014), each of which has documented extensive evidence of ceremonial architecture. At the site of Santa Ana–La Florida in Loja, Ecuador, Francisco Valdez (2008, 2013a) discovered the foundations of circular stone structures located on top of an alluvial terrace. One of these structures featured curvilinear walls that ended in a spiral near the center of a terrace (Valdez 2008:878–879). A hearth was identified in the center of the spiral and below it was a finely carved stone bowl and several greenstone artifacts. Close to the hearth, but at a

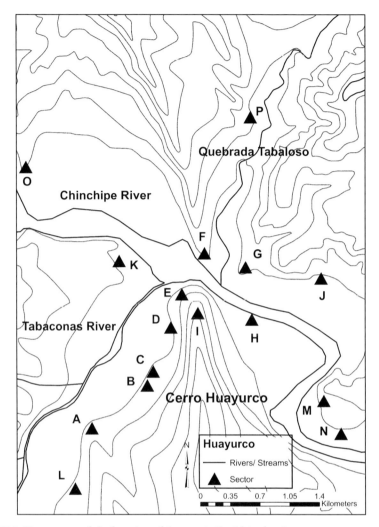

FIGURE 10.2. Huayurco and the location of Sectors A–P within the site.

greater depth, excavators identified a shaft tomb that contained *Strombus* shell, greenstone pendants, stone bowls, and pottery, including four types of stirrup-spout vessels (Valdez 2008:878–884). A series of radiocarbon dates (Valdez 2013a:109–110, table 1, fig. 1) place this feature and the architecture within the Central Andean Late Preceramic, suggesting that the Jaén region had formed unique ceremonial complexes, established local industries, and engaged in long-distance relationships with coastal populations before 2000 BC.

Quirino Olivera's (2013, 2014) investigations at Montegrande, a mound site with artificial platforms and located just outside the city of Jaén, support these findings. Excavation revealed evidence of concentric circular stone footings, many covered in a light-colored plaster, split by a stone staircase. Excavation of the northeastern sector of the mound also revealed a spiral-shaped stone structure (Olivera 2013:183–184, 2014). Although radiocarbon dates are unavailable, the similarity of the spiral architecture to Santa Ana–La Florida, as well as the lack of associated ceramics, suggests that Montegrande may also correspond to the Late Preceramic. More research is needed, but both sites speak to an early ceremonial architectural tradition in the Jaén region.

In western Jaén, along the Huancabamba River, Atsushi Yamamoto (2007, 2008, 2011, 2013) conducted excavations at the site of Ingatambo, where he discovered a large ceremonial platform mound complex surrounding an open plaza. The complex was associated with at least three major construction phases pertaining to the Initial Period and the Early Horizon that resulted in the gradual expansion of the mounds. By the latter Ingatambo phase, the principal mound featured rectangular structures with yellow plastered walls and a central stone staircase. Yamamoto shows, through ceramic style and exotic materials such as seashell, that Ingatambo was integrated into long-distance exchange networks with the coast, highlands, and tropical forest by the late Initial Period. These networks were likely expanded during the Early Horizon, since excavations identified Janabarriu-style pottery as well as cinnabar and obsidian from the southern Peruvian highlands (Yamamoto 2013), which indicate participation within the Chavín sphere of interaction (see Burger 1992).

Huayurco

From 2007 to 2012, I investigated the site of Huayurco to expand on Rojas's original findings. These investigations used survey and excavation to understand the type of site at Huayurco, the nature of its interregional relationships, and changes in culture and social organization over time. Huayurco is located along the Chinchipe–Tabaconas confluence at roughly 415 masl (Figure 10.2). The confluence is met by the Quebrada Tabaloso, which flows from the north. These investigations show that Huayurco is a large site complex made up of sixteen discontinuous components. These components cover 350 ha and correspond to natural terraces along the edges of the rivers and *quebrada* (gullies) that make up confluence (Figure 10.3). The boundaries of the components were defined by the spatial distribution of surface materials as well as the natural contours of the landscape. Based on these demarcations, the components were divided into sectors (A through P) forming the larger Huayurco complex (see Figure 10.2).

Huayurco was occupied between 800 BC and AD 550, with subsequent reoccupation sometime around AD 1200. Each sector features a unique occupational history often with considerable time depth. Huayurco's occupational history was divided into eight phases according to ceramic style, architectural association, and radiocarbon support (Clasby 2014b). The Early Horizon at Huayurco corresponds to the three earliest identified phases: the Ambato Phase (800–600 BC), the Tabaloso Phase (600–400 BC), and the Las Juntas Phase (400–1 BC). The Ambato and Tabaloso Phases are each supported by two radiocarbon dates, whereas seven were obtained for Las Juntas (Table 10.1). All dates (AMS) were produced from charcoal taken from floors, burial contexts, or within hearths associated with specific architectural features.

The Ambato Phase (800–600 BC)

The Ambato Phase is known exclusively from Sector E along the northeastern edge of the Tabaconas River. This sector is defined by a narrow stretch of flat river terrace that sits di-

TABLE 10.1. Radiocarbon dates (AMS) supporting the Early Horizon phases at Huayurco.

Phase	Lab no.	Sector	Context	^{14}C BP	2 σ (ShCal 04)
Ambato	Beta: 320432	E	Interior of a hearth	2440 ± 30	732–390 BC
	D-AMS:1217-405		Interior of a hearth	2394 ± 25	516–262 BC
Tabaloso	Beta: 320436	E	Burials below initial construction phase	2470 ± 30	750–398 BC
	D-AMS:1180	G	Floor associated with exterior wall	24220 ± 31	727–382 BC
Las Juntas	Beta: 320433	G	Hearth interior to the structure	2440 ± 30	732–390 BC
	Beta: 320434	G	Hearth interior to the structure	2270 ± 30	386–196 BC
	Beta: 320435	G	Hearth interior to the structure	2400 ± 30	700–261 BC
	D-AMS:1179	G	Hearth interior to the structure	2148 ± 29	203–2 BC
	D-AMS:1181	G	Hearth near front of middle platform	2169 ± 23	431–47 BC
	D-AMS:1183	G	Hearth interior to the structure	2219 ± 32	762–96 BC
	D-AMS:1184	G	From along exterior wall of structure	2413 ± 28	718–376 BC

rectly below Cerro Huayurco to the east. Four of the eight ceramic phases from Huayurco were identified in Sector E, with Ambato the only one pertaining to the Early Horizon.

Ambato Phase Architecture

The Ambato Phase in Sector E is associated with a small domestic occupation. Although horizontal excavation was limited (six 2 by 2 m units), the investigation identified two successive floor levels, P1 and P2, belonging to Ambato. Both floors featured stone footings of river cobbles that likely formed the edges of rectangular structures. The footings associ-

Figure 10.3. A view of the Chinchipe Valley and Quebrada Tabaloso from the south. One of the components, Sector G, is visible in the image (arrow).

ated with the more recent floor (P2) were superimposed over the previous structure, suggesting a degree of rebuilding and continuation of architectural patterns during Ambato. For the earlier floor, excavation identified a large unlined hearth (30 by 30 cm) adjacent to one of the footings (Figure 10.4A). A second, oval stone-lined hearth was found roughly 5 m to the south and contained dark black ash and many river cobbles inside it, suggesting it likely functioned as an earth oven (Figure 10.4B).

Ambato Phase Economy

The Ambato Phase is characterized by a relatively diverse subsistence economy dependent on agriculture, mixed game hunting, and possibly pastoralism. Starch grain analysis (Víctor F. Vásquez Sánchez and Teresa E. Rosales Tham, 2012 unpublished report, "Análisis de los Restos de Fauna de Huayurco," Centro de Investigaciones Arqueobiológicas y Paleoecológicas Andinas ARQUEOBIOS) recovered evidence of manioc (*Manihot esculenta*), corn (*Zea mays*), beans (*Phaseolus* sp.), and potatoes (*Solanum tuberosum*), all of which can be grown locally either along the edges of the floodplains or the upper reaches of the valleys.

Agricultural products were supplemented through the mixed game hunting of local forest and riverine species (such as rodents, amphibians, lizards, fish, crabs, deer, among others; Vásquez Sánchez and Rosales Tham, 2012 unpublished report). However, exotic species, including camelids (*Lama* sp.), guinea pig (*Cavia porcellus*), and marine fishes (*Paralonchurus peruanus,* Serranidae) are also present in the faunal assemblage, with the camelids likely introduced as the result of the expansion of the Chavín religious cult (Burger 1984b, 1992, 2003b).

FIGURE 10.4. Ambato Phase architecture from Sector E. **A.** Floor levels (P1, P2) with stone footings. **B.** Stone-lined hearth from the Ambato Phase occupation.

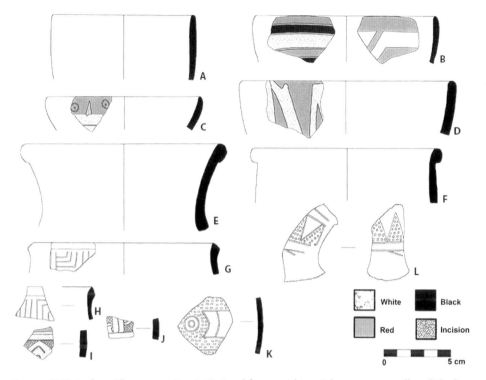

FIGURE 10.5. Ambato Phase ceramics. **A–D.** Bowl forms with straight or convex walls polished on both sides and simple geometric incision or painting on the exterior. **E–H.** Jar forms with short to medium necks and globular bodies. **I, J.** Jar forms with complex geometric and figurative zoned polychrome incision. **K, L.** Jar forms with punctation with incision on highly polished dark surfaces.

Huayurco imported marine shell to be manufactured into beads and pendants. Excavation recovered twenty-two fragments of pearl oyster (*Pinctada mazatlanica*, MNI = 4 [minimum number of individuals]) and three individual beads/pendants made of conch (*Strombus gracilior*, MNI = 2) and rice shell (*Prunum curtum*, MNI = 1) (Gladys Paz, 2011 unpublished report, "Análisis Malacológico: Proyecto de investigación arqueológico Huayurco: Bellavista, Jaén-Huarango, San Ignacio Cajamarca"). The presence of both carved and uncarved pendants indicates that manufacturing was completed at the site. Other types of local industries during the Ambato Phase are less understood, but excavation recovered evidence of bone needles and simple stone tools (scrapers and pestles) (Edwin Silva, 2011 unpublished report, "Informe del Análisis del Material Lítico del Proyecto de Investigación Arqueológica Huayurco: Bellavista, Jaén-Huarango, San Ignacio, Cajamarca"). Fossilized remains of both plants and snail shells were recovered as well, and that their presence continued during the subsequent Tabaloso and Las Juntas Phases possibly suggests that they were desirable ritual items.

Ambato Phase Ceramics

The Ambato Phase ceramics primarily consist of open bowls and necked jars (Figure 10.5A–K). Neckless jars and bottles are also present, but in much smaller frequencies, the latter in the form of stirrup-spout bottles (Figure 10.5L). Most bowl forms featured straight or convex walls and were polished on both sides (Figure 10.5A–D). Incision or painting was often present on the exterior. The incision typically consisted of simple geometric lines or shapes (Figure 10.5B, C) and was sometimes applied over areas of bichrome painting (Figure 10.5C) or used to divide zones of different colors (red, white, and sometimes black; Figure 10.5B). The incision was occasionally painted red or white. A notable type of decoration was the use of post-fired white-painted designs on the red slipped exterior of bowls (Figure 10.5D). Interior painting was also identified, in the form of simple bands (Figure 10.5B).

Jar forms typically featured short to medium necks and globular bodies (Figure 10.5E–H). The necks were straight or concave, whereas rims were often reinforced on the exterior. These reinforced rims were often painted red and sometimes scored on the lower half of the reinforcement. Surfaces were matte with a dark gray color from being fired in a reduced atmosphere. Vertical red-painted bands resembling finger impressions were sometimes applied to the body of jars. The bands usually extend to the junction between the body and neck. Highly polished jar forms with beveled rims also appear (Figure 10.5G, H), sometimes featuring incised geometric designs. Other techniques include zoned polychrome incision with complex geometric and figurative designs (Figure 10.5I, J), the negative space filled in by crosshatching. Punctation also occurs in combination with incision, usually on highly polished dark surfaces (Figure 10.5K, L). Some jars also featured corrugation and nicked appliqué bands along the exterior, traits that would become more prominent during the subsequent Tabaloso Phase.

The Tabaloso Phase (600–400 BC)

Surface survey around the Chinchipe–Tabaconas confluence identified Tabaloso Phase ceramics in five different sectors (C, F, G, J, and P), most of which were concentrated along the north bank of the Chinchipe River or within the Quebrada Tabaloso.

Tabaloso Phase Architecture

The Tabaloso Phase is known primarily from Sector G along the northern edge of the Chinchipe River, just east of the Quebrada Tabaloso (see Figure 10.2). This sector, more than 3 ha in area, consists of a terraced hill with three natural platforms (Figure 10.6A). Intact stratigraphic deposits were limited to the middle platform (Figure 10.6B) where excavation uncovered a large rectangular roughly 370 m² structure (Figure 10.7) comprised of several stone footings and walls. This structure is related to two major Early Horizon phases, Tabaloso (600–400 BC) and Las Juntas (400–1 BC).

The Tabaloso Phase, identified along the eastern edge of the platform (Rooms R11, R13, R14, and R15 of the Las Juntas Phase structure; see Figure 10.7), is associated with an initial floor and at least three freestanding walls. Each wall was made from river cobbles packed in mortar and covered in yellow plaster. Although exposure was limited, the walls likely formed a large rectangular structure similar to the later Las Jas Phase construction. In fact, many of the Las Juntas walls and footings were built in alignment directly over the initial Tabaloso Phase construction, indicating a similar floor plan (Figure 10.8A).

Most interestingly, the Tabaloso construction was preceded by a stratigraphic layer containing the remains of at least twenty-four human individuals (Figure 10.8B), nineteen of which were children or infants (J. Marla Toyne, 2012 unedited report, "Final report of

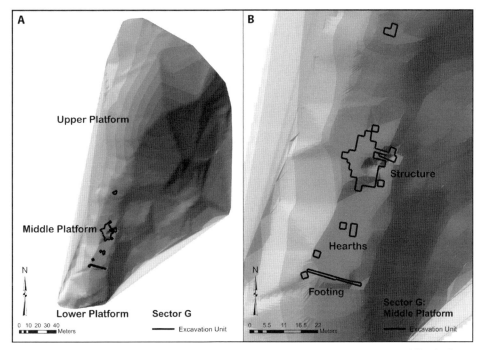

FIGURE 10.6. Location of Sector G excavation units at Huayurco. **A.** Huayurco. **B.** Middle Platform.

the human osteological analysis from the Huayurco Archaeological Project, Jaén-Peru"). Most of the remains were incomplete, primarily crania or long bones, and were secondary burials added to the terrace before the initial floor was laid down. Grave goods were scarce, with the exception of a rose-colored quartz axe (Figure 10.8C) and bead fragments made of stone and pearl oyster shell. The stratigraphic layer containing the burials was covered by a thin layer of rose-colored quartz, mined from other parts of the Sector G hill, used to create a level terrace before application of the initial floor.

Tabaloso Phase Economy

As in the previous Ambato Phase, the inhabitants at Huayurco maintained a diverse subsistence economy dependent on agriculture, mixed game hunting, and possibly pastoralism. Corn was identified through residue analysis. The presence of manioc, beans, and potatoes in later phases (Vásquez Sánchez and Rosales Tham, 2012 unpublished report) suggests that Huayurco continued to produce these crops during the Tabaloso Phase. The mixed game diet again included local riverine and forest fauna (birds, amphibians, rodents, reptiles, crabs, and deer) as well as camelids. New introductions to the faunal assemblage include paca (*Agouti* sp.) and capybara (*Hydrochaeris* sp.), both associated with wetter environments and almost certainly imported into the site, possibly from nearby cloud forest or lowland environments.

Huayurco maintained strong relationships with the coast during the Tabaloso Phase, continuing to import pearl oyster, conch, and rice shell for the production of beads and pendants. As mentioned, small bead fragments of pearl oyster were associated with one of the burials found underneath the floor level. Little is known of other industries at Huayurco, although bone needles and simple stone tools were also recovered (E. Silva,

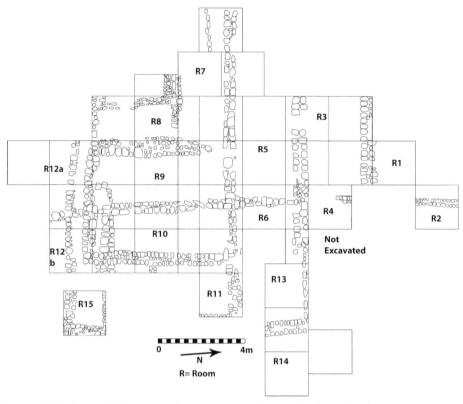

FIGURE 10.7. Plan of the Las Juntas Phase structure in Sector G and associated rooms.

FIGURE 10.8. Tabaloso Phase features. **A.** Architecture from the eastern edge of the middle platform in Sector G showing original Tabaloso Phase wall and subsequent Las Juntas Phase addition. **B.** Tabaloso Phase burials. **C.** Hand axe associated with Tabaloso Phase burials.

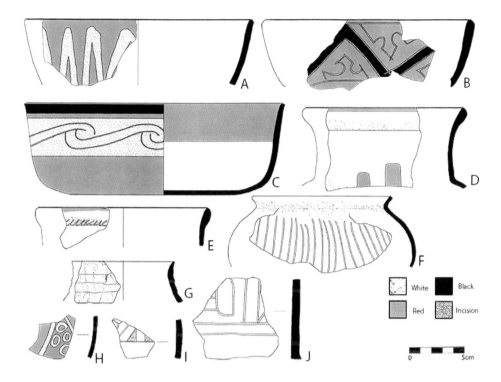

Figure 10.9. Tabaloso Phase ceramics showing characteristics retained from the Ambato Phase. **A–C.** Painted and incised straight-walled or convex bowls with hemispherical bodies. **D.** Jars with reinforced rims and matte surfaces with vertical red-painted bands. **E.** Jars with red painting and rim scoring. **F.** Jars with highly polished exterior surfaces with either fine incision or painting. **G.** Jars with corrugated necks featuring horizontal bands with vertical impressions. **H.** Jars with post-fired white-painted designs on red-slipped exteriors. **I.** Highly polished jars with beveled rims and complex incised designs. **J.** Bi-corn eyes decoration.

2011 unpublished report). The rose-colored quartz hand axe and stone pendants recovered from burial contexts suggest that some local stone working was for the production of ornaments or ritual items.

Tabaloso Phase Ceramics

Tabaloso Phase ceramics retained many characteristics from the previous Ambato Phase. Bowls and necked jars again dominated the assemblage, but stirrup-spout bottles also appear. Bowls were usually straight-walled or convex with hemispherical bodies (Figure 10.9A–C). Decoration typically consisted of painting, incision, or both. The most notable decoration was post-fired white-painted designs (bands, triangles, circles, and L shapes) on red-slipped exteriors (Figure 10.9A, H). In some cases, geometric designs (trapezoids and double helixes) were incised and then covered in post-fired white paint (Figure 10.9C). Zoned polychrome incision (red, black, and white paint) was also popular (Figure 10.9B).

Jar forms were similar to the Ambato Phase, but more varied. Many jars continued to feature reinforced rims and matte surfaces with vertical red-painted bands (Figure

FIGURE 10.10. The Las Juntas Phase structure viewed from the north.

FIGURE 10.11. Hearths found in Room R3 of the Las Juntas Phase structure.

10.9D). Both red painting and rim scoring on reinforced rims increased in frequency (Figure 10.9E). A few jar forms, usually with nonreinforced rims, had highly polished exterior surfaces with either fine incision or painting (Figure 10.9F). Painted incision continued as well. Some jars featured post-fired, white-painted designs over a highly polished red slip. Highly polished jars with beveled rims and complex incised designs (Figure 10.9I) carried over from the Ambato Phase, with bi-corn eyes in small quantities (Figure 10.9J). Jars with corrugated necks were also popular and featured horizontal bands with vertical impressions (Figure 10.9G).

The Las Juntas Phase (400–1 BC)

The Las Juntas Phase was identified in eight of the sixteen sectors that constitute Huayurco. As in the Tabaloso Phase, most sectors were located north of the Chinchipe River or within the Quebrada Tabaloso.

Las Juntas Phase Architecture
During the Las Juntas Phase, the original Tabaloso architecture was covered over and replaced by a new structure that was at least 370 m^2 in area (Figures 10.7, 10.10). This structure largely followed the plan of the Tabaloso Phase architecture, with new footings and walls built in direct alignment over previous features. These new features were also made of river cobbles packed in mortar and covered by a yellow plaster.

As in the Tabaloso Phase, a layer of rose-colored quartz was applied to the platform before application of the initial floor. Two burials, an adult and a child (Toyne, 2012 unedited report), were deposited within this layer as dedicatory offerings. The adult lacked associated grave goods and was partially interred underneath a footing. The child was found in the center of a room, accompanied by a stone mortar fragment and the partial skeleton of a camelid.

The Las Juntas Phase structure was comprised of at least fifteen rectangular rooms (see Figure 10.7), most of which featured multiple unlined hearths (Figure 10.11). The hearths were usually found close together, with some superimposed over previous pits. This pattern suggests that burning activities were frequent and each hearth was used only for a brief period before being replaced. Most hearths contained dark black soot, indicating high firing temperatures, and a few yielded small amounts of marine shell and animal bone, the latter corresponding to a medium-sized feline species (*Felis* cf. *tigrina*; see Vásquez Sánchez and Rosales Tham, 2012 unpublished report). The focus on exotic items suggests that the hearths were intended for ritual rather than domestic activities.

The ritual importance of the structure is supported by offerings left along the interior floor, including large ceramic jars and fairly complete necklaces or bracelets made of marine shell and rose-colored quartz. As mentioned, the rose-colored quartz was also used in the foundational stratum that preceded each of the initial Tabaloso and Las Juntas construction episodes.

Las Juntas Phase Economy
The Las Juntas Phase subsistence economy changed very little from the previous phase. Huayurco continued to grow corn and manioc (Vásquez Sánchez and Rosales Tham, 2012 unpublished report) while also exploiting a mixed game diet of local forest and riverine

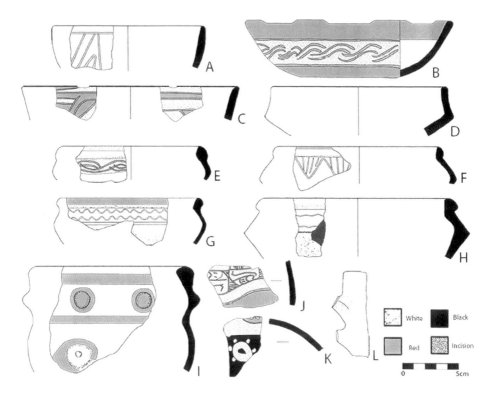

FIGURE 10.12. Las Juntas Phase bowls and necked jars. **A.** Incised triangle design. **B.** Rim castellation. **C.** Zoned polychrome incision and bichrome painting. **D.** Vessel carination. **E–H.** Sharply carinated jars. **I.** Appliqué and modeling. **J, K.** Complex incised motifs featuring serpent and anthropomorphic images.

fauna in addition to nonlocal species such as camelids, guinea pig, paca, capybara, and marine fishes (*Trachurus symmetricus, Rhinobatos planiceps*) and crab (*Platyxanthus orbignyi*). Huayurco also continued to import pearl oyster, conch, and rice shell for the production of beads and pendants (Paz, 2011 unpublished report), as evidenced by the recovery of two mostly complete shell necklaces and several fragments of unworked shell. An array of bone (needles and pendants) and lithic (rose-colored quartz necklaces, ceramic polishers, stone spindle whorls, axes, blades, and mortars) tools and ornaments were also identified (E. Silva, 2011 unpublished report).

Las Juntas Phase Ceramics
Las Juntas Phase ceramics retain many Tabaloso traits, but with some variation. Bowls and necked jars (Figure 10.12A–K) again dominate the assemblage, whereas neckless jars and double-spout-and-bridge-vessels (Figure 10.12L) are present in small quantities. Most bowl forms (Figure 10.12A–D) carried over from the previous phase, although there is a greater presence of straight-walled vessels during Las Juntas. Rim castellation (Figure 10.12B) and vessel carination (Figure 10.12D) also become more prominent. In terms of decoration, post-fired white-painted bands on red-slipped exteriors continue, but give way to incised designs, particularly the double helix motif (Figure 10.12B, C). This motif

FIGURE 10.13. Example of a Las Juntas Phase jar.

was usually applied to a red-slipped or buff-colored surface and then covered in post-fired white paint (Figure 10.12B). Other types of incised designs include triangles (Figure 10.12A), crosshatching, and trapezoids. Zoned polychrome incision and bichrome painting are also present, featuring red, white, black, and purple (Figure 10.12C).

Jars with matte finishes, reinforced rims, and red-painted vertical bands continued in Las Juntas (Figure 10.12E–G), although rim scoring faded in use. Sharply carinated jars (Figures 10.12E–H, 10.13) became more popular, often featuring incised designs (triangles, waves, stamped circles,and double helixes) in post-fired white paint on the exterior. Highly polished jars with nonreinforced rims were less prominent than in earlier phases. The complex incised motifs featuring serpent and anthropomorphic images (Figure 10.12J, K) continued, along with polychrome painting (Figure 10.12K) and appliqué and modeling techniques (Figure 10.12I) during Las Juntas. Corrugation largely declined in frequency.

Discussion

A reconstruction of Huayurco during the Early Horizon speaks to a pattern of considerable cultural stability for some eight hundred years. This period is marked by civic constructions, platform terracing, large populations, agriculture, craft production, and participation in intensive interregional exchange networks. All these features support the idea that the people of the eastern slopes were tied to larger cultural developments occurring in the highlands and on the coast. In fact, a diachronic examination of the architecture, local economy, and local ceramics shows that Huayurco established long-distance exchange relationships with the coast, highlands, and tropical lowlands by at least 800 BC and that these relationships were maintained throughout the Early Horizon.

Surveys of Huayurco reveal that its inhabitants settled on the river terraces that lined the Chinchipe and Tabaconas Rivers. Investigations by Yamamoto (2007, 2008, 2013) and Shady Solis (1973, 1987, 1999; Shady and Rosas 1979) have documented similar site distribution patterns for the Huancabamba and Bagua, respectively. Further investigation is needed on the function of each sector, but a linear pattern of settlement implies similarities with the type of societies that developed in the Amazon. Most sectors with Early Horizon components are located north of the Chinchipe and within the Quebrada Tabaloso. However, this pattern might reflect sampling errors, because some sectors feature deep cultural deposits (e.g., 8 m in Sector D) that would not be visible without excavation.

The terraces were frequently altered to create level platforms for the construction of both domestic and public architecture. All buildings were rectilinear, made of short stone footings (river cobbles in mortar) and capped by a perishable superstructure. The earliest known architectural features at Huayurco, located in Sector E, date to 800 BC and consist of simple rectilinear domestic structures. Excavation of these structures shows that the inhabitants also used river cobbles to create earth ovens.

Public architecture appears at Huayurco by at least 600 BC in the form of a large rectangular structure in Sector G. The footings for this Tabaloso Phase structure, wider and higher than their domestic Ambato Phase counterparts, were typically covered in a bright yellow plaster. The building's function can be inferred from the ritual activities that took place in the later Las Juntas Phase structure, which as mentioned was built directly aligned over the earlier structure, suggesting a continuity of tradition. The Las Juntas Phase ritual activities were centered on brief but frequent burning events, as evidenced by the many hearths located within the structure. Wild feline bone and marine shell within the hearths indicate that these burning events may have focused on the disposal of sacred exotic goods, possibly as a way to reinforce the importance of interregional exchange to the site.

In addition to shared architectural features, for both the Tabaloso Phase and Las Juntas Phase structures construction was preceded by the interment of human remains. In the case of the Tabaloso structure, at least twenty-four individuals were identified, many secondary burials of children and infants. As Burger (1992:74) has noted, there is a long tradition within the Andes of placing burials below the foundation of civic architecture as a way to ensure the success of the activities inside the structure (Burger 1992:74). Huayurco's use of this tradition could reflect broader ideological ties with other contemporary Andean societies or connections with earlier Jaén region sites, or both, since Olivera (2014:96) noted a similar pattern at Montegrande where two individuals were found buried below or within walls associated with the spiral architecture.

Curiously, both the initial Tabaloso Phase and Las Juntas Phase floors were built over a layer of rose-colored quartz mined from other areas of Sector G. Whereas the application of this layer could have been solely related to creating strong foundations for the buildings, the raw material and its distinctive bright red color may have had a special ritual importance within the society. This raw material was used to produce a hand axe as part of a burial offering in the Tabaloso Phase and a stone bead necklace in the Las Juntas Phase.

From a broader perspective, the Early Horizon public architecture at Huayurco and the type of activities that occurred within the interior seem to be local developments, distinct from the contemporary public architecture known in the Central Andes. Huayurco lacks the platform mound complexes and central plazas that defined the Early Horizon in many regions and even elsewhere in Jaén at sites such as Ingatambo. The architectural pattern at Huayurco seems to be focused inward, with little available space for an open plaza of any kind. Even the rituals focused on frequent burning activities are distinct from the earlier Kotosh religious tradition (Burger and Salazar-Burger 1980, 1985; Burger 1992), where a single, central hearth with subfloor flues was placed within a square or round structure.

The ceremonial architecture at Huayurco likewise shares little with other known public architectural traditions elsewhere in the eastern slopes, such as the mound patterns (groups of four) from the Upano Valley (Rostain 1999a, 1999b; E. Salazar 2008; Rostain and Pazmiño 2013; Rostain and Saulieu 2013). There are some similarities with sites from the Ecuadorian highlands, such as Catamayo (Guffroy 2004) and Challuabamba (Grieder 2009), as both used river cobble footings to form rectilinear structures. However, the function of these buildings is little understood and it remains unclear whether they were ceremonial or domestic structures.

The closest comparison to the Huayurco public constructions may be the architecture identified at the sites of Montegrande and Santa Ana–La Florida in the Jaén region (Valdez 2007, 2008, 2013a, 2013b; Olivera 2013), both of which seem to date to the Central Andean Late Preceramic Period. As at Huayurco, river cobble footings were the primary method of construction and the yellow plaster used on some of the ceremonial architecture at Montegrande (Olivera 2014:78) suggests a continuity of tradition. Although Huayurco lacks spiral or concentric circle architectural patterns, it shares similarities with these other sites in that the architecture was focused inward. Large open plazas do not seem to have been significant. If Huayurco is a continuation of these patterns, it would speak to a unique eastern slope architectural tradition in the Jaén region. Of course, the question remains of why a shift to a rectangular architectural arrangement occurred.

As with the architectural patterns, Huayurco's subsistence economy remained relatively stable throughout the Early Horizon with a focus on both agriculture and a mixed game economy. Although the inhabitants of the site primarily exploited locally available riverine and forest fauna, they also took advantage of long-distance exchange networks to bring in nonlocal species from the highlands (camelid, guinea pig), cloud forest and tropical lowlands (paca, capybara), and the coast (marine fishes). Because of the type of marine species found at Huayurco, interregional relationships with the coast were likely aligned most strongly toward the warmer waters of the far north of Peru and southern Ecuador, where the distance between the regions would have been shortest. For camelids, as Burger (1984b, 1992, 2003b) notes, their spread into northern Peru and southern Ecuador is likely associated with the spread of the Chavín religious cult during the Early Horizon.

The continued importance of a mixed game subsistence economy at Huayurco during the latter part of the Early Horizon contrasts with events elsewhere in the Central Andes, where the introduction of domesticated camelids reduces the reliance on hunting (Burger 1992; Miller and Burger 1995). Camelids, which were likely being raised at the site despite the unfavorable hot and dry conditions of the region, do begin to play a more significant role in the subsistence patterns at Huayurco during the Early Intermediate Period. Nevertheless, the hunting of animals such as white-tailed deer remains an important component (Clasby 2014b).

The appearance of felines during all three Early Horizon phases at Huayurco is also intriguing. At least some of the remains correspond to small cat species with striped coats, such as the oncilla. Although it is possible that species were brought to Huayurco for consumption or as pets, the identification of feline remains within some of the ceremonial hearths from the Las Juntas Phase structure indicates that they may have also been considered sacred and served important ritual functions. This tradition likely continued into the Early Intermediate Period at Huayurco, as excavations uncovered an offering of twin modeled stirrup-spout vessels in the shape of felines, one male and one female. The former featured painted pelage marks and a tail that transitions into a serpent as it wraps up the spout.

About industry at Huayurco, much remains unknown. This is particularly true of the idea that Huayurco was a local production center for fine stone bowls. As mentioned, Rojas seems to have discovered an offering or burial rather than evidence of production (see Clasby 2014b). Despite extensive survey and excavation at the site, my own investigations have so far yielded only a single example, a fragment of an elliptical bowl featuring incised volutes on the exterior. It was recovered during the survey of Sector J on the north side of the Chinchipe. Although Huayurco may have engaged in the production of these stone bowls, the practice was not likely exclusive to the site. Several examples now in local Jaén area museums have been discovered in different parts of the region and apparently the production of these stone vessels was a regional phenomenon (Clasby 2014b). Furthermore, research by Valdez (2008) at Santa Ana–La Florida suggests that some of these vessels date to the Central Andean Late Preceramic, well before the earliest known occupation at Huayurco.

More research is necessary to assess the interregional spread of these vessels, but at least some made their way to distant regions, including Chavín de Huántar. For example, a stone bowl in the shape of a fish was identified in the Ofrendas Gallery at Chavín de Huántar (Lumbreras 1993, 2007) in a context that is typically thought to date to the late Initial Period or beginning of the Early Horizon (Burger 1992:138–140). This stone vessel is similar to other known examples found in the Jaén region (see Clasby 2014b), including one that was supposedly recovered from Huayurco (Bushnell 1966). The dating of the Ofrendas Gallery example would make these fish-shaped vessels contemporary with or slightly earlier than the Ambato Phase.

Huayurco does show clear evidence of an industry based around the working of marine shell into pendants. The persistence of this tradition in all three Early Horizon phases indicates that Huayurco maintained strong connections with coastal populations, especially in the far north coast of Peru and southern Ecuador. The primary purpose of the marine shell pendants at Huayurco could have been for use in ritual activities considering that at least two mostly complete marine shell bracelets or necklaces were found as offerings within the Las Juntas Phase structure, and a single pendant was also found within one of the hearths. In fact, Paz (2011 unpublished report) argues that Huayurco favored the importation of smaller shell species precisely for the production of small pendants or ornaments. These findings relate to the initial discoveries by Rojas, who identified conch trumpets and a marine shell necklace with fish-shaped pendants as part of the cache. The flow of marine shell through the Jaén region would support theories (Hocquenghem et al. 1993) that the long-distance exchange of *Spondylus* and *Strombus* shell entered Peru by inland routes rather than through the Sechura Desert along the Pacific coast. Although *Spondylus* is not present at Huayurco, it is found at Ingatambo along the Huancabamba River during the Early Horizon (Yamamoto 2013).

Other industries at Huayurco are even less understood. However, the inhabitants seem to have used local stone for ornaments (beads and pendants), tools (scrapers, blades, polishers, pestles, hafted axes, spindle whorls, and fish hooks), and mortars. Boneworking was present in the form of needles and pendants. Canine teeth pendants were also identified.

A comparative review of the Early Horizon ceramics suggests that Huayurco participated in various long-distance exchange networks with coastal, highland, and eastern slope populations from areas in both Ecuador and Peru. Similarities in ceramic form and style are particularly strong with other sites in the Jaén region, including Bagua (Shady Solís 1973, 1987, 1999) and Ingatambo (Yamamoto 2008, 2013), as well as the far north coast of Peru (Piura, Tumbes), and the southern Ecuadorian highlands. These areas are sometimes collectively referred to as the Transitional Zone between the northern and central Andes. Similarities include general assemblages based on necked jars and bowls as well as a variety of decorative techniques (incision, zoned polychrome painting, polychrome painting, and white-on-red painting) and motifs (zoomorphic monster or spirals, vertical red-painted bands resembling fingers, framed geometric incised designs, and crosshatching in zoned texturing).

One of the most notable aspects of the pottery was the infrequent presence of neckless jars. This vessel form dominates many contemporary assemblages along the coast and highlands of Peru. Warren DeBoer (2003) has shown that the neckless jar tends to decline in favor of the necked jar the more closely located the ceramic assemblage is to Ecuador. Nevertheless, the Early Horizon ceramics at Huayurco share many decorative techniques with contemporary assemblages from the Northern Highlands, including highly polished monochrome ceramics, incision, and zoned polychrome incision. These broad similarities are also found in Janabarriu ceramics at Chavín, although Huayurco lacks the characteristic decorative motifs of the S shape or circle-and-dot.

Similarities between the Early Horizon ceramics at Huayurco and the pottery of the tropical forest are difficult to assess because few investigations have been carried out to the east of the Jaén region. The Huayurco corrugated ware does show some similarities to ceramics from the Upano region and particularly to the undated Chiguaza materials that feature reinforced rims with rim scoring and early corrugated pottery (Porras 1987:255–266). Similarities to the Sangay Phase ceramics include repeating spiral designs that are reminiscent of motifs in Ambato and the double helix motifs found in the Tabaloso and Las Juntas Phases.

Despite Huayurco's participation in broad exchange networks spanning the coast, highlands, and tropical forest during the Early Horizon, its relationship to Chavín de Huántar seems to have been indirect, especially when compared to other sites in the Jaén region, such as Ingatambo. As mentioned above, ceremonial architecture at Huayurco is fairly distinct from other known coastal and highland traditions. However, Ingatambo with its emphasis on platform mounds and open plazas more closely reflects the architectural patterns identified at highland ceremonial centers involved with the Chavín cult, such as Pacopampa and Kuntur Wasi. A similar pattern is noted in the pottery, as the Early Horizon Ingatambo Phase at Ingatambo features polished, monochrome black pottery with Janabarriu-like S shapes and circle-and-dot motifs that are absent from the Huayurco ceramic assemblage.

Excavations at Ingatambo also yielded evidence of the long-distance exchange of obsidian, including flakes from the Quispisisa source (Yamamoto 2013), and cinnabar, both of which come from the southern Peruvian highlands. Trade in these materials increased dramatically during the Chavín Horizon (Burger 1992, 2012; Burger, Lane, and

Cooke 2016) and are widely attributed to its spread. Although sampling issues cannot be ignored, the absence of obsidian and cinnabar at Huayurco may suggest that its level of participation within the Chavín cult was small in comparison to the neighboring Ingatambo. Indeed, note that Ingatambo is abandoned shortly before or around the same time Chavín collapses, while Huayurco continues to be occupied without disruption during the remainder of the Early Horizon.

Huayurco may have been less connected to Chavín than other contemporary sites in the Jaén region, such as Ingatambo, but still probably benefited from the increased activity in exchange networks, possibly indirectly, such as by the arrival of camelids into the region or in the increased trade of seashell such as *Spondylus* and *Strombus*. Although the former type of shell was not identified in either Rojas's or my excavations, this absence could have been a conscious rejection of the material by the Huayurco community, because the trade routes with the coast were certainly open to them, as evident from the marine shell present at Huayurco.

Significant changes in culture and sociopolitical organization do not occur at Huayurco until the beginning of the Early Intermediate Period and even then a degree of cultural continuity is maintained at the site. For example, the subsequent Higuerones Phase (AD 100–200) architecture is more suitable for defense, with large 2 m high walls erected on top of a modified hill with two terraced platforms (Clasby and Meneses Bartra 2013; Clasby 2014b). The walls were built along the western edge of the hill and at the front edge of the upper platform to provide some access restriction. Nevertheless, although the Sector D architecture was different in nature from the large Las Juntas Phase rectangular structure in Sector G, there was no clear technological break given that both were built using river cobbles. In addition, small unlined hearths were identified along the upper platform, suggesting that the frequent burning rituals may have continued in the Higuerones Phase as well. Even the pottery, although less varied, retained many of the previous Las Juntas Phase traits. This pattern is significantly different from the coast and highlands, where the dissolution of Chavín around 400 BC seems to result in a significant cultural upheaval (Burger 1992:228–229).

Conclusions

The investigations at Huayurco reveal that the site had a long occupational history with complex cultural developments beginning as early as 800 BC. These developments likely came out of broader Jaén region cultural traditions that were underway as early as the Late Preceramic Period. During the Early Horizon at Huayurco, the inhabitants of the site took advantage of the natural river terraces that lined each side of the confluence to construct both domestic and ceremonial structures. They engaged in farming and mixed game hunting while also becoming specialists in the production of ceramics and finely carved stone bowls.

The sociopolitical developments at Huayurco and other sites in the Jaén region reflected local traditions, yet they were also part of the larger cultural processes occurring in the Central Andean highlands and coast during the Early Horizon. Ceramic style, faunal remains, and exotic goods such as marine shell indicate that Huayurco had established and maintained long-distance exchange networks with populations from the coast, highlands, and tropical forest during the Early Horizon and that these relationships had a significant influence on local developments. A comparison of Huayurco with other sites in the Jaén region, such as Ingatambo, shows that there was also considerable local variation in the nature of these interregional relationships.

As a whole, the excavation results from Huayurco further support the idea that the eastern slopes were deeply involved in the historical processes that led to the development of complex societies in the Central Andes. It also highlights the need for additional research to better understand the type of societies that developed in the eastern slopes and their larger role within Andean prehistory.

Acknowledgments. The investigations at Huayurco were carried out under the generous financial support of the National Science Foundation (Doctoral Dissertation Improvement Grant BCS-0951661) and the Macmillan Center at Yale University (Dissertation Research Grant). I would like to thank Richard Burger, Lucy Salazar, and Yuji Seki for inviting me to participate in this publication. Richard Burger and Jason Nesbitt were also very helpful in reviewing the manuscript and providing comments and suggestions.

CHAPTER ELEVEN

South of Chavín

Initial Period and Early Horizon Interregional Interactions between the Central Highlands and South Coast

Yuichi Matsumoto

For more than a half century, the role of Chavín de Huántar and its influence over other regions have been important in the study of the Central Andes during the late Initial Period and Early Horizon (e.g., Tello 1943, 1960; Burger 1988, 1992, 2012; Lumbreras 1989, 2007; Kembel and Rick 2004; Rick 2008). During this time, investigations at Chavín de Huántar have advanced and discussion about the "Chavín Phenomenon" continues to be active, incorporating recent data from the North Coast and Northern Highlands (e.g., Burger 1992, 2008, 2012; Inokuchi 1998; Elera 1998; Rick 2008). On the other hand, archaeological investigations in the south coast and central highlands focused on the late Initial Period and Early Horizon have been scarce, and thus it has been difficult to evaluate the nature of the Chavín phenomenon in the regions to the south of Chavín de Huántar (Figure 11.1).

Archaeological data in these areas are increasing (e.g., DeLeonardis 1991, 1997, 2005; Burger and Matos 2002; Isla and Reindel 2006; Reindel and Wagner 2008; Kaulicke et al. 2009; Matsumoto 2010; Matsumoto and Tsurumi 2011), yet have not been fully evaluated in relation to the recent data from Chavín de Huántar and other contemporary sites to the north. The scarcity of large-scale public architecture has given us a general impression that these areas were culturally isolated from the northern regions where socioeconomic development was expressed through the creation of large-scale public ceremonial centers.

Therefore, I will attempt to discuss the nature of the Chavín phenomenon in the central highlands and south coast by integrating available data from these regions. Though the nature of the Chavín phenomenon is controversial, archaeologists seem to agree that the time period crucial to this issue is approximately 1200–500 cal BC (e.g., Inokuchi 1998; Mesía-Montenegro 2007; Matsumoto 2009, 2010; Rick et al. 2009). For the purpose of considering the Chavín phenomenon in these regions and periods from a diachronic perspective, I will divide this review into two sections: the late Initial Period (1200–800 cal BC) and the early Early Horizon (800–500 cal BC).

Late Initial Period (1200–800 cal BC)

According to John Rick and his colleagues, the history of Chavín de Huántar as a ceremonial center began around 1200 cal BC, which corresponds to the late Initial Period

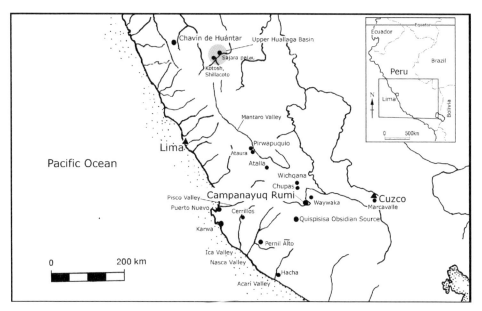

FIGURE 11.1. Location of archaeological sites in the central highlands and south coast of Peru.

(Kembel and Rick 2004; Mesía-Montenegro 2007; Kembel 2008; Rick 2008). Richard Burger (2008) is more conservative in estimating the time of its inception, placing its beginnings around 1000 cal BC. During the late Initial Period, the architecture of Chavín de Huántar was expanding and seems to have been associated with the ceramic style called the Urabarriu Phase defined by Burger (Burger 1984a, 1992; Mesía-Montenegro 2007; Kembel 2008:69).

The Upper Huallaga Basin

In the Upper Huallaga Basin of the central highlands, the late Initial Period corresponds to the Kotosh Kotosh Period (Izumi and Terada 1972). This period is characterized by a unique ceramic style with strong similarities to styles of the contemporary tropical forest known as the Late Tutishcainyo and Shakimu (Lathrap 1962, 1970). In addition to the excavations of three sites (Kotosh, Shillacoto, and Waira-jirca) during the 1960s (Onuki 1994), our 2001 survey in this region (Inokuchi et al. 2002), identified five sites pertaining to this period (Figure 11.2). Although it is premature to discuss the relationships among them, their sizes and material styles suggest that Shillacoto was the largest and most important among these sites (Izumi, Cuculiza, and Kano 1972; Kano 1979; Inokuchi et al. 2002). The excavations at Kotosh and Shillacoto (Izumi, Cuculiza, and Kano 1972; Izumi and Terada 1972) show that this region had some kind of contact with Chavín de Huántar. The most obvious evidence is the two curved bone artifacts, excavated from a funeral context at Shillacoto (Tomb 4), with iconographies similar to the famous Lanzón sculpture of Chavín de Huántar (Kano 1979; Bischof 2008:112). In addition, a few Kotosh style ceramic sherds were recovered from Urabarriu Phase contexts at Chavín de Huántar (Burger 1984a:78–79; see also Tello 1960:227–239).

These data imply that interregional interactions between Chavín de Huántar and the Upper Huallaga Basin existed during the late Initial Period, yet the overall differences in ceramic styles between them seem to suggest that their interactions were sporadic and did not create strong cultural ties. Apparently, important sites such as Kotosh and Shillacoto interacted with Chavín de Huántar, but the sites in the Upper Huallaga Basin generally maintained local traditions that were represented in material styles and religious iconographies.

The South Coast

The ceramic styles of the Initial Period south coast are not well known. Although no contemporary ceremonial centers are identified, there are data from residential sites such as Puerto Nuevo in the Pisco drainage (Engel 1966; García and Pinilla 1995; García 2009), Pernil Alto in the Palpa Valley (Reindel and Isla 2009), and Hacha in the Acarí Valley (Riddel and Valdéz 1987–1988; Robinson 1994). According to these data, it seems possible to define two distinct ceramic styles. The first is distributed in the area between the Pisco and Nazca drainage and is characterized by the use of negative painting and resin painting as representative decorative techniques. This style is recognized in Puerto Nuevo and Pernil Alto (García 2009; Reindel and Isla 2009).

The second is represented by the ceramics from the site of Hacha and is probably distributed in the area to the south of the Nazca Valley (Riddel and Valdéz 1987–1988; Robinson 1994; Neira and Cardona 2000–2001). This style is characterized by neckless jars painted in red and adorned with appliqué decorations (Figure 11.3). Although this style is poorly understood, the basic vessel shapes and decorative technique show some similarities to those of the south-central highlands, such as the Marcavalle Phase material in Cuzco (Mohr Chávez 1980, 1981a, 1981b) and Muyu Moqo Phase material in Andahuaylas (Grossman 1972). What makes things more complicated is that the second style shares some basic vessel forms and decorative techniques, such as the red-painted neckless jar, with the first one. However, two specific decorative techniques, negative painting and resin painting, seem to effectively differentiate the styles from each other since they are not recognized in the area to the south of the Nazca drainage. In any case, these ceramic styles do not show clear similarities to those of the Urabarriu Phase at Chavín de Huántar (Burger 1984a) or to contemporary North Coast styles such as Cupisnique (e.g., Elera 1998).

The South-Central Highlands

During the late Initial Period, possible ceremonial centers as well as village sites appeared in the south-central highlands (e.g., Casafranca 1960; Lumbreras 1974b; MacNeish et al. 1981). Generally, these sites are small in scale compared to the coeval centers to the north. The ceramic styles of this region are composed of several local ones showing a mosaic-like distribution, such as Pirwapukio in the Mantaro Valley (Browman 1970), Wichqana in Ayacucho (Casafranca 1960; Lumbreras 1974b, 1981; Ochatoma 1985), Muyu Moqo in Andahuaylas (Grossman 1972), and Marcavalle in Cuzco (Mohr Chávez 1980, 1981a, 1981b). These share some of the basic vessel forms and surface treatment, but their decorative techniques and motifs suggest that they can be treated as different local styles that were distributed independently.

Compared to other sites in the south-central highlands, the situation at Campanayuq Rumi is exceptionally complex. Campanayuq Rumi is a ceremonial center in Peru's Department of Ayacucho situated at an elevation of 3,600 masl. It is located just 600 m to the east of the main plaza of Vilcashuaman, and about 110 km to the south of the department capital of Ayacucho, Huamanga (Matsumoto 2010; Matsumoto and Cavero

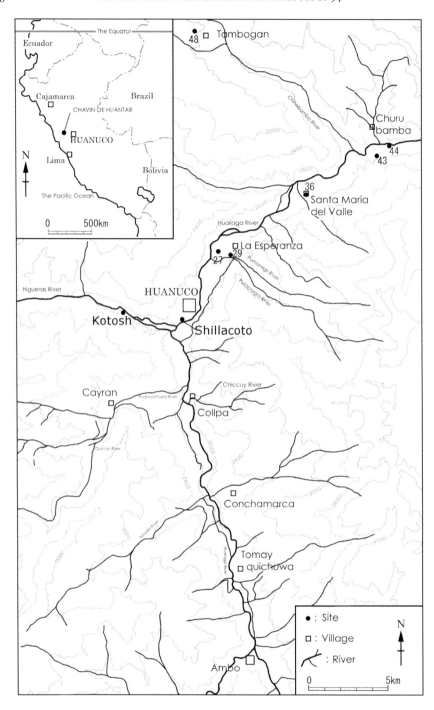

Figure 11.2. Site distribution of the Kotosh Kotosh Period (1200–700 cal BC) in the Upper Huallaga Basin of Peru.

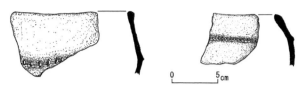

FIGURE 11.3. Initial Period ceramics from the Hacha site. Redrawn from Robinson (1994, fig. 14).

2009). Radiocarbon dates suggest that the first monumental ceremonial architecture at Campanayuq Rumi was constructed around 1000 cal BC. It followed a U-shaped layout with a sunken rectangular plaza, which is similar to the public architecture of Chavín de Huántar (Figure 11.4). The architectural technique and style used for the site are quite different from those of contemporary centers in the south-central highlands. The presence of a stone-lined gallery (Figure 11.5), similar to the ones used in specific ritual activities with limited access at Chavín de Huántar, suggest that the designer of Campanayuq Rumi must have been aware of the architectural technique (and unique ritual practice) of Chavín de Huántar.

On the other hand, the ceramic style of Campanayuq Rumi does not show any clear relationship to that of the Urabarriu Phase at Chavín de Huántar. During the late Initial Period (Campanayuq I Phase), the ceramic assemblage at Campanayuq Rumi (Figure 11.6) consisted of a mix of different styles that were distributed in the south-central highlands and south coast, such as Pirwapukio in the Mantaro Valley (Browman 1970; Figure 11.6G–I, K), Hacha in the Acari Valley (Riddel and Valdéz 1987–1988; Robinson 1994; Neira and Cardona 2000–2001; Figure 11.6E, L), Marcavalle in Cuzco (Mohr Chávez 1977; Figure 11.6B, C, J), and Muyu Moqo in Andahuaylas (Grossman 1972; Figure 11.6F). Importantly, these are the areas where monumental ceremonial architecture is scarce.

These data seem to suggest that interregional interactions between the south coast and highlands already existed during the late Initial Period. Although the similarities in architectural style imply that the center at Campanayuq Rumi emerged in relation to Chavín de Huántar, the material culture of the famous northern center was not accepted in the south-central highlands, including at Campanayuq Rumi. The variety of ceramic styles recognized at Campanayuq Rumi seems to suggest that this ceremonial center functioned independently as a node of interregional interactions between groups in the south-central highlands and south coast during the late Initial Period. Campanayuq Rumi might have connected groups from areas where people did not carry out large-scale monumental construction projects.

Before my research at Campanayuq Rumi, I had imagined that the south-central highlands could be considered peripheral to Chavín de Huántar and that its relationships should be interpreted through world-systems perspectives (e.g., Burger and Matos 2002; Kardulias and Hall 2008). Using this approach, Campanayuq Rumi might be interpreted as a "gateway community" (Hirth 1978) for a prestige goods economy based on Quispisisa obsidian (Burger and Glascock 2000, 2002; see Figure 11.1). Recent studies of the obsidian sources of Campanayuq Rumi indicate that approximately 90% of the obsidian of the late Initial Period (Campanayuq I Phase) came from the Quispisisa source (Nesbitt et al. 2015; Matsumoto et al. 2018). Moreover, it became clear that the obsidian sources identified in Campanayuq Rumi are distributed in the wide geographic area covering the

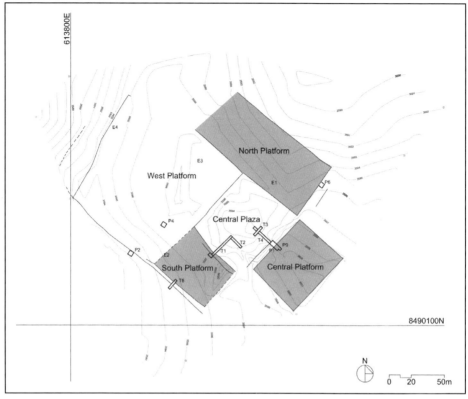

FIGURE 11.4. Architectural layout of the ceremonial center at Campanayuq Rumi.

Peruvian south-central highlands. Notably, the locations of the sources at least partially conform to the pattern of interregional interactions recognized through the analysis of ceramic styles.

Campanayuq Rumi is the closest known center to the important obsidian source at Quispisisa, yet only a small amount of obsidian was recovered from the late Initial Period (the Urabarriu Phase) contexts at Chavín de Huántar. At that time obsidian trade in general was sporadic in the Central Andes to the north of Campanayuq Rumi. These data made it impossible to interpret Chavín de Huántar and these regions using a core-periphery or world-systems approach based on the obsidian trade. On the contrary, the south-central highlands and south coast seemed to have formed part of an interaction sphere independent from that of Chavín de Huántar during the late Initial Period.

Early Horizon (800–500 cal BC)

As a result of the recent research on the Central Coast, North Coast, and Northern Highlands, it seems obvious that around 800–700 cal BC the Central Andes experienced a radical change in interregional interactions that is expressed in material styles, including ceramics and architecture. At several sites this change was associated with socioeconomic transformations represented by the emergence of marked hierarchical social organiza-

FIGURE 11.5. A gallery in the south platform at Campanayuq Rumi.

tions (e.g., Burger 1992; Onuki 1995; Seki et al. 2008). At Chavín de Huántar, this period corresponds to the Janabarriu Phase (Burger 1984a, 1992) or Black and White Portal Phase (Mesía-Montenegro 2007; Kembel 2008; Rick 2008) and can be characterized by the completion of construction activities and changes in ceramic styles. Accordingly, the data from the central highlands and south coast imply that several changes in both social organizations and material styles occurred simultaneously.

The Upper Huallaga Basin

In the Upper Huallaga Basin, the date of 800–700 cal BC corresponds to the transition from the Kotosh Kotosh Period to the Kotosh Chavín Period (Izumi and Terada 1972; Matsumoto 2009, in press; Matsumoto and Tsurumi 2011). Several radical changes occurred simultaneously in ceramic style, architectural techniques used in monumental architecture, and settlement patterns. The ceramic style of the Kotosh Chavín Period is completely different from that of the former Kotosh Kotosh Period (Onuki 1972), and shows close similarities to that of the Janabarriu Phase at Chavín de Huántar (Burger 1984a). The ceremonial centers of the Kotosh Chavín Period adopted new architectural styles and techniques, such as rectangular platforms and sunken plazas (Izumi and Terada 1972; Matsumoto and Tsurumi 2011). The sites of the Kotosh Kotosh Period were abandoned or destroyed to build new public centers with these new architectural conventions (Figure 11.7).

Despite these radical changes recognized in the Upper Huallaga Basin, it seems dangerous to assume that these changes occurred simply as a result of coercive influence

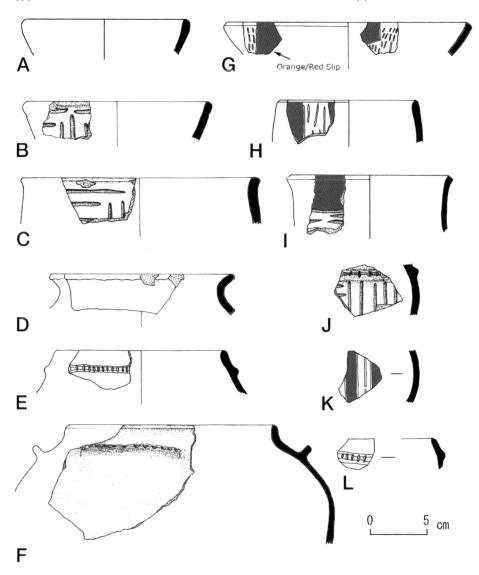

FIGURE 11.6. Representative variations of ceramics of the Campanayuq I Phase (1000–700 cal BC) at Campanayuq Rumi.

or acculturation from Chavín de Huántar. The ceremonial centers of the Upper Huallaga Basin seem to have maintained autonomy by manipulating this external influence in their own ways. For example, the Kotosh groups emulated the cultural elements of Chavín de Huántar, from the architectural technique to the ceramics styles and religious iconographies (Izumi and Terada 1972). However, in the case of Sajara-patac 20 km to the east of Kotosh, although some general architectural concepts such as sunken plazas and platforms were accepted, architectural technique and layout remained quite local (Matsumoto and Tsurumi 2011; Figure 11.8).

The ceramic styles of these two sites show close parallels with that of the Janabarriu

Phase. This seems to suggest intensive interactions with Chavín de Huántar. However, Kotosh and Sajara-patac could have emulated the Janabarriu Phase ceramic style in quite different ways. The group associated with Kotosh intended to emulate or even copy the Janabarriu Phase ceramic assemblage, including not only vessel forms, but decorations and iconographies (Izumi and Sono 1963; Izumi and Terada 1972). For example, religious iconography similar to that at Chavín de Huántar can be recognized in the ceramic assemblage of the Kotosh Chavín Period at Kotosh. In the case of the Sajara-patac site, the ceramic assemblage only partially emulates that of the Janabarriu Phase in vessel forms and decorative motifs. In the ceramic assemblage from Sajara-patac most of the decorative motifs are composed of geometric designs represented by typical circle-and-dot motifs or concentric circles (Figure 11.9A–C, G, I, K–N) and religious iconography is rare and looks local (Matsumoto 2009; Matsumoto and Tsurumi 2011; Figure 11.9E, H). These differences could mean that each center accepted or interpreted the new religious ideology of Chavín de Huántar quite differently.

These data indicate that in the Upper Huallaga Basin the influence from Chavín de Huántar was a radical change and caused abandonment of local religious traditions. However, this does not necessarily signify either a total socioeconomic change or political integration at the regional level. Each center seems to have negotiated, made their own active decisions, and manipulated the religious ideology of Chavín de Huántar. These processes of negotiation functioned to consolidate the political autonomy of each center rather than result in political integration or unification at a regional level in the Upper Huallaga Basin.

The South Coast

On the south coast, the changes in ceramic style suggest that the area between the Pisco and Nasca Valleys accepted the influence from Chavín de Huántar (e.g., García and Pinilla 1995). The local decorative techniques, such as resin painting and negative painting, were applied to new vessel forms such as the stirrup-spout bottle and new decorative motifs related to the religious iconography of Chavín de Huántar (e.g., Menzel, Rowe, and Dawson 1964). One of the popular local motifs of the late Initial Period, *el dios de Puerto Nuevo*, seems to have been replaced by Chavín-related iconography (García and Pinilla 1995; Silverman 1996; Isla and Reindel 2006; Garcia 2009). A ceremonial center built at Cerrillos in the Ica Valley (Wallace 1962; Splitstoser, Wallace, and Delgado 2009) and the famous Chavin-style painted textiles recovered from the Karwa site near Independencia Bay (e.g., Cordy-Collins 1976; Burger 1988) correspond to this period.

The scarcity of excavation data prevents us from understanding the first half of the Early Horizon in the regions to the south of the Nazca drainage, such as the Acarí Valley. Some ceramic sherds decorated by circle-and-dot motifs are recognized (e.g., Neira and Cardona 2000–2001:53), but no clear evidence of Paracas style, characterized by resin painting and negative painting, has been confirmed. For now, it seems reasonable to assume that local traditions continued in the southern part of the south coast. This situation contrasts with the cases of the Nasca and Pisco drainages, where the influence of Chavín de Huántar is obvious in ceramic styles and appeared as an intrusive change.

The frontier dividing the Paracas style and the local one that had continued from the late Initial Period might have coincided with the distribution border between the Puerto Nuevo and Hacha styles in the late Initial Period. This stylistic diversity seen in the south coast at the beginning of the Early Horizon could represent different reactions to the influence from Chavín de Huántar. That is, whereas the northern groups that had shared

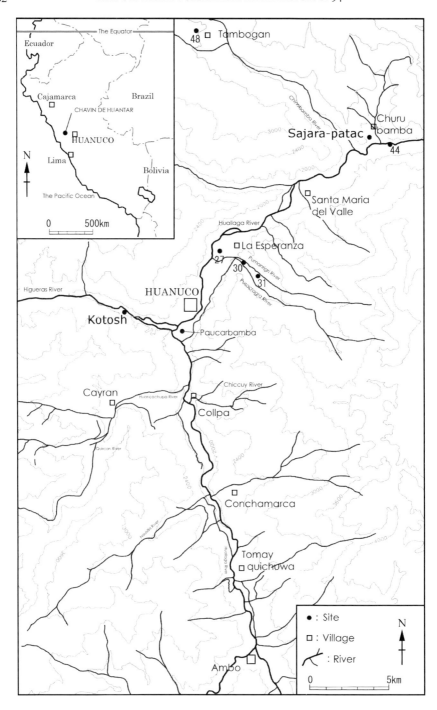

FIGURE 11.7. Site distribution of the Kotosh Chavín Period (700–250 cal BC) in the Upper Huallaga Basin of Peru.

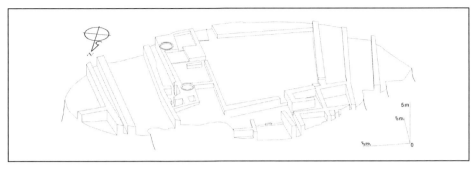

FIGURE 11.8. Early Horizon ceremonial architecture at the Sajara-patac site.

the Puerto Nuevo ceramic style accepted the religious ideology of Chavín de Huántar, the groups that lived to the south of the Nasca drainage refused to adopt the new ideology and maintained local ceramic styles.

The South-Central Highlands

In the south-central highlands local reactions varied, as was the case on the south coast. In the Mantaro drainage, Huancavelica, and Ayacucho, ceramic style transformed into the "Janabarriu-related" style, which is very similar to that of the contemporary Chavín de Huántar (e.g., Cruzatt 1971; Matos 1971, 1972; Ochatoma 1985, 1998; Burger and Matos 2002). In these regions, the changes in ceramic style seem to have occurred in tandem with socioeconomic transformations. Monumental ceremonial centers such as Ataura (Matos 1971, 1972), Chupas (Cruzatt 1971), and Atalla (Burger and Matos 2002) probably indicate the emergence of hierarchical social organization, which had been less marked during the late Initial Period. In contrast, in the regions farther south, such as at Cuzco and Anda-huaylas, large-scale monumental ceremonial architecture was not constructed and local ceramic styles derived from the former period (e.g., Grossman 1972). These data seem to indicate that the groups in Cuzco and Andahuaylas refused to accept the new religious ideology. Considering the geographic proximity of these regions to other centers, such as Chupas and Campanayuq Rumi, these differences do not seem to be caused by distance. Moreover, as mentioned earlier, ceramic examples of these local styles are recognized in the late Initial Period contexts at Campanayuq Rumi (see Figure 11.6). Therefore, this sty-listic border rather represents active decision-making on a regional level.

The data from Campanayuq Rumi provide an important perspective to interpret these variations in ceramic styles and different reactions to the influence from Chavín de Huántar (Matsumoto 2010). Four important changes occurred at Campanayuq Rumi around 700 cal BC. First, social organization became more hierarchical. Personal adorn-ments such as exotic stone beads, elaborate bone ornaments, ear spools, and gold jewelry appeared in this period (Matsumoto 2010; Matsumoto and Cavero 2012; Matsumoto and Palomino 2012; Figure 11.10). Moreover, fine elaborate vessels were associated with buri-als as offerings, a pattern not seen in the Initial Period contexts at the site (Figure 11.11).

Second, there was new construction activity at the monumental ceremonial struc-tures. The use of cut and polished stones, called "ashlars," is especially important (Figure 11.12), because this may have been a new technique invented at the contemporary Chavín de Huántar (Kembel 2001, 2008).

Third, the amount of obsidian among the chipped stone at Campanayuq Rumi in-

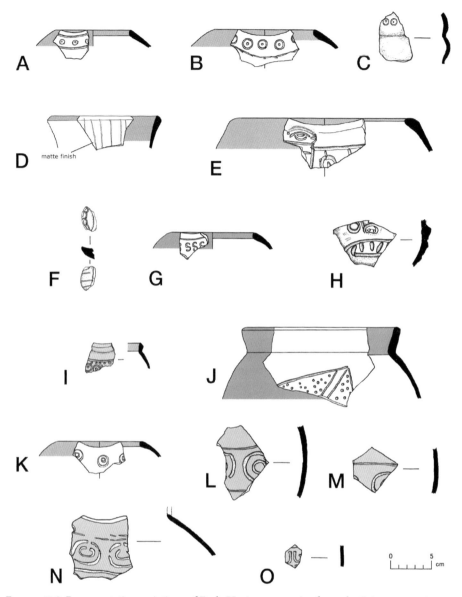

Figure 11.9. Representative variations of Early Horizon ceramics from the Sajara-patac site.

creased from 70% to 90% (Matsumoto 2010), of which roughly 80% came from Quispisisa (Matsumoto et al. 2018:18, table 2). This change is quite suggestive, because in this period the percentage of Quispisisa obsidian at Chavín de Huántar increased to more than 90% of the chipped stone artifacts (e.g., Burger, Asaro, and Michel 1984; Burger and Glascock 2009).

    Fourth, the ceramic style changed radically. The styles similar to those of Cuzco and the Mantaro Valley were replaced by a style related to the Janabarriu Phase ceramics of Chavín de Huántar, and the Early Paracas style of the south coast. Although these data

FIGURE 11.10. A pierced gold ornament from Campanayuq Rumi.

imply that the relationship with Chavín de Huántar was closer than during the Initial Period, the new ceramic style at Campanayuq Rumi might reflect the changes in its sphere of interaction, incorporating Chavín de Huántar, the south-central highlands, and south coast. It is interesting that Campanayuq Rumi accepted elements of the Early Paracas style that emerged in the region between the valleys of Pisco and Nasca, given that the material styles of Campanayuq Rumi do not seem to show marked similarities with this zone during the late Initial Period.

In sum, this change in ceramic and architectural styles at Campanayuq Rumi suggests that Campanayuq Rumi reinforced its relationship with Chavín de Huántar. The interaction between Campanayuq Rumi and the regions where the new religious ideology was rejected could have been weakened or lost while Campanayuq Rumi created new ties with other regions where new ideology was accepted. The latter is represented by the south coast of Ica and Paracas, where societies accepted elements of Janabarriu-style ceramics and Chavín religious iconography represented by the ceramic style of Mollake Chico in the Palpa Valley Chico (Isla and Reindel 2006), the possible monumental architecture and Janabrriu-related ceramics at Cerrillos in the Ica Valley (Splitstoser, Wallace, and Delgado 2009), and the well-known textiles from the Karwa site (Cordy-Collins 1976).

The Chavín Phenomenon in the South

The data presented here sheds light on two aspects of the "unity and heterogeneity" (Burger 1988) of the so-called Chavín phenomenon. An observation in support of unity in the central highlands and south coast is that this phenomenon was produced by an abrupt change that occurred in several regions almost simultaneously. The intrusive influence of Chavín de Huántar reached these areas around 800–700 cal BC and probably each had to make its own decision on whether to accept or refuse the new religious ideology from Chavín de Huántar. These decisions were not necessarily dichotomous and could have been arrived at through complex historical processes of negotiated and contested rela-

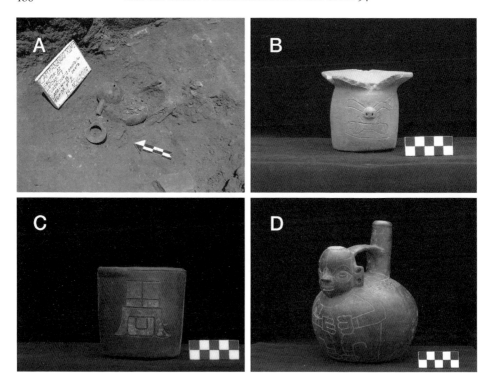

Figure 11.11. An Early Horizon burial from Campanayuq Rumi and its associated vessels. **A.** Vessels in situ. **B.** Cup with flaring rim. **C.** Cup with pouring lip. **D.** Bridge-spout bottle representing a human figure.

tionships between local and new religious ideologies and among autonomous polities on a regional level. These processes seem to have generated the heterogeneity of the Chavín phenomenon. For example, in the case of the Upper Huallaga Basin, the acceptance of new religious ideology did not cause a political integration of the region, but could have consolidated the intraregional interactions among "peer polities" (Renfrew 1986) surviving from the late Initial Period (Matsumoto 2009; Matsumoto and Tsurumi 2011). The ceremonial centers and societies associated with them modified and selected the cultural elements from Chavín de Huántar through their particular decision-making processes.

The data from the south coast and south-central highlands provide examples of heterogeneity at interregional levels. On the south coast, two different zones seem to have made distinct decisions and ended up reacting differently to the influences generated from Chavín de Huántar. The Early Paracas culture accepted the new ceramic style and religious iconographies from Chavín de Huántar though monumental construction activities were rarely carried out. Notably, both in the Early Paracas culture and at Campanayuq Rumi burials with rich offerings appeared around 800–700 cal BC and these offerings show clear stylistic affiliation with Chavín de Huántar.

The cultural elements of Chavín de Huántar and the early Paracas culture appeared simultaneously at Campanayuq Rumi, raising the question of whether it was the early Paracas culture that caused the transition from the Campanayuq I Phase to Campanayuq II Phase at the site. However, although the Early Paracas culture shares a ceramic style and

FIGURE 11.12. A cut stone ashler staircase at Campanayuq Rumi.

iconography with Chavín de Huántar, no public architecture similar to the site has been discovered in the south coast. In contrast, the data from Campanayuq Rumi suggest that not only ceramic (and possibly textile) style, but architectural style and technique, and the ritual activities carried out there show strong similarities between Chavín de Huántar and Campanayuq Rumi. Therefore, it seems more appropriate to consider the relationship among Chavín de Huántar, Campanayuq Rumi, and the Early Paracas culture in the wider context of the sphere of influence centered on Chavín de Huántar (Burger 2008) than interpret the Early Paracas remains at Campanayuq Rumi as the influence from the south coast to the south-central highlands. In any case, the acceptance of the new religious ideology caused a radical change in both regions.

On the other hand, the regions where societies did not accept the new religious ideology and associated material styles do not seem to have experienced these changes. These data probably suggest that the acceptance of new religious ideology caused radical socioeconomic transformations, including the adoption of hierarchical social systems that had not been clearly marked during the late Initial Period.

The data from Campanayuq Rumi could suggest that this ceremonial center became more structured in its relationship with Chavín de Huántar during the Early Horizon. The presence of large amounts of Quispisisa obsidian artifacts at Chavín de Huántar seems to imply that their relationship involved economic factors, which might be explained by the world-systems approach (e.g., Burger and Matos 2002; Kardulius and Hall 2008). Campanayuq Rumi may have decreased its contacts with the regions where the new religious ideology was not accepted because it was more integrated within the pan-regional interaction sphere centered on Chavín de Huántar. Campanayuq Rumi was abandoned around 500 cal BC, a date that coincides with the collapse of Chavín de Huántar (e.g., Kembel 2008). This seems to suggest that Campanayuq Rumi was deeply involved in the relationship with Chavín de Huántar during the Early Horizon.

On the other hand, note that the rejection of the new pan-regional ideology did not necessarily mean the end of other kinds of ties that had been existed from the Initial Period among the different areas. For example, the obsidian provenience data from Campanayuq Rumi show that in the Early Horizon (Campanayuq II Phase) the diversity of obsidian proveniences at Campanayuq Rumi was greater than the previous phase; that is, obsidian came to Campanayuq Rumi from the areas where the new religious ideology was not accepted, such as Andahuaylas (Matsumoto et al. 2018). These data suggest that local economic ties could have survived despite the emergence of a pan-regional religious network, and also show the multiple levels of heterogeneity in the Chavín Phenomenon.

Conclusions

This chapter is a preliminary synthesis of the Chavín phenomenon in the regions to the south of Chavín de Huántar. When we consider the Chavín phenomenon, there seems to be a notable contrast between the areas to the south and north of Chavín de Huántar. Although a comprehensive review of the recent debate about this is beyond the focus of this chapter, one important point in dispute is whether this phenomenon should be interpreted as a regional development or radical socioeconomic transformation at a pan-regional level (Burger 1988, 1992, 2008; Inokuchi 1998; Kembel 2001, 2008; Kembel and Rick 2004; Rick 2005, 2008; Burger and Salazar 2008).

In the case of the North Coast and the Northern Highlands, several cultural continuities can be pointed out, especially in material styles and iconographies between the late Initial Period and Early Horizon. For example, the feline deity and the stirrup-spout bottle can be recognized both in the late Initial Period cultures such as Cupisnique on the North Coast (e.g., Larco Hoyle 1941; Elera 1998) or the Late Huacaloma Phase at Huacaloma in Cajamarca (Terada and Onuki 1982, 1985), and the Early Horizon cultures, such as the Kuntur Wasi Phase at Kuntur Wasi (e.g., Inokuchi 1998) or the Janabarriu Phase at Chavín de Huántar (Burger 1984a). These general continuities from the late Initial Period to the Early Horizon in areas to the north of Chavín complicate this debate. This is why I dealt with the "south of Chavín" as the area that received "intrusive influence from Chavín de Huántar" and not vice versa.

The Chavín phenomenon appeared as radical changes in the central highlands and south coast, around 800–700 cal BC. As discussed here, material styles show rejection of preceding local ones, and in many cases social organizations seem to have transformed to more hierarchical. New data from these regions suggest that this phenomenon was not a unidirectional process of acculturation. Rather, we should consider this process in relation to the active decision-making of different agents, which could have ranged from a few persons such as leaders to a reasonably large geographic area. In this perspective, archaeologists need to focus on local reactions to the Chavín phenomenon to understand how societies manipulated and negotiated with the new religious ideology and were transformed by their decisions.

CHAPTER TWELVE

CHANGING INTERPRETATIONS
OF EARLY CENTRAL ANDEAN CIVILIZATION

Richard L. Burger

The session at the Fifty-fourth International Congress of Americanists in Vienna in 2012 that inspired this publication concluded with a lively discussion, but without a final commentary or synthesis. However, the reviewers of the draft manuscript of this edited volume believed that adding a concluding cqhapter would enhance its overall coherence and value. In this spirit, I have put together some final remarks that I hope will serve this purpose and serve to stimulate additional discussion and debate.

This book is the product of a resurgence of interest in the archaeology of the second and first millennium BC in the Central Andes. As in all academic fields, topics rise and fall in popularity. Perhaps because of the enduring influence of Julio C. Tello, the study of the Initial Period and Early Horizon (also known as the Formative) was especially popular in the 1960s, 1970s, and early 1980s, but over the following decades as his influence faded the number of investigations declined. At the same time, there was increasing focus by archaeologists on later Andean prehistory, such as the Moche and Inca cultures.

Despite the shifting interests, progress continued to be made on the Formative. The efforts of Yoshio Onuki and his colleagues at Kuntur Wasi and sites in the Cajamarca Valley, Tom and Shelia Pozorski's research in Casma, and the Yale University investigations in the lower Lurín Valley are examples of the continuing research on the Formative in the late 1980s and 1990s despite the climate of violence that pervaded Peru. Yet compared to the work on other areas of Peruvian prehistory, the volume of research was small.

Fortunately, research interest in the Initial Period and Early Horizon has revived. In recent years, other than this book, three collections of essays have been published summarizing much current research on the Formative, and include essays written by dozens of Peruvian and foreign scholars (Kaulicke and Onuki 2008, 2009; Seki 2014). Other projects were begun too recently to be incorporated into this publication, including Jalh Dulanto's investigations at Puerto Nuevo in Paracas, Oscar Gabriel Prieto's work at Gramalote in the Moche Valley, Rebecca Bria's studies at Hualcayán in Caraz, Michelle Young's excavations at Atalla in Huancavelica, Jason Nesbitt's research at Canchas Urko and Reparín in the Puccha drainage, Kimberly Munro's investigations at Cosmos in the mid-Nepeña Valley, and the Universidad Nacional Mayor Santiago Antúnez de Mayolo's project at Pallka in Casma. This list is by no means exhaustive and it leaves little doubt that widespread investigation into the emergence of early central Andean civilization has returned in force.

Problems of Terminology

Before discussing the content of these essays, a potential source of confusion should be addressed. As noted in the preface, two schools of research are represented in this book: one consists of Japanese researchers linked to the investigations directed by Seiichi Izumi and Kazuo Terada at the University of Tokyo. The other school is comprised of researchers tied to the archaeological studies program at Yale University and the investigations in the Lurín Valley begun by Burger and Salazar. Here the Yale scholars use the chronological framework proposed by John Howland Rowe (1962), whereas those belonging to the Japanese school of scholarship have adopted a variant of the evolutionary terminological framework first popularized by Luis Lumbreras (1969, 1974a). Because these two systems are based on differing principles, they are not fully comparable, but from a practical perspective there is a rough correlation among the early and middle Initial Period and Lower Formative, the late Initial Period and the Middle Formative, the early Horizon and the early portion of the Late Formative, and the late Early Horizon and the final portion of the Late Formative (called the Final Formative by Shibata). Although there is no consensus on the terminology, there is increasing agreement about the "absolute" or chronometric dating of the cultural sequences in calibrated radiocarbon years. This is reflected in a general consistency of the age estimates found throughout this book.

Cultural Stages, Cultural Identity, and Scale of Analysis

The neo-evolutionary models of explanation that were popularized by processual archaeology in the late twentieth century are almost completely absent in this collection of essays. No space is dedicated to debating whether the prehistoric societies in question are chiefdoms or archaic states (e.g., see Chapter 3 for an explicit rejection of this approach). Rather than focus on idealized cultural stages, the efforts here are aimed at trying to understand the nature of the organization of specific societies from the evidence available.

In the spirit of post-processualism, the ideological or cosmological principles that underlie or justify these social systems are also considered to be fair game for research, and there are discussions of subjects such the creation and meaning of landscapes (see Chapter 2), ancestor worship (see Chapters 2 and 8), and dualism (see Chapter 4), topics once viewed by most archaeologists as overly speculative. These ideological elements are appreciated as fundamental to cultural perception and the concrete decisions that they shaped in antiquity.

At the same time, there seems to be a diminishing interest in the cultural identity or affiliation of specific archaeological sites or assemblages. This is especially true of the chapters written by the scholars of the Japanese school. In the 1960s and 1970s, literature on the Formative was dominated by discussions of archaeological cultures such as Chavín, Cupisnique, and Paracas. This is not the case here. For example, Eisei Tsurumi (see Chapter 2) provides a detailed consideration of the cultural landscape of the Tembladera section of the middle Jequeteque Valley during the Initial Period (i.e., Early and Middle Formative) without reference to Cupisnique, the culture traditionally considered to characterize the North Coast during the time in question. Should we consider the Hamacas complex described by Tsurumi as an expression of Cupisnique culture or, given its distinctive burial towers and sequentially occupied mounds, should we treat it as a distinctive culture in its own right, perhaps one that characterizes the middle valley environment?

The lack of reference to the Cupisnique culture in this context may be liberating, particularly considering the ambiguity surrounding its definition, but could it also have negative consequences? For example, the narrow focus on the Hamacas Plain in this case makes it possible to discuss the functioning of the Tembladera sites without considering their relationship to Limoncarro and other Cupisnique sites located downstream (Salazar-Burger and Burger 1983; Sakai and Martinez 2010) or the highland center of Kuntur Wasi, situated up-valley (see Chapter 6).

Similarly, the chapters in this volume that discuss Kuntur Wasi and Pacopampa (the former once referred to as a "colony of Chavín" [Carrión Cachot 1948]), do so largely without reference to Chavín de Huántar and the pan-regional transformations linked to it during the late Initial Period and Early Horizon. Although there is value in understanding each archaeological site on its own terms, can we really hope to fully grasp the profound changes that occurred at these centers without reference to the larger cultural universe?

As Yuichi Matsumoto's overview (see Chapter 11) of cultural and socioeconomic developments in the south-central highlands shows, during the late Initial Period and Early Horizon societies in a wide range of geographical settings experienced a series of social, economic, and technological changes that were not limited to one locale, but occurred at a pan-regional scale. In this collection, Matsumoto's essay is unique in the broad scope of his analysis and his explicit consideration of the Chavín, Paracas, and Cupisnique cultures in his discussion of the transformations that occurred at Campanayuq Rumi.

It is significant that gold jewelry was encountered in the Early Horizon tomb of the "Lady of Pacopampa" on the eastern slopes of the Andes (see Chapter 8) and that its presence aids in tracing the emergence of inequality and centralized power at the site, yet it also is relevant that analogous precious metal objects have also been unearthed in situ at coeval tombs at Kuntur Wasi on the western Andean slopes, at Campanayuq Rumi in the south-central highlands of Ayacucho, and at a host of looted sites such as Chongoyape on the North Coast (Lothrop 1941; Alva 1992). Significantly, many of the precious metal objects from these elite burials were adorned with religious imagery related to the style and themes of the Chavín de Huántar stone sculptures and the Cupisnique pottery of the North Coast (Burger 1992:203–207). In addition, there is evidence of gold-working at Pacopampa and Campanayuq Rumi, a pattern also documented at Cerrillos, an early Paracas site in the Ica Valley (Splitstoser, Wallace, and Delgado 2010; Matsumoto and Cavero Palomino 2012).

The gold jewelry recovered in elaborate burials and the apparent fabrication of technologically sophisticated gold objects at Early Horizon civic-ceremonial sites must be linked to each other. This does not, however, indicate that the production of precious metal emblems for religious leaders was imposed by one center on the others. On the contrary, the apparent local production of the items and their considerable stylistic variation imply a degree of agency in each center. It does, however, suggest that the existence of elite individuals associated with the precious metal objects were part of a larger process of increased cultural interaction and social differentiation that was pan-regional rather than local in scale.

The spread of exchange networks for rare raw materials such as cinnabar, obsidian, sodalite, and *Strombus* and *Spondylus* shell reinforces the argument for maintaining a pan-regional perspective that transcends a narrow focus on the archaeological site, particularly for the first millennium BC. Thanks to trace element analysis, isotopic studies, and other scientific sourcing techniques, it is now possible to describe the movement of these raw materials in antiquity with unprecedented precision and confidence (e.g., Burger and Glascock 2009; Cooke et al. 2013). The spike in the movement of these exotics during the late Initial Period and the first centuries of the Early Horizon is striking (Burger 2013) and new evidence of the pan-regional movement of goods appears in many of these chapters (e.g., Chapters 3 and 8) even though their significance is discussed mainly in terms of each site's local history.

In contrast, Uzawa's discussion of the appearance of domesticated camelid remains at Kuntur Wasi (2,300 masl) in an ecological zone outside of the natural habitat of llamas and alpacas (see Chapter 7) considers pan-regional factors like climate change as well as local forces, such as changing strategies of cervid hunting around Kuntur Wasi and the use of these animals in religious rituals. Ultimately, Uzawa concludes that the introduction of domesticated camelids cannot be adequately explained by changing patterns of deer hunting or climate change and that it is best interpreted as the result of "social developments such as trade between remote societies." Although he does not explicitly discuss this in relation to the emergence of the Chavín sphere of interaction, his conclusion is consistent with earlier models linking the spread of llamas to the appearance of llama caravans responsible for moving goods between distant centers such as Chavín de Huántar, Pacopampa, and Kuntur Wasi (Burger 1992:210; Miller and Burger 1995).

Power and Inequality: Some Caveats

Throughout this volume it is clear that the authors are not satisfied with describing new archaeological evidence from their investigations of Initial Period and Early Horizon sites. Virtually all of them marshal this data to address larger anthropological questions, especially those dealing with sociopolitical organization, inequality, and power. In some cases, this proves problematic because of the specific nature of the archaeological remains or the type of analysis used. Is there really a relationship between elite power and the changing patterns of ceramic paste identified through petrography? And what does the shifting orientation of a site's axis tell us about the nature of leadership and the consolidation of authority? If the bridging arguments between the evidence and the interpretations are unconvincing, the conclusions may seem overly speculative even if such ideas can be taken as working hypotheses to be reexamined in the future.

The essays here address the social and political changes over nearly two millennia, and it is during this block of time that significant inequality and powerful leaders emerged for the first time in the Central Andes (Burger 1992:203–207). How and when this occurred remains a subject of active debate. Some scholars have argued that sharp socioeconomic stratification is absent for most of the Initial Period (Patterson 1983; Burger 2009a; Burger and Salazar 2014), but others have concluded that the many monumental constructions of this time imply the presence of powerful leaders with coercive power and a socioeconomic status commensurate with their political role (T. Pozorski and S. Pozorski 1993a, 2012).

In this volume, two of the chapters present new evidence supporting the former position. Nesbitt's contribution (see Chapter 1) is particularly significant in this regard because he is reporting on a site, Caballo Muerto (150 masl) in the Moche Valley that was formerly presented as providing evidence in support of the latter position (T. Pozorski 1982, 1995). Caballo Muerto is a large complex with eight mounds covering some 200 ha. Nesbitt focuses his attention on two of the site's larger mounds, Huaca Cortada and Huaca Herederos Grande, both terraced platforms built in the early Initial Period (Lower Formative), but occupied into the late Initial Period (Middle Formative). Nesbitt's new research at these mounds revealed that the platforms had been constructed in many episodes spaced over a long span of time. He argues that building the two constructions would have required some two million person-days, but that this could have been accomplished by one to two hundred people working over the twenty generations represented in the building sequence. Although each of these edifices eventually grew to over 20 m in height, he found no evidence that they had been produced as an act of personal aggrandizement or as the product of elite direction. Moreover, close study of the two platform complexes, located only 300 m apart, indicated that they are not architecturally integrated with each other and were probably built by different and perhaps competing social groups. Nesbitt interprets their construction as expressing community identity inspired and maintained through collective action and shared religion. Like Burger and Salazar (2014) in the Lurín Valley, Nesbitt argues that the motivation for the building of Huaca Cortada and Huaca Herederos Grande at Caballo Muerto was the result of piety and social solidarity rather than coercion by powerful leaders.

Nesbitt also presents the idea that wealth in these unstratified nonstate Initial Period societies on the North Coast would have been conceptualized as wealth in people, a concept popularized by Scottish social anthropologist Jane Guyer (1995). This provocative idea merits additional exploration.

The essay by Burger and Salazar (Chapter 4) likewise presents additional evidence supporting their earlier conclusion that the Initial Period centers of the Manchay culture of the central coast were characterized by weakly stratified groups lacking powerful leaders (Burger and Salazar-Burger 1992; Burger 2009a). The new investigations at Cardal in the Lurín Valley found that although there were "restricted" inner chambers on the summit of the main terraced platform for ceremonies invisible to those in the plazas below, there also were rituals carried out in open or "unrestricted" summit spaces oriented toward the general public. The research also revealed many secondary axes of public activity linked to public spaces that were designed to hold social groups of different sizes. The work on the lateral platforms (or "arms") of the U-shaped complex at Cardal supported the interpretation that the society was dually organized and that these dual groups or moieties had separate built environments for their rituals.

Thus, a more detailed understanding of Cardal's architecture suggests a complex architectural arrangement designed to accommodate the activities of the different social units that collectively constituted the larger community responsible for building Cardal. This layout suggests a diffuse distribution of power. Although religious leaders existed, their authority resided at the level of moieties and even smaller units such as lineages or sodalities as well as the community social unit as a whole. In many respects, when the U-shaped architectural complex at Cardal is analyzed in detail, it is more consistent with a pattern of hetararchy than hierarchy.

The study of inequality in the Formative has been hampered by the lack of research on the isolated residences, hamlets, and villages that sustained the centers with public architecture. The difficulty of locating these types of residential sites using traditional archaeological surface survey is partly responsible for this bias in investigation. A rare exception to the focus on civic-ceremonial sites is presented by Christopher Milan (see Chapter 5) from his excavations at Anchucaya in the middle Lurín Valley. He shows that Anchucaya, which had been incorrectly identified as a U-shaped public center, was actually a small village or hamlet dating to the early Initial Period. Milan contrasts the cultural assemblage and practices of Anchucaya with those of the nearby coeval civic-ceremonial center of Malpaso. He concludes that neither of the two sites offers evidence of powerful leaders or inequality.

The situation is very different for the sites dating to the Early Horizon (Late Formative). Even before the discoveries of the rich Early Horizon tombs at Kuntur Wasi and Pacopampa (discussed in Chapter 8), it was suggested on the basis of looted material from Chongoyape, Chavín de Huántar, and other sites, as well as other evidence such as faunal remains and household debris, that socioeconomic inequality had emerged by the outset of the Early Horizon and that this fundamental socioeconomic change underlay the Chavín phenomenon (Burger 1992; see also Patterson 1983). The recent archaeological discoveries at Pacopampa and elsewhere seem to confirm this observation about the social transformations occurring during the Early Horizon, but they raise other questions. Who were the emergent leaders and how were they able to consolidate power sufficient to acquire personal wealth, ignoring what must have been long-standing moral conventions forbidding such inequality? Unfortunately, as Shibata observes (Chapter 3), few households from the Early Horizon have been located or excavated, so that our understanding of power relationships are necessarily based on evidence unearthed at the public centers that were dominated by the elite, thereby biasing the models proposed.

The elite burials at Kuntur Wasi and Pacopampa are located on the summits of these sites and are placed along the central axes of these religious complexes. This mortuary pattern implies that religious authority provided the foundation for their extraordinary status, as does the religious iconography that decorates the precious metal crowns, nose ornaments, earspools, pendants, and snuff spoons that were buried with them. In contrast, weapons are absent from the interments and there is no evidence of violence. Judging from the evidence available, it can be concluded that physical coercion did not play a central role in establishing the authority of leaders in these centers (compare Burger 1992:225; Arkush and Tung 2013). If not, what were the mechanisms used to implement and maintain the legitimacy of authority?

In an earlier discussion of this question, I suggested that at Chavín de Huántar the use of new technologies and materials that instilled awe would have played such a role in the success of the Chavín cult and its religious leaders. I also argued that the recycling and fusion of prestigious architectural styles taken from older coastal and highland centers could also have lent legitimacy to the claims of temple's leadership (Burger 1988:130–131, 1992:202). The emotional and aesthetic power of religious ceremonies based in the esoteric cosmology of the tropical forest that featured the consumption of lowland hallucinogenic snuff must have likewise reinforced the ideological control and claims of Chavín's religious authorities (Burger 1992, 2011). In his writings, John Rick (2008) has likewise emphasized the role of architectural conventions and new technologies to strengthen authority at Chavín de Huántar.

Ultimately, the power of the religious leaders must have rested on the religious ideology of Chavín de Huántar and its claims of authority deriving from links with and understanding of the supernatural. This religious ideology must have been embraced by its adherents, including pilgrims traveling to Chavín de Huántar from other regional centers of power, and been considered an adequate explanation for the unprecedented inequality of power and wealth that emerged during the first millennium BC.

In these chapters, several strategies, some related to those identified at Chavín de Huántar, are ascribed to the emergent leaders of other Early Horizon centers. For example, Seki and colleagues (Chapter 8) suggest that the use of earlier building techniques and the reuse of carved blocks from older structures would have suggested continuity with the past and helped to legitimize Pacopampa's new elite. Similarly, the repeated burial of important ancestors along the central axis of the site is interpreted as strengthening the authority by the site's leaders.

In the same spirit, Matsato Sakai and his colleagues (Chapter 9) argue that the shift of Pacopampa's axis from an orientation pointing toward the rising of the Pleiades to an orientation toward La Capilla hill in the Pacopampa I Phase, and the subsequent decisions to keep this orientation during the Pacopampa II Phase, can best be understood as strategies related to maintaining the legitimacy of the authorities at the site. This may be the case, yet other motivations could also account for these axial shifts, and it is not evident how to determine which, if any, of them is correct.

In their contribution to this collection, Kinya Inokuchi and Isabel Druc (see Chapter 6) confront a similar conundrum. Using petrography, they show that, although the residents of Kuntur Wasi mainly consumed local pottery during the late Initial Period Idolo Phase, they also acquired small quantities of imported pottery from the lower valley potters and from adjacent highland groups, possibly in Cajamarca (see also Druc et al. 2017). In the subsequent Kuntur Wasi Phase, at the outset of which the site was transformed architecturally, this pattern of mainly consuming local pottery continues although the amount of ceramics from the lower valley seems to increase. This pattern changes, however, in the following Copa Phase when a new local production source began to function and all of the pottery consumed was produced within 6 km of Kuntur Wasi.

As the authors acknowledge, the meaning of the changes in consumption patterns is difficult to interpret since pottery was never produced at Kuntur Wasi itself and it cannot be determined whether it was ever under the control of temple authorities or reflects the self-interest of independent suppliers. Nonetheless, the authors argue, from evidence at the site, that the Copa leaders had more power than in earlier phases and probably supervised the production of goods, including ceramics. The decline in ceramic variability, along with the shift to local production during the Copa Phase, is considered to be "a disguised form of power exercised by the religious and economic center of Kuntur Wasi at that time, imposing decorative and formal canons displaying a specific ideology" (Chapter 6, page 95). Although this may be the case, I remain skeptical of this interpretation, because the degree of power being attributed to the Copa Phase leaders at Kuntur Wasi is substantial. In fact, few rulers in later prehistoric central Andean states were able to control ceramic production to the degree hypothesized in Inokuchi and Druc's model for the Early Horizon.

Cultural and Sociopolitical Heterogeneity in the Initial Period and Early Horizon

The strategies for consolidating and exercising power during the Initial Period and Early Horizon may be elusive, but other subjects are perhaps more amenable to analysis. One that warrants closer scrutiny is the increasing evidence for substantial cultural and social heterogeneity throughout the Initial Period and Early Horizon. For example, the settlement pattern in many coastal valleys during the Initial Period is characterized by a multitude of centers with monumental architecture, often built close to each other. No comparable pattern occurs in later prehistoric times. What is the relationship between the multiple Initial Period public centers within a single valley? This question was studied in the Lurín Valley and it was concluded that each center was autonomous and corresponded to a small-scale social unit with its own leaders and public architecture. As a result of community fission, additional centers were established over the centuries, resulting in many culturally similar coeval centers in a single relatively small valley (Burger and Salazar 2014).

Significantly, Tsurumi (see Chapter 2) presents a very different model of Initial Period settlement for the middle Jequetepeque Valley. He concludes that the early Initial Period (Early Formative) centers on the Hamacas Plain represent a diachronic series with new centers constructed around the time of the abandonment of the previous center. Thus, the pattern of construction, utilization, and abandonment of civic-ceremonial centers in Jequetepeque seems to be fundamentally different from the pattern documented in the Lurín Valley, although the two cultural trajectories are roughly contemporary.

An equally dramatic difference between the two areas is the importance of constructing burial towers and the apparent centrality of ancestor worship for Jequetepeque. A cultural practice focusing on highly visible funerary structures, so prominent in the middle Jequetepeque Valley, seems to be absent in Lurín and the lower sections of all other coastal valleys at this time. On the other hand, it was present in the midsection of the Virú Valley and has been well documented by the research of Thomas Zoubek (1997, 1998).

As Uzawa (Chapter 7) shows, the evidence for substantial heterogeneity during the Formative extends to the economic realm. Although Kuntur Wasi's faunal assemblage consists almost exclusively of cervids during the late Initial Period (Middle Formative), wild and domesticated camelids are already featured prominently at Chavín de Huántar. Llamas constituted the predominant source of meat there during the early and middle Early Horizon (Late Formative), but the hunting of deer continued to provide over 70% of the meat consumed at Kuntur Wasi (see Figure 7.2). Other Formative sites where faunal analysis has been done, such as Huaricoto, Huacaloma, and Kotosh, each have distinctive but different patterns of animal utilization as a result of both ecological and cultural factors.

The issue of sociocultural heterogeneity is particularly important for the period from 800 to 500 cal BC, the time during the Early Horizon corresponding to the zenith of the Chavín phenomenon. It is characterized by the strengthening of a sphere of interaction that is manifested archaeologically in the long-distance circulation of exotic raw materials (such as cinnabar, obsidian, *Spondylus,* and sodalite) and finely manufactured crafts (bone snuff tablets, ceramics) as well as the emulation of a ceramic style popular at Chavín de Huántar during the Chakinani and Janabarriu Phases. It is also linked to the spread of a distinctive iconographic style and religious imagery interpreted as expressions of the Chavín cult. This period has sometimes been interpreted as characterized by a high degree of cultural homogeneity (Rowe 1960). However, as shown by many of the contributions to this volume, this assumption is incorrect. This period in question (800–500 cal BC) was characterized by a great diversity of cultures—some emulating traits popular at Chavín de Huántar, some absorbing and reinterpreting them, and some ignoring them entirely, perhaps as an expression of resistance or local cultural autonomy, or both.

This point is illustrated nicely by Matsumoto (Chapter 11) by his contrast of the reactions to the Chavín phenomenon between the south coast and the south-central highlands of Ayacucho. Whereas the residents of Campanayuq Rumi during the Campanayuq II Phase accepted the architectural style and building techniques of Chavín de Huántar and emulated many elements of the ceramic style, the peoples of the south coast, while accepting the religious ideology and elements of the pottery style, show no evidence of having produced public architecture inspired by the highland center in Ancash. Elsewhere Matsumoto has shown how even within a relatively small area of the Upper Huallaga Valley the residents of the small Early Horizon site of Sajarapatac reacted to the Chavín phenomenon very differently than those living in the larger center at Kotosh in terms of its architectural layout and rituals (Matsumoto 2009).

This same phenomenon is highlighted by Ryan Clasby's excavations at Huayurco on the lower eastern slopes of the Andes (see Chapter 10). The public architecture built at Huayurco during the Early Horizon consisted of a large multi-room rectangular building of cobbles and yellow clay mortar without a supporting platform or other "monumental" elements. The rituals carried out there involved local practices, with such evidence as multiple small pits for burning offerings, layers of crushed pink quartz, and burials of young children. The pottery sequence was equally distinctive with little emulation of the Chavín-related pottery style so popular throughout much of the Central Andes. Although the residents of Huayurco were able to obtain Pacific shell from the warm waters off the coast of far northern Peru and southern Ecuador, the species acquired was mainly pearl oyster (*Pinctada mazatlanica*) rather than the *Spondylus* shell that was so sought after by Chavín-related sites.

As Clasby observes, the distinctively local pattern is in sharp contrast to the coeval occupation at Ingatambo, a site 80 km to the north. Although Ingatambo is farther from Chavín de Huántar than Huayurco, it manifests strong Chavín affinities in its architecture and cultural assemblage and clearly participated in the Chavín sphere of interaction (Yamamoto 2008). Curiously, although Huayurco was culturally dissimilar from Ingatambo, Pacopampa, and other Chavín-related sites, finely carved stone bowls produced at or near Huayurco were brought to Chavín de Huantar and were recovered there in the Ofrendas Gallery (see Chapter 10; Lumbreras 1971, fig. 27A).

Final Thoughts

As this collection of essays shows, considerable progress has been made toward understanding the nature of the cultures and societies of the Initial Period and Early Horizon (or Formative). Advances in the study of the Formative in some cases have not only raised new questions, but have forced us to reevaluate earlier debates and conclusions. In the past, following the path cut by Tello, studies of the Early Horizon were usually dominated by the work that had been done at Chavín de Huántar and sites were frequently organized by their similarities to that famous site. A widely disseminated version of this approach was the proposal of the existence of a "Chavín horizon." Discussed by Alfred Kroeber (1944:81–90, 108) and further developed by Gordon Willey (1945), its most detailed presentation appeared in Gordon Willey's 1951 essay "The Chavín Problem: A Review and Critique." Willey concentrated on reducing the confusion regarding Chavín that had been introduced as a result of Tello's lack of a rigorous definition for Chavín culture (Tello 1939, 1943), and he decided to focus on the value of using Chavín as a horizon style, which is to say a tool designed to serve as an integrating mechanism for Peruvian chronology. A horizon style, by definition, can be used to identify a short period of time over a broad geographical area. To achieve this, Willey defined the Chavín horizon style on the basis of the style of the site's stone sculpture and then used it as a standard of comparison to determine whether other sites should be considered part of the Chavín horizon. It was assumed that the Chavín style was historically unique and would have spread with sufficient rapidity as to be considered approximately contemporary wherever it happened. Other cultural elements, such as architecture, ceramics, and metallurgy, were not considered. The archaeological sites that were linked together by the style of the Chavín sculpture, often on the basis of a small number of objects, were defined as constituting a "Chavín horizon." Even with Willey's efforts to apply this definition rigorously, problems were encountered in applying it and serious errors were made in the analyses of Willey, Peter Roe (1974), and others. As a result of this approach, the cultural homogeneity of this period was emphasized; at the same time, the cultural unity of this period was contrasted with the balkanization that characterized the epochs preceding and following the "Chavín horizon."

In 1960, John Rowe drew on the idea of a "Chavín horizon" to name the Early Horizon, one of the blocks of time in his relative chronological framework (Rowe 1960, 1962). Defined by Rowe as beginning with the arrival of Chavín influence in the Ica Valley and ending with the adoption of the slip painting of ceramics in the Ica Valley, the term Early Horizon was fundamentally different in definition and purpose from the terminological tool advocated by Willey, who consistently maintained an interest in classification issues, chronological and otherwise, throughout his career (e.g., Willey and Phillips 1958). Despite the efforts of Willey and Rowe, the term Early Horizon became confused with Chavín in the work of some scholars.

The Rowe terminology is designed to define a large block of time using specific occurrences in the Ica Valley, the place designated for what Rowe called the Master Sequence. The Early Horizon was always assumed to have had a substantial duration (almost a thousand years), and cultures as diverse as Paracas, Chanapata, and Salinar, as well as Chavín, can all fall within the Early Horizon using Rowe's definition. Although the Rowe terminological system has limitations, in my opinion it remains less ambiguous than the multiple and sometimes contradictory Formative terminologies proposed by Lumbreras, Kaulicke, and others (Kaulicke 2010:360–384).

The term Chavín horizon, however, is now harder to defend given advances in the archaeology of the Initial Period and Early Horizon. At the time the Chavín horizon style was proposed, and in the following decades, little was known about Kuntur Wasi, Pacopampa, or any of the other contemporary centers. When I was a university student we were still using textbooks, such as those by Geoffrey Bushnell and Luis Lumbreras, that treated villages such as Ancon and Curayacu and public centers like Moxeke, Caballo Muerto, Kuntur Wasi, and Pacopampa as "Chavínoid" (Bushnell 1963:51–53; Lumbreras 1974a:67–71). This same ambiguous adjective was applied to the varied ceramic assemblages from these and other sites.

Yet as we have come to better understand the Chavín phenomenon, it seems less and less like a horizon in the classic sense. With the improvement in radiocarbon dating and its widespread application at numerous sites, it seems that what has been called the Chavín horizon lasted for five hundred years or more. And many of the centers, such as Kuntur Wasi and Pacopampa, once believed on the basis of a few sculptures to belong to the Chavín culture, have proved to be independent centers, each with a long and unique history that contrasts with that of the famous coeval center in the Mosna Valley.

Before the extensive excavations by Japanese archaeologists at Kuntur Wasi and Pacopampa, it was unclear what the relationship was between these famous sites and Chavín de Huántar. A small sample of stone sculptures carved with iconography resembling that of Chavín de Huántar had impressed archaeologists, as had the presence of cut and polished stone blocks in the architecture and the existence of large stone-lined galleries or canals. Yet without extensive excavations, it could not be determined how similar these sites were to Chavín de Huántar and how each site's development paralleled or differed from that of the Mosna center.

With over a decade of research at each of the sites, it is now clear how fundamentally different each of the centers is from Chavín de Huántar and from each other. At both Kuntur Wasi and Pacopampa, stone sculpture proved to be scarce and was not used in the same way that it was at Chavín de Huántar, where hundreds of carvings decorate the exterior of platform mounds and the interior of sunken courtyards. Many of the distinctive features of Chavín de Huántar, such as tenoned heads and a complex maze of interior galleries and chambers, are absent from both Kuntur Wasi and Pacopampa. Similarly, each of these centers had elements that were totally alien to Chavín de Huántar. For example, the large circular platform on the summit of Pacopampa has few known parallels outside of this site. And although detailed architectural sequences are now available for both Kuntur Wasi and Pacopampa, it is not possible to explain them in terms of architectural developments that were occurring at the Chavín de Huántar complex at roughly the same time.

There are also important socioeconomic contrasts between Chavín de Huántar and the two other northern centers. Neither Kuntur Wasi nor Pacopampa has the quantity of exotic materials found at Chavín de Huántar. Chavín de Huántar seems to be a center of pan-regional importance, but the other two sites might be better characterized as regional centers. Perhaps as a function of this contrast, only the Chavín de Huántar civic-ceremonial center seems to be associated with a large "proto-urban" population. Most relevant to the question of evaluating the Chavín horizon concept, no single architectural phase at either site can be identified as the result of the spread of Chavín influence.

The lack of a relatively short and fixed chronological unit linked to the Chavín phenomenon at Kuntur Wasi and Pacopampa is not consistent with a horizon terminology, and the situation is no more convincing elsewhere. For example, in the lower Nepeña Valley, as shown by Shibata (see Chapter 3), Chavín influence (in public art as well as other areas) seems to be strongest at the end of Initial Period, roughly 1000–800 cal BC, but it nearly disappears in this area during the following centuries. In contrast, as Matsumoto describes (see Chapter 11), influence is significant from 1000–800 cal BC at Campanayuq Rumi in Ayacucho, but strengthens rather than diminishes between 800 and 500 cal BC.

With the introduction of increasingly more reliable radiocarbon measurements and the likelihood of developing even more precise chronometric techniques, such as archaeomagnetism, perhaps it is time to acknowledge that the term Chavín horizon has outlived its usefulness and that the confusion it causes is no longer justified by its value as a chronological marker. Yet abandoning this term should not be equated with relinquishing the pan-regional analytical perspective that remains crucial for understanding the complex socioeconomic and cultural dynamics of the first half of the first millennium BC.

Clearly, we have come a long way in recent decades. Given the surge in research on the Initial Period and Early Horizon by a new generation of archaeologists, both Peruvian and foreign, there is reason to be optimistic about the future study of this crucial period of Peru's past.

References

ABRAMS, ELLIOT M. 1994. *How the Maya Built Their World: Energetics and Architecture.* Austin: University of Texas Press. 176 pp.

ALCOCK, SUSAN E. 2002. *Archaeology of the Greek Past: Landscape, Monuments, and Memories.* Cambridge: Cambridge University Press. 222 pp.

ALLEN, CLABON W. 1973. *Astrophysical Quantities.* 3rd ed. London: Athlone Press. 310 pp.

ALVA, WALTER. 1988. Investigaciones en el Complejo Formativo con Arquitectura Monumental de Purulén, Costa Norte del Perú. *Beiträge zur Allgemeinen und Vergleichenden Archäologie* 8:283–300.

—1992. Orfebrería del Formativo. In: José Antonio de Lavalle, ed. *Oro del Antiguo Perú.* Lima: Banco de Crédito del Perú en la Cultura. pp. 17–116.

ARKUSH, ELIZABETH AND TIFFANY A. TUNG. 2013. Patterns of war in the Andes from the Archaic to the Late Horizon: insights from settlement patterns and cranial trauma. *Journal of Archaeological Research* 21(4):307–369. https://doi.org/10.1007/s10814-013-9065-1.

ASTROARTS. 2006. StellaNavigator, Version 8. Tokyo; http://www.astroarts.co.jp/products/software.shtml.

AVENI, ANTHONY F. 1981. Horizon astronomy in Incaic Cuzco. In: Ray A. Williamson, ed. *Archaeoastronomy in the Americas.* Los Altos, CA: Ballena Press. pp. 305–368. (Anthropological Papers 22.)

AVILA, FRANCISCO DE. 1966. *Dioses y hombres de Huarochirí* [1608]. Lima: Instituto de Estudios Peruanos. 278 pp.

BANDY, MATTHEW S. 2004. Fissioning, scalar stress, and social evolution in early village societies. *American Anthropologist* 106(2):322–333. https://doi.org/10.1525/aa.2004.106.2.322.

BENDER, BARBARA. 2001. Introduction. In: Barbara Bender and Margot Winer, eds. *Contested Landscapes: Movement, Exile and Place.* Oxford: Berg. pp. 1–18.

BENFER, ROBERT A., JR. 1990. The Preceramic Period site of Paloma, Peru: bioindications of improving adaptation to sedentism. *Latin American Antiquity* 1(4):284–318. https://doi.org/10.2307/971812.

BILLMAN, BRIAN R. 1996. "The Evolution of Prehistoric Political Organization in the Moche Valley, Peru" [dissertation]. Santa Barbara: University of California, Department of Anthropology. 385 pp. Order no. 9708060, https://search.proquest.com/docview/304232703?accountid=15172.

—1999. Reconstructing prehistoric political economies and cycles of political power in the Moche Valley, Peru. In: Brian R. Billman and Gary M. Feinman, eds. *Settlement Pattern Studies in the Americas: Fifty Years since Virú.* Washington, DC: Smithsonian Institution Press. pp. 131–159. (Smithsonian Series in Archaeological Inquiry.)

—2001. Understanding the timing and tempo of the evolution of political centralization on the central Andean coastline and beyond. In: Jonathan Haas, ed. *From Leaders to Rulers.* New York: Kluwer Academic/Plenum Publishers. pp. 177–204.

—2002. Irrigation and the origins of the Southern Moche state on the north coast of Peru. *Latin American Antiquity* 13(4):371–400. https://doi.org/10.2307/972222.

BINFORD, LEWIS R. 1968. Post-pleistocene adaptations. In: Sally R. Binford and Lewis R. Binford, eds. *New Perspectives in Archaeology.* Chicago: Aldine. pp. 313–341.

BISCHOF, HENNING. 1994. Towards the definition of pre- and early Chavin art styles in Peru. *Andean Past* 4(art. 13):169–228. https://digitalcommons.library.umaine.edu/andean_past/vol4/iss1/13.

—1997. Cerro Blanco, valle de Nepeña, Perú: un sitio del Horizonte Temprano en emergencia. In: Elizabeth Bonnier and Henning Bischof, eds. *Archaeologica Peruana 2: Arquitectura y Civilización en los Andes Prehispánicos.* Mannheim: Sociedad Arqueológica Peruano-Alemana, Reiss-Engelhorn-Museum. pp. 202–234.

—2008. Context and contents of early Chavín art. In: William J. Conklin and Jeffrey Quilter, eds. *Chavín: Art, Architecture and Culture.* Los Angeles: Cotsen Institute of Archaeology, University of California. pp. 35–81. (Monograph 61.) https://doi.org/10.2307/j.ctvdmwx21.

—2009 [2010]. Los Períodos Arcaico Tardío, Arcaico Final y Formativo Temprano en el valle de Casma: evidencias e hipótesis. In: Peter Kaulicke and Yoshio Onuki, eds. El Período Formativo: enfoques y evidencias recientes. Cincuenta años de la Misión Arqueológica Japonesa y su vigencia. *Boletín de Arqueología PUCP* 13(2009):9–54. http://revistas.pucp.edu.pe/index.php/boletindearqueologia/article/view/977.

BOSERUP, ESTER. 1965. *The Conditions of Agricultural Growth: The Economics of Agrarian Change under Population Pressure.* 7th ed. Chicago: Aldine. 124 pp.

BRADLEY, RICHARD. 1998. *The Significance of Monuments: On the Shaping of Human Experience in Neolithic and Bronze Age Europe.* London: Routledge. 179 pp.

BROWMAN, DAVID L. 1970. "Early Peruvian Peasants: The Culture of a Central Highland Valley" [dissertation]. Cambridge: Harvard University, Department of Anthropology. 2 vols.

BURGER, RICHARD L. 1983. Pojoc and Waman Wain: two Early Horizon villages in the Chavín heartland. *Ñawpa Pacha* 20(1):3–40. https://doi.org/10.1179/naw.1982.20.1.002.

—1984a. *The Prehistoric Occupation of Chavín de Huántar, Peru.* Berkeley: University of California Press. 403 pp. (University of California Publications in Anthropology 14.)

—1984b. Archaeological areas and prehistoric frontiers: the case of Formative Peru and Ecuador. In: David L. Browman, Richard L. Burger, and Mario A. Rivera, eds. *Social and Economic Organization in the Prehispanic Andes.* Oxford: British Archaeological Reports. pp. 33 71. (BAR International Series 194.)

—1987. The U-shaped pyramid complex, Cardal, Peru. *National Geographic Research* 3(3):363–375.

—1988. Unity and heterogeneity within the Chavín Horizon. In: Richard Keatinge, ed. *Peruvian Prehistory.* Cambridge: Cambridge University Press. pp. 99–144.

—1992. *Chavín and the Origins of Andean Civilization.* New York: Thames and Hudson. 248 pp.

—2003a. El Niño, Civilización Peruana Temprana, y Agencia Humana: Algunos pensamientos del valle Lurín. In: Jonathan Haas and Michael O. Dillon, eds. *El Niño en Perú: Biología and Cultura sobre 10,000 años.* Chicago: The Field Museum. pp. 90–107. (Fieldana Botany New Series 43.)

—2003b. Conclusions: cultures of the Ecuadorian Formative in their Andean contexts. In: Scott Raymond and Richard L. Burger, eds. *Archaeology of Formative Ecuador.* Washington, DC: Dumbarton Oaks Research Library and Collection. pp. 465–486.

—2008. Chavín de Huántar and its sphere of influence. In: Helaine Silverman and William H. Isbell, eds. *Handbook of South American Archaeology.* New York: Springer. pp. 681–703.

—2009a. Los Fundamentos sociales de la arquitectura monumental del Período Inicial en el valle de Lurín. In: Richard L. Burger and Krysztof Makowski, eds. *Arqueología del Período Formativo en la Cuenca Baja de Lurín,* Volume 1. Lima: Fondo Editorial de la Pontificia Universidad Católica del Perú. pp. 17–36.

—2009b. The intellectual legacy of Julio C. Tello. In: Richard L. Burger, ed. *The Life and Writing of Julio C. Tello: America's First Indigenous Archaeologist.* Iowa City: University of Iowa Press. pp. 65–88.

—2011. What kind of hallucinogenic snuff was used at Chavín de Huántar? An iconographic identification. *Ñawpa Pacha* 31(2):123–140. https://doi.org/10.1179/naw.2011.31.2.123.

—2012. Central Andean language expansion and the Chavín sphere of interaction. In: Paul Heggarty and David Beresford-Jones, eds. *Archaeology and Language in the Andes: A Cross-disciplinary Exploration of Prehistory.* Oxford: Published for the British Academy by Oxford University Press. pp. 135–161. (Proceedings of the British Academy 173.)

—2013. In the realm of the Incas: an archaeological reconsideration of household exchange, long-distance trade, and marketplaces in the pre-hispanic Andes. In: Kenneth G. Hirth and Joanne Pillsbury, eds. *Merchants, Markets, and Exchange in the Pre-Columbian World.* Washington, DC: Dumbarton Oaks Research Library and Collection. pp. 319–334.

BURGER, RICHARD L., FRANK ASARO, AND HELLEN MICHEL. 1984. Appendix E. In: Richard L. Burger, ed. *The Source of Obsidian Artifacts at Chavín de Huántar, Peru.* Berkeley: University of California Press. pp. 263–270.

BURGER, RICHARD L. AND MICHAEL D. GLASCOCK. 2000. Locating the Quispisisa obsidian source in the Department of Ayacucho, Peru. *Latin American Antiquity* 11(3):258–268. https://doi.org/10.2307/972177.

—2002. Tracking the source of Quispisisa Type obsidian from Huancavelica to Ayacucho. In: William Isbell and Helaine Silverman, eds. *Andean Archaeology I. Variations in Sociopolitical Organization.* New York: Kluwer Academic/Plenum Publishers. pp. 341–368.

—2009. Intercambio prehistórico de obsidiana a larga distancia en el norte Peruano. *Revista del Museo de Arqueología, Antropología e Historia* 11:17–50.

BURGER, RICHARD L., KRIS E. LANE, AND COLIN A. COOKE. 2016. Ecuadadorian cinnabar and the prehispanic trade in vermilion pigment: viable hypothesis or red herring? *Latin American Antiquity* 27(1):22–35. https://doi.org/10.7183/1045-6635.27.1.22.

BURGER, RICHARD L. AND KRZYSZTOF MAKOWSKI, EDS. 2009. *Arqueología de Período Formativo en la Cuenca Baja de Lúrin,* Volume 1. Lima: Fondo Editorial de la Pontificia Universidad Católica del Perú. 530 pp. (Colección Valle de Pachacamac 1.)

BURGER, RICHARD L. AND RAMIRO MATOS. 2002. Atalla: a center on the periphery of the Chavín Horizon. *Latin American Antiquity* 13(2):153–177. https://doi.org/10.2307/971912.

BURGER, RICHARD L. AND LUCY C. SALAZAR. 2008. The Manchay culture and the coastal inspiration for Highland Chavín civilization. In: William J. Conklin and Jeffrey Quilter, eds. *Chavín: Art, Architecture and Culture.* Los Angeles: Cotsen Institute of Archaeology, University of California. pp. 85–105. (Monograph 61.) https://doi.org/10.2307/j.ctvdmwx21.

—2009. Investigaciones Arqueológicas en Mina Perdida, valle de Lurín. In: Richard L. Burger and Krzysztof Makowski, eds. *Arqueología del Período Formativo en la Cuenca Baja de Lurín,* Volume 1. Lima: Fondo Editorial de la Pontificia Universidad Católica del Perú. pp. 37–58.

—2012. Monumental public complexes and agricultural expansion on Peru's Central Coast during the second millenium B.C. In: Richard L. Burger and Robert M. Rosenswig, eds. *Early New World Monumentality.* Gainesville: University Press of Florida. pp. 399–430. https://doi.org/10.5744/florida/9780813038087 .003.0014.

—2014. ¿Centro de qué? Los sitios con arquitectura pública de la cultura Manchay en la costa central del Perú. In: Yuji Seki, ed. *Êl Centro Ceremonial Andino: Nuevas Perspectivas para los Periodos Arcaico y Formativo.* Osaka: National Museum of Ethnology. pp. 291–313. (Senri Ethnological Studies 89.)

BURGER, RICHARD L. AND LUCY C. SALAZAR-BURGER. 1980. Ritual and religion at Huaricoto. *Archaeology* 33(6):26–32. https://www.jstor.org/stable/41726522.

—1985. The early ceremonial center of Huaricoto. In: Christopher B. Donnan, ed. *Early Ceremonial Architecture in the Andes: A Conference at Dumbarton Oaks, 8th to 10th October 1982.* Washington, DC: Dumbarton Oaks Research Library and Collection. pp. 111–138.

—1991. The second season of investigations at the Initial Period center of Cardal, Peru. *Journal of Field Archaeology* 18(3):275–296. https://doi.org/10.2307/529934.

—1992. La Segunda Temporada de Investigaciones en Cardal, valle de Lurín (1987). In: Duccio Bonavia, ed. *Estudios de Arqueología Peruana.* Lima: FOMCIENCIAS. pp. 123–147.

—1994. La organización dual en el ceremonial andino temprano: un repaso comparativo. In: Luis Millones and Yoshio Onuki, eds. *El Mundo Ceremonial Andino.* Lima: Editorial Horizonte. pp. 97–116. (Etnología y Antropología 8.)

—1998. A sacred effigy from Mina Perdida and the unseen ceremonies of the Peruvian Formative. *Res: Anthropology and Aesthetics* 33:28–53. https://www.jstor.org/stable/20167000.

BUSHNELL, GEOFFREY H. S. 1963. *Peru.* Revised edition. London: Thames and Hudson, Ltd. 216 pp.

—1966. Some archaeological discoveries from the frontier region of Peru and Ecuador, near Jaén. In: Alfredo Jiménez Núñez, ed. *XXXVI Congreso Internacional de Americanistas, España, 1964: Actas y Memorias,* Volume 1. Seville: Ed. Católica Española. pp. 501–507.

CARCELÉN SILVA, JOSÉ. 1984. Los trabajos realizados en la Huaca Campos de Montegrande. *Beiträge zur Allgemeinen und Vergleichenden Archäologie* 6:519–540.

CARRIÓN CACHOT, REBECA. 1948. La cultura Chavín: dos nuevas colonias Kuntur Wasi y Ancón. *Revista del Museo Nacional de Antropología y Arqueología* 2(1):99–172.

CARRIÓN SOTELO, LUCÉNIDA. 1998. Excavaciones en San Jacinto, templo en "U" en el valle de Chancay. In: Peter Kaulicke, ed. Perspectivas Regionales del Período Formativo en el Perú. *Boletín de Arqueología PUCP* 2(1998):239–250. http://revistas.pucp.edu.pe/index.php/boletindearqueologia/article/view/755.

CASAFRANCA, JOSÉ. 1960. Los nuevos sitios Chavinoides en el departamento de Ayacucho. In: Ramiro Matos Mendieta, ed. *Antiguo Perú: Espacio y Tiempo.* Lima: Libreria Editoria Juan Mejia Baca. pp. 325–334.

CAUGHLEY, GRAEME. 1966. Mortality patterns in mammals. *Ecology* 47(6):906–918.

—1977. *Analysis of Vertebrate Populations.* London: John Wiley and Sons. 234 pp.

CHAUCHAT, CLAUDE, JEAN GUFFROY, AND THOMAS POZORSKI. 2006. Excavations at Huaca Herederos Chica, Moche Valley, Peru. *Journal of Field Archaeology* 31(3):233–250. https://www.jstor.org/stable/40023490.

CHICOINE, DAVID. 2008 [2010]. Cronología y secuencias en Huambacho, valle de Nepeña, costa de Ancash. In: Peter Kaulicke and Yoshio Onuki, eds. El Período Formativo: enfoques y evidencias recientes. Cincuenta años de la Misión Arqueológica Japonesa y su vigencia. *Boletín de Arqueología PUCP* 12(2008):317–347. http://revistas.pucp.edu.pe/index.php/boletindearqueologia/article/view/973.

CHILDE, V. GORDON. 1951. *Man Makes Himself.* New York: New Academy Library. 272 pp.

CLARK, JOHN E. 2013. Review of *Early New World Monumentality* by Richard L. Burger and Robert M. Rosenswig. *Latin American Antiquity* 24(2):233–235. http://www.jstor.org/stable/43746220.

CLARK, JOHN E., JON L. GIBSON, AND JAMES ZEIDLER. 2010. First towns in the Americas: searching for agriculture, population growth, and other enabling conditions. In: Matthew S. Bandy and Jake R. Fox, eds. *Becoming Villagers: Comparing Early Village Societies.* Tucson: University of Arizona Press. pp. 205–245. (Amerind Studies in Archaeology 6.)

CLASBY, RYAN P. 2014a. Early ceremonial architecture in the Ceja de Selva (800–100 B.C.): a case study from Huayurco, Jaén Region, Peru. In: Stéphen Rostain, ed. *Antes de Orellana. Actas del 3er Encuentro Internacional de Arqueología Amazónica.* Quito: Instituto Francés de Estudios Andinos. pp. 233–242. (Actes et Mémoires de l'Institut Français d'Études Andines 37.)

—2014b. "Exploring Long Term Cultural Developments and Interregional Interaction in the Eastern Slopes of the Andes: A Case Study from the Site of Huayurco, Jaén Region, Peru" [dissertation]. New Haven: Yale University, Department of Anthropology. 885 pp. Order no. 3582159, https://search.proquest.com/docview/1658811370?accountid=15172.

CLASBY, RYAN AND JORGE MENESES BARTRA. 2013. Nuevas investigaciones en Huayurco: resultados iniciales de las excavaciones de un sitio de la ceja de selva de los Andes peruanos. *Arqueología y Sociedad* 25(2012):303–326. https://revistasinvestigacion.unmsm.edu.pe/index.php/Arqueo/article/view/12364/11074.

CLASTRES, PIERRE. 1987. *Society Against the State: Essays in Political Anthropology.* Robert Hurley, translator. New York: Zone Books. 218 pp.

COMAROFF, JOHN L. AND JEAN COMAROFF. 2001. On personhood: an anthropological perspective from Africa. *Social Identities* 7(2):267–283. https://doi.org/10.1080/13504630120065310.

CONKLIN, WILLIAM J. 1985. The architecture of Huaca los Reyes. In: Christopher B. Donnan, ed. *Early Ceremonial Architecture in the Andes: A Conference at Dumbarton Oaks, 8th to 10th October 1982.* Washington, DC: Dumbarton Oaks Research Library and Collection. pp. 139–164.

COOKE, COLIN A., HOLGER HINTELMANN, JAY J. AGUE, RICHARD BURGER, HARALD BIESTER, JULIAN P. SACHS, AND DANIEL R. ENGSTROM. 2013. Use and legacy of mercury in the Andes. *Environmental Science and Technology* 47(9):4181–4188. https://doi.org/10.1021/es3048027.

CORDELL, LINDA S. 1997. *Archaeology of the Southwest.* 2nd ed. San Diego: Academic Press. 522 pp.

CORDY-COLLINS, ALANA K. 1976. "An Iconographic Study of Chavín Textiles from the South Coast of Peru: The Discovery of a Pre-columbian Catechism" [dissertation]. Los Angeles: University of California. 307 pp. Order no. 7622180, https://search.proquest.com/docview/288214623?accountid=15172.

CRUZATT, V. AUGUSTO. 1971. Horizonte Temprano en el valle de Ayacucho. *Anales Científicos* 1:603–631.

DAVID, NICHOLAS AND JUDY STERNER. 1999. Wonderful society: the Burgess Shale creatures, Mandara polities, and the nature of prehistory. In: Susan Keech McIntosh, ed. *Beyond Chiefdoms: Pathways to Complexity in Africa.* Cambridge: Cambridge University Press. pp. 97–109. (New Directions in Archaeology.)

DEBOER, WARREN R. 2003. Ceramic assemblage variability in the Formative of Ecuador and Peru. In: J. Scott Raymond and Richard L. Burger, eds. *Archaeology of Formative Ecuador.* Washington, DC: Dumbarton Oaks Research Library and Collection. pp. 465–486.

DE LA VERA CRUZ CHÁVEZ, PABLO. 1987. Cambio en los Patrones de Asentamiento y el Uso y Abandono de los Andenes en Cabanaconde, Valle de Colca, Perú. In: William M. Denevan, Kent Mathewson, and Gregory W. Knapp, eds. *Pre-Hispanic Agricultural Fields in the Andean Region,* Volume 1; proceedings, 45th International Congress of Americanists, Congreso Internacional de Americanistas, Bogotá, Colombia, 1985. Oxford: British Archaeological Reports. pp. 89–128. (BAR International Series 359.)

DELEONARDIS, LISA. 1991. "Settlement History of the Lower Ica Valley, Peru. Vth–Ist Centuries, B.C." [master's thesis]. Washington, DC: The Catholic University of America. 234 pp.

—1997. "Paracas Settlement in Callango, Lower Ica Valley, 1st Millennium, B.C., Peru" [dissertation]. Washington, DC: The Catholic University of America. 683 pp. Order no. 9829294, https://search.proquest.com /docview/304363610?accountid=15172.

—2005. Early Paracas cultural contexts: new evidence from Callango. *Andean Past* 7(art. 7):27–55. https:// digitalcommons.library.umaine.edu/andean_past/vol7/iss1/7.

DEMARRAIS, ELIZABETH, LUIS JAIME CASTILLO, AND TIMOTHY EARLE. 1996. Ideology, materialization, and power strategies. *Current Anthropology* 37(1):15–31. https://www.jstor.org/stable/2744153.

DILLEHAY, TOM D. 2004. Social landscape and ritual pause: uncertainty and integration in Formative Peru. *Journal of Social Archaeology* 4(2):239–268. https://doi.org/10.1177%2F1469605304042396.

—2007. *Monuments, Empires, and Resistance: The Araucanian Polity and Ritual Narratives.* Cambridge: Cambridge University Press. 484 pp.

—2008 [2010]. Sociedades, Sectores y Sitios Formativos en los Valles de Zaña y Jequetepeque, Costa Norte del Perú. In: Peter Kaulicke and Yoshio Onuki, eds. El Período Formativo: enfoques y evidencias recientes. Cincuenta años de la Misión Arqueológica Japonesa y su vigencia. *Boletín de Arqueología PUCP* 12(2008):119–139. http://revistas.pucp.edu.pe/index.php/boletindearqueologia/article/view/882/845.

DRUC, ISABELLE C. 2011. Tradiciones alfareras del valle de Cajamarca y cuenca alta del Jequetepeque, Perú. *Bulletin de l'Institut Français d'Études Andines* 40(2):307–331. https://doi.org/10.4000/bifea.1438.

DRUC, ISABELLE C., SILVANA BERTOLINO, ANDRÉE VALLEY, KINYA INOKUCHI, FRANCISCO RUMICHE, AND JOHN FOURNELLE. The Rojo Grafitado case: production of an early fine-ware style in the Andes. *Boletín de Arqueología PUCP.* In press.

DRUC, ISABELLE C., KINYA INOKUCHI, VICTOR CARLOTTO, AND PEDRO NAVARRO. 2017. Looking for the right outcrop: ceramic petrography in the Peruvian Andes. In: Mary F. Ownby, Isabelle C. Druc, and Maria A. Masucci, eds. *Integrative Approaches in Ceramic Petrography.* Salt Lake City: University of Utah Press. pp. 144–156. https://muse.jhu.edu/chapter/1946299/pdf.

DRUC, ISABELLE C., KINYA INOKUCHI, AND LAURE DUSSUBIEUX. 2017. LA-ICP-MS and petrography to assess ceramic interaction networks and production patterns in Kuntur Wasi, Peru. *Journal of Archaeological Science: Reports* 12:151–160. https://doi.org/10.1016/j.jasrep.2017.01.017.

DRUC, ISABELLE C., KINYA INOKUCHI, AND ZHIZHANG SHEN. 2013. Análisis de arcillas y material comparativo por medio de difracción de rayos X y petrografía para Kuntur Wasi, Cajamarca, Perú. *Arqueología y Sociedad* 26(2013):91–109. https://revistasinvestigacion.unmsm.edu.pe/index.php/Arqueo/article/view/12389/11092.

DUELLMAN, WILLIAM E. AND JENNIFER B. PRAMUK. 1999. *Frogs of the Genus* Eleutherodactylus *(Anura: Leptodactylidae) in the Andes of Northern Peru.* Lawrence, KS: Natural History Museum, University of Kansas. 78 pp. (Scientific Papers 13.) https://doi.org/10.5962/bhl.title.16169.

ELERA, CARLOS G. 1993. El Complejo Cultural Cupisnique: antecedentes y desarrollo de su ideología religiosa. In: Luis Millones and Yoshio Onuki, eds. *El Mundo Ceremonial Andino.* Osaka: National Museum of Ethnology. pp. 229–257. (Senri Ethnological Studies 37.)

—1998. "The Puemape Site and the Cupisnique Culture: A Case Study on the Origin and Development of Complex Society in the Central Andes, Peru" [dissertation]. Calgary, Alberta, Canada: University of Calgary. 679 pp. Order no. NQ38464, https://search.proquest.com/docview/304495437?accountid=15172.

—2009. La cultura Cupisnique a partir de los datos arqueológicos de Puémape. In: Luis Jaime Castillo and Cecilia Pardo, eds. De Cupisnique a los Incas: El Arte del Valle de Jequetepeque. Lima: Asociación Museo de Arte de Lima. pp. 34–61.

ENGEL, FREDERIC. 1966. Paracas: Cien Siglos de Cultura Peruana. Lima: Editorial Juan Mejía Baca. 228 pp.

ERASMUS, CHARLES. 1965. Monument building: some field experiments. Southwestern Journal of Anthropology 21(4):277–301. https://doi.org/10.1086/soutjanth.21.4.3629433.

EVANS-PRITCHARD, EDWARD E. 1935. The Nuer: tribe and clan. VII. Sudan Notes and Records 18(1):37–87. https://www.jstor.org/stable/41716096.

ESRI. 2004. ArcGIS, Version 9.0.1. Redlands, CA; esri.com.

FALCÓN, VICTOR AND MÓNICA SUÁREZ. 2009. El felino en la emergencia de la civilización en los Andes Centrales. In: Marcela Sepúlveda R., Luís E. Briones Morales, and Juan Chacama, eds. Crónicas Sobre la Piedra: Arte Rupestre de las Américas. Arica, Chile: Ediciones Universidad de Tarapacá. pp. 331–348.

FARRINGTON, IAN. 1974. Irrigation and settlement pattern: preliminary research results from the north coast of Peru. In: Theodore Downing and McGuire Gibson, eds. Irrigation's Impact on Society. Tucson: University of Arizona Press. pp. 83–94.

—1985. Operational strategies, expansion, and intensification within the prehistoric irrigation system of the Moche Valley, Peru. In: Ian Farrington, ed. Prehistoric Intensive Agriculture in the Tropics. Oxford: British Archaeological Reports. pp. 621–652. (BAR International Series 232.)

FELDMAN, ROBERT A. AND ALAN L. KOLATA. 1978. Archaeology in the electronics age. Field Museum of Natural History Bulletin 49(7):4–8. https://biodiversitylibrary.org/page/4348952.

FELTHAM, JANE. 1983. "The Lurin Valley, Peru: A.D. 1000–1532" [dissertation]. London: University of London, Institute of Archaeology. 1097 pp. Order no. U339672, https://search.proquest.com/docview/301483384?accountid=15172.

—2010. La arqueología de Sisicaya. In: Frank Salomon, Jane Feltham, and Sue Grosboll. La revisita de Sisicaya, 1588: Huarochirí veinte años antes de Dioses y Hombres. Lima: Fondo Editorial de la Pontificia Universidad Católica del Perú. pp. 57–101.

FLORES, ISABEL. 1975. Excavaciones en El Mirador, Pacopampa. In: Rosaura Andazabal Cayllahua. Publicaciones del Seminario de Historia Rural Andina. Lima: Seminario de Historia Rural Andina, Universidad Nacional Mayor de San Marcos. pp. 109–140.

FLORES OCHOA, JORGE A. 1979. Pastoralists of the Andes: The Alpaca Herders of Paratía. Ralph Bolton, translator. Philadelphia: Institute for the Study of Human Issues. 134 pp.

FONSECA MARTEL, CESAR. 1972. La economía vertical y la economía de mercado en las comunidades Alteñas del Perú. In: John V. Murra, ed. Visita de La Provincia de Leon de Huánuco en 1562, Volume 2. Huánuco, Peru: Universidad Nacional Hermilio Valdizan. pp. 315–337.

FRISON, GEORGE C. 1991. Hunting strategies, prey behavior and mortality data. In: Mary C. Stiner, ed. Human Predators and Prey Mortality. Boulder, CO: Westview Press. pp. 15–30.

FUENTES SADOWSKI, JOSÉ LUIS. 2009. "La secuencia cronológica de la Huaca La Florida, valle Del Rímac, Perú" [bachelor's thesis]. Lima: Universidad Nacional Mayor de San Marcos, Facultad de Ciencias Sociales.

FUNG PINEDA, ROSA. 1975. Excavaciones en Pacopampa, Cajamarca. Revista del Museo Nacional 41:129–207.

GAMBOA VELÁSQUEZ, JORGE AND JASON NESBITT. 2012. La Ocupación Moche en la Margen Norte del Valle Bajo de Moche, Costa Norte del Perú. Arqueología y Sociedad 25(2012):115–142. https://revistasinvestigacion.unmsm.edu.pe/index.php/Arqueo/article/view/12357/11067.

GARCÍA, RUBÉN. 2009 [2010]. Puerto Nuevo y los orígenes de la tradición estilístico-religiosa Paracas. In: Peter Kaulicke and Yoshio Onuki, eds. El Período Formativo: enfoques y evidencias recientes. Cincuenta años de la Misión Arqueológica Japonesa y su vigencia. Boletín de Arqueología PUCP 13(2009):187–208. http://revistas.pucp.edu.pe/index.php/boletindearqueologia/article/view/1000.

García, Rubén and José Pinilla. 1995. Aproximación a una sequencia de fases con cerámica temprana de la región Paracas. *Journal of the Steward Anthropological Society* 23:43–81.

Gibson, Jon. 2004. The power of beneficent obligation in first mound-building societies. In: Jon Gibson and Philip Carr, eds. *Signs of Power: The Rise of Cultural Complexity in the Southeast.* Tuscaloosa: University of Alabama Press. pp. 254–269.

Goldstein, Paul. 2000. Exotic goods and everyday chiefs: long-distance exchange and indigenous sociopolitical development in the south central Andes. *Latin American Antiquity* 11(4):335–361. https://doi.org/10.2307/972001.

Graeber, David. 2001. *Toward an Anthropological Theory of Value: The False Coin of Our Own Dreams.* New York: Palgrave. 337 pp.

Grieder, Terence. 2009. *Art and Archaeology of Challuabamba, Ecuador.* With James D. Farmer, David V. Hill, Peter W. Stahl, and Douglas H. Ubelaker. Austin: University of Texas Press. 221 pp.

Grossman, Joel W. 1972. "Early Ceramic Cultures of Andahuaylas, Apurimac, Peru" [dissertation]. Berkeley: University of California. 191 pp. Order no. 0281531, https://search.proquest.com/docview/302589169 ?accountid=15172.

Guffroy, Jean. 1999. *El Arte Rupestre del Antiguo Perú.* Lima: Instituto Francés de Estudios Andinos. 147 pp.

—2004. *Catamayo Precolombino: Investigaciones Arqueológicas en la provincia de Loja (Ecuador).* Paris: Institut de Recherche pour le Développement éditions. 191 pp.

—2008. Cultural boundaries and crossings: Ecuador and Peru. In: Helaine Silverman and William H. Isbell, eds. *Handbook of South American Archaeology.* New York: Springer. pp. 889–902.

Gutiérrez, Belkys. 1998. Menocucho, un complejo ceremonial del Formativo Inferior en el valle de Moche. *Revista de Ciencias Sociales* 5:341–364.

Guyer, Jane I. 1993. Wealth in people and self-realization in equatorial Africa. *Man, New Series* 28(2):243–265. https://doi.org/10.2307/2803412.

—1995. Wealth in people, wealth in things—introduction. *Journal of African History* 36(1):83–90. https://doi.org/10.1017/S0021853700026980.

Guyer, Jane I. and Samuel M. Eno Belinga. 1995. Wealth in people as wealth in knowledge: accumulation and composition in equatorial Africa. *Journal of African History* 36(1):91–120. https://doi.org/10.1017/S0021853700026992.

Haas, Jonathan. 1987. The exercise of power in Early Andean state development. In: Jonathan Haas, Shelia G. Pozorski, and Thomas G. Pozorski, eds. *The Origins and Development of the Andean State.* Cambridge: Cambridge University Press. pp. 31–35.

Haas, Jonathan and Winifred Creamer. 2012. Why do people build monuments? Late Archaic platform mounds in the Norte Chico. In: Richard L. Burger and Robert M. Rosenswig, eds. *Early New World Monumentality.* Gainesville: University of Florida Press. pp. 289–312.

Hastings, C. Mansfield and M. Edward Moseley. 1975. The adobes of Huaca del Sol and Huaca de la Luna. *American Antiquity* 40(2, pt. 1):196–203. https://doi.org/10.2307/279615.

Helms, Mary. 1988. *Ulysses's Sail: An Ethnographic Odyssey of Power, Knowledge, and Geographical Distance.* Princeton: Princeton University Press. 297 pp.

—1993. *Craft and Kingly Ideal: Art, Trade, and Power.* Austin: University of Texas Press. 287 pp.

Hirth, Kenneth G. 1978. Interregional trade and the formation of prehistoric gateway communities. *American Antiquity* 43(1):35–45. https://doi.org/10.2307/279629.

Hocquenghem, Anne-Marie, Jaime Idrovo, Peter Kaulicke, and Dominique Gomis. 1993. Bases del intercambio entre las sociedades norperuanas y surecuatorianas: una zona de transición entre 1500 A.C. y 600 D.C. *Bulletin de l'Institut Français d'Études Andines* 22(2):443–466.

Hogg, Alan G., Quan Hua, Paul G. Blackwell, Mu Niu, Caitlin E. Buck, Thomas P. Guilderson, Timothy J. Heaton, Jonathan G. Palmer, Paula J. Reimer, Ron W. Reimer, et al. 2013. ShCal13 Southern Hemisphere calibration, 0–50,000 years cal BP. *Radiocarbon* 55(4):1889–1903. https://doi.org/10.2458/azu_js _rc.55.16783.

IKEHARA, HUGO. 2007. "Festines del Período Formativo Medio y Tardío en Cerro Blanco de Nepeña" [bachelor's thesis]. Lima: Pontificia Universidad Católica del Perú, Facultad de Letras y Ciencias Humanas. 331 pp. http://hdl.handle.net/20.500.12404/432.

IKEHARA, HUGO AND KOICHIRO SHIBATA. 2005 [2008]. Festines e integración social en el Periodo Formativo: nuevas evidencias de Cerro Blanco, valle bajo de Nepeña. In: Peter Kaulicke and Tom D. Dillehay, eds. Encuentros: identidad, poder y manejo de espacios públicos. Boletín de Arqueología PUCP 9(2005):123–159. http://revistas.pucp.edu.pe/index.php/boletindearqueologia/article/view/1709.

IMAMURA, KEIJI. 1996. Prehistoric Japan: New Perspectives on Insular East Asia. Honolulu: University of Hawaii Press. 320 pp.

INOKUCHI, KINYA. 1998. La cerámica de Kuntur Wasi y el problema Chavín. In: Peter Kaulicke, ed. Perspectivas Regionales del Período Formativo en el Perú. Boletín de Arqueología PUCP 2(1998):161–180. http://revistas.pucp.edu.pe/index.php/boletindearqueologia/article/view/746.

—2008 [2010]. La arquitectura de Kuntur Wasi: secuencia constructiva y cronología de un centro ceremonial del Período Formativo. In: Peter Kaulicke and Yoshio Onuki, eds. El Período Formativo: enfoques y evidencias recientes. Cincuenta años de la Misión Arqueológica Japonesa y su vigencia. Boletín de Arqueología PUCP 12(2008):219–247. http://revistas.pucp.edu.pe/index.php/boletindearqueologia/article/view/968.

INOKUCHI, KINYA, YOSHIO ONUKI, EISEI TSURUMI, YUICHI MATSUMOTO, AND ARTURO RUIZ. 2002. Preliminary report of the general survey in Huánuco, Peru. America Antigua 5: 69–88. [In Japanese.]

INOMATA, TAKESHI, JESSICA MacLELLAN, AND MELISSA BURHAM. 2015. The construction of public and domestic spheres in the Preclassic Maya lowlands. American Anthropologist 117(3):519–534. https://doi.org/10.1111/aman.12285.

ISBELL, WILLIAM H. 1976. Cosmological order expressed in prehistoric ceremonial centers. In: Jacques Lafaye, ed. Actes du XLIIe Congrès International des Américanistes, Congrés du Centenaire, Paris, 2–9 Septembre 1976, Volume 4. [Paris]: Société des Américanistes. pp. 269–299.

ISLA, JOHNY AND MARKUS REINDEL. 2006. Una tumba Paracas temprano en Mollake Chico, valle de Palpa, costa sur del Perú [Ein grab der frühen Paracas-Zeit in Mollake Chico, Palpa-Tal, südküste Perus]. Zeitschrift für Archäologie Außereuropäischer Kulturen 1:153–181.

IZUMI, SEICHI, PEDRO CUCULIZA, AND CHIAKI KANO. 1972. Excavations at Shillacoto, Huánuco, Peru. Tokyo: University of Tokyo Press. 82 pp. (The University Museum Bulletin 3.)

IZUMI, SEICHI AND TOSHIHIKO SONO. 1963. Andes 2: Excavations at Kotosh, Peru 1960. Tokyo: Kadokawa Publishing Co. 210 pp.

IZUMI, SEICHI AND KAZUO TERADA, EDS. 1972. Andes 4: Excavations at Kotosh, Peru, 1963 and 1966. Tokyo: University of Tokyo Press. 375 pp.

JOYCE, ROSEMARY A. 2003. Concrete memories: fragments of the past in the Classic Maya Present (500–1000 AD). In: Ruth M. Van Dyke and Susan E. Alcock, eds. Archaeologies of Memory. Malden, MA: Blackwell. pp. 104–125.

—2004. Unintended consequences? Monumentality as a novel experience in Formative Mesoamerica. Journal of Archaeological Method and Theory 11(1):5–29. https://doi.org/10.1023/B:JARM.0000014346.87569.4a.

KADWELL MIRANDA, MATILDE FERNANDEZ, HELEN F. STANLEY, RICARDO BALDI, JANE C. WHEELER, RAUL ROSADIO, AND MICHAEL W. BRUFORD. 2001. Genetic analysis reveals the wild ancestors of the llama and the alpaca. Proceedings of the Royal Society of London Series B, Biological Sciences 268(1485):2575–2584. https://doi.org/10.1098/rspb.2001.1774.

KANO, CHIAKI. 1979. The Origins of the Chavín Culture. Washington, DC: Dumbarton Oaks Trustees for Harvard University. 87 pp.

KARDULIAS, P. NICK AND THOMAS D. HALL. 2008. Archaeology and world-systems analysis. World Archaeology 40(4):572–583. http://www.jstor.org/stable/40388295.

KATO, YASUTAKE. 2014. Kuntur Wasi: un centro ceremonial del período Formativo Tardío. In: Yuji Seki, ed. El Centro Ceremonial Andino: Nuevas Perspectivas para los Períodos Arcaico y Formativo. Osaka: National Museum of Ethnology. pp. 159–174. (Senri Ethnological Studies 89.)

KAULICKE, PETER. 2010. Las Cronologías del Formativo: 50 Años de Investigaciones japoneses en perspectiva. Lima: Fondo Editorial de la Pontificia Universidad Católica del Perú. 438 pp.

—2014. Memoria y temporalidad en el Período Formativo centroandino. In: Yuji Seki, ed. *El Centro Ceremonial Andino: Nuevas Perspectivas para los Períodos Arcaico y Formativo*. Osaka: National Museum of Ethnology. pp. 21–50. (Senri Ethnological Studies 89.)

KAULICKE, PETER, LARS FEHREN-SCHMITZ, MARÍA KOLP-GODOY, PATRICIA LANDA, ÓSCAR LOYOLA, MARTHA PALMA, ELSA TOMASTO, CINDY VERGEL, AND BURKHARD VOGT. 2009 [2010]. Implicancias de un área funeraria del Período Formativo Tardío en el departamento de Ica. In: Peter Kaulicke and Yoshio Onuki, eds. El Período Formativo: enfoques y evidencias recientes. Cincuenta años de la Misión Arqueológica Japonesa y su vigencia. *Boletín de Arqueología PUCP* 13(2009):289–322. http://revistas.pucp.edu.pe/index.php/boletindearqueologia /article/view/1006.

KAULICKE, PETER AND YOSHIO ONUKI, EDS. 2008 [2010]. El Período Formativo: enfoques y evidencias recientes. Cincuenta años de la Misión Arqueológica Japonesa y su vigencia. *Boletín de Arqueología PUCP* 12(2008). http://revistas.pucp.edu.pe/index.php/boletindearqueologia/issue/view/218.

—2009 [2010]. El Período Formativo: enfoques y evidencias recientes. Cincuenta años de la Misión Arqueológica Japonesa y su vigencia. *Boletín de Arqueología PUCP* 13(2009):289–322. http://revistas.pucp .edu.pe/index.php/boletindearqueologia/issue/view/219.

KEATINGE, RICHARD W. 1980. Archaeology and development: the Tembladera sites of the Peruvian north coast. *Journal of Field Archaeology* 7(4):467–477. https://doi.org/10.1179/009346980791505284.

KEMBEL, SILVIA. 2001. "Architectural Sequence and Chronology at Chavín de Huántar, Perú" [dissertation]. Stanford: Stanford University, Department of Anthropological Sciences. 317 pp. Order no. 3026846, https:// search.proquest.com/docview/304727155?accountid=15172.

—2008. The architecture at the monumental center of Chavín de Huántar: Sequence, transformations, and chronology. In: William J. Conklin and Jeffrey Quilter, eds. *Chavín: Art, Architecture and Culture*. Los Angeles: Cotsen Institute of Archaeology, University of California. pp. 35–81. (Monograph 61.) https://doi.org/10.2307 /j.ctvdmwx21.

KEMBEL, SILVIA AND JOHN RICK. 2004. Building authority at Chavín de Huántar. In: Helaine Silverman, ed. *Andean Archaeology*. Malden, MA: Blackwell. pp. 51–75.

KOCH, CLAUDIA, PABLO VENEGAS, AND WOLFGANG BÖHME. 2006. A remarkable discovery: description of a big-growing new gecko (Squamata: Gekkonidae: Phyllopezus) from northwestern Peru. *Salamandra* 42(2/3):145–150. http://www.salamandra-journal.com/index.php/home/contents/2006-vol-42/132-koch-c-p-j-venegas -w-boehme/file.

KOIKE, HIROKO. 1992. Nihonretto niokeru sensijidai no shuryou katsudo [Prehistoric hunting activities in the Japanese archipelago]. In: *Shūzō Koyama, ed. Shuryō to Gyorō—Nihon bunka no genryū o saguru [Hunting and Fishing—Exploring the Origin of Japanese Culture]*. Tokyo: Yuzankaku. [In Japanese.]

KOIKE, HIROKO AND NORIYUKI OHTAISHI. 1985. Prehistoric hunting pressures estimated by the age composition of excavated sika deer (*Cervus nippon*) using the annual layer of tooth cement. *Journal of Archaeological Science* 12(6):443–456. https://doi.org/10.1016/0305-4403(85)90004-4.

KOYAMA, SHŪZŌ. 1978. *Jomon Subsistence and Population*. Osaka: National Museum of Ethnology. 65 pp. (Senri Ethnological Studies 2.)

—1984. *Jomon Jidai (Jomon Period)*. Tokyo: Chuo Koron-sha. 206 pp. [In Japanese.]

KRAHTOPOULOU, ATHANASIA AND CHARLES FREDERICK. 2008. The stratigraphic implications of long-term terrace agriculture in dynamic landscapes: polycyclic terracing from Kythera Island, Greece. *Geoarchaeology* 23(4):550–586. https://doi.org/10.1002/gea.20231.

KROEBER, ALFRED L. 1944. *Peruvian Archaeology in 1942*. New York: The Viking Fund. 151 pp. (Viking Fund Publications in Anthropology 4.)

LARCO HOYLE, RAFAEL. 1941. *Los Cupisniques: Trabajo presentado al Congreso Internacional de Americanistas de Lima XXVII Sesion*. Lima: Casa editora "La Crónica" y "Variedades" S. A. 259 pp.

LATHRAP, DONALD W. 1962. "Yarinacocha: Stratigraphic Excavations in the Peruvian Montaña" [dissertation]. Cambridge: Harvard University. 1032 pp. Order no. 0258437, https://search.proquest.com/docview/302095256 ?accountid=15172.

—1970. *The Upper Amazon*. London: Thames and Hudson. 256 pp.

—1985. Jaws: the control of power in the early nuclear American ceremonial center. In: Christopher B. Donnan, ed. *Early Ceremonial Architecture in the Andes: A Conference at Dumbarton Oaks, 8th to 10th October 1982.* Washington, DC: Dumbarton Oaks Research Library and Collection. pp. 241–267.

LOTHROP, SAMUEL. 1941. Gold ornaments of Chavín style from Chongoyape, Peru. *American Antiquity* 6(3):250–262. https://doi.org /10.2307/275542.

LUDEÑA RESTAURE, HUGO. 1973. "Investigaciones Arqueológicas en el Sitio de Huacoy, Valle del Chillón" [dissertation]. Lima: Universidad Nacional Mayor de San Marcos, Programa Académico de Ciencias Sociales. 177 pp.

LUMBRERAS, LUIS G. 1969. *De los pueblos, las culturas, y las artes del Antiguo Perú.* Lima: Moncloa-Campodónico. 377 pp.

—1971. Towards a re-evaluation of Chavín. In: Elizabeth P. Benson, ed. *Dumbarton Oaks Conference on Chavin, October 26th and 27th, 1968.* Washington, DC: Dumbarton Oaks Research Library and Collection, Trustees for Harvard University. pp. 1–28.

—1974a. *The Peoples and Cultures of Ancient Peru.* Betty J. Meggers, translator. Washington, DC: Smithsonian Insitution Press. 248 pp.

—1974b. *Las Fundaciones de Huamanga: Hacia una Prehistoria de Ayacucho.* Lima: Editorial Nueva Educación. 238 pp.

—1977. Excavaciones en el Templo Antiguo de Chavín (Sector R); informe de la sexta campaña. *Ñawpa Pacha* 15(1):1–38. https://doi.org/10.1179/naw.1977.15.1.001.

—1981. The stratigraphy of the open sites. In: Richard S. MacNeish, Angel G. Cook, Luis G. Lumbreras, Robert Vierra, and Antoinette Nelken-Terner, eds. *Prehistory of the Ayacucho Basin, Peru.* Volume 2, Excavations and Chronology. Ann Arbor: University of Michigan Press. pp. 167–198.

—1989. *Chavín de Huántar en el nacimiento de la Civilización Andina.* Lima: Instituto Andino de Estudios Arqueológicos. 245 pp.

—1993. *Chavín de Huántar: Excavaciones en la Galería de las Ofrendas.* Meinz am Rhein: Verlag Philipp von Zabern. 461 pp. (Materialien zur Allgemeinen und Vergleichenden Archäologie 51.)

—2007. *Chavín: Excavaciones Arqueológicas.* Lima: Universidad ALAS Peruanas. 753 pp.

LYON, PATRICIA. 1978. Female supernaturals in ancient Peru. *Ñawpa Pacha* 16(1):95–144. https://doi.org /10.1179/naw.1978.16.1.006.

MACNEISH, RICHARD S., ANGEL G. COOK, LUIS G. LUMBRERAS, ROBERT VIERRA, AND ANTOINETTE NELKIN-TERNER. 1981. *Prehistory of the Ayacucho Basin, Peru.* Volume 2, Excavations and Chronology. Ann Arbor: University of Michigan Press. 279 pp.

MALPASS, MICHAEL. 1986. Prehistoric agricultural terracing at Chijra in the Colca Valley, Peru: preliminary report II. In: William. M. Denevan, Kent Mathewson, and Gregory W. Knapp, eds. *Pre-Hispanic Agricultural Fields in the Andean Region.* Volume 1, proceedings, 45th International Congress of Americanists, Congrèso Internacional de Américanistas, Bogotá, Colombia, 1985. Oxford: British Archaeological Reports. pp. 45–66. (BAR International Series 359.)

MATOS, RAMIRO. 1971. El período Formativo en el valle del Mantaro. *Revista del Museo Nacional* 37:41–51.

—1972. Ataura: un centro Chavín en el valle del Mantaro. *Revista del Museo Nacional* 38:93–108.

MATSUMOTO, YUICHI. 2009 [2010]. El manejo del espacio ritual en el sitio de Sajara-patac y sus implicancias para el "fenómeno Chavín." In: Peter Kaulicke and Yoshio Onuki, eds. El Período Formativo: enfoques y evidencias recientes. Cincuenta años de la Misión Arqueológica Japonesa y su vigencia. *Boletín de Arqueología PUCP* 13(2009):133–158. http://revistas.pucp.edu.pe/index.php/boletindearqueologia/article/view/998.

2010. "The Prehistoric Ceremonial Center of Campanayuq Rumi: Interregional Interactions in the Peruvian South-Central Highlands" [dissertation]. New Haven: Yale University, Department of Anthropology. 602 pp. Order no. 3440573, https://search.proquest.com/docview/847555915?accountid=15172.

—2012. Recognising ritual: the case of Campanayuq Rumi. *Antiquity* 86(333):746–759. https://doi.org/10.1017 /S0003598X0004789X.

—Reconsideración de la cronología radiocarbónica del Período Formativo en la cuenca de Alto Huallaga. In: Hernán Amat Olazábal, ed. *Homenaje al 50 Aniversario de la Misión Japonesa a los Andes*. Lima: Universidad Nacional Mayor de San Marcos. In press.

MATSUMOTO, YUICHI AND YURI CAVERO PALOMINO. 2009 [2010]. Una aproximación cronológica del centro ceremonial de Campanayuq Rumi, Ayacucho. In: Peter Kaulicke and Yoshio Onuki, eds. El Período Formativo: enfoques y evidencias recientes. Cincuenta años de la Misión Arqueológica Japonesa y su vigencia. *Boletín de Arqueología PUCP* 13(2009):323–346. http://revistas.pucp.edu.pe/index.php/boletindearqueologia/article /view/1020.

—2012. Early Horizon gold metallurgy from Campanayuq Rumi in the Peruvian south-central highlands. *Ñawpa Pacha* 32(1):115–130. https://doi.org/10.1179/naw.2012.32.1.115.

MATSUMOTO, YUICHI, JASON NESBITT, MICHAEL D. GLASCOCK, YURI I. CAVERO PALOMINO, AND RICHARD L. BURGER. 2018. Interregional obsidian exchange during the Late Initial Period and Early Horizon: new perspectives from Campanayuq Rumi, Peru. *Latin American Antiquity* 29(1):44–63. https://doi.org/10.1017 /laq.2017.64.

MATSUMOTO, YUICHI AND EISEI TSURUMI. 2011. Archeological investigations at Sajara-patac in the Upper Huallaga Basin, Peru. *Ñawpa Pacha* 31(1):55–110. https://doi.org/10.1179/naw.2011.31.1.55.

MAUSS, MARCEL. 1990. *The Gift: The Form and Reason for Exchange in Archaic Societies*. New York: W. W. Norton. 164 pp.

MCFADYEN, LESLEY. 2008. Building and architecture as landscape practice. In: Bruno David and Julian Thomas, eds. *Handbook of Landscape Archaeology*. Walnut Creek, CA: Left Coast Press. pp. 307–314. (World Archaeological Congress Research Handbooks in Archaeology 1.)

MCINTOSH, SUSAN KEECH, ED. 1999. *Beyond Chiefdoms: Pathways to Complexity in Africa*. Cambridge: Cambridge University Press. 176 pp. (New Directions in Archaeology.)

MENGONI GOÑALONS, GUILLERMO L. AND HUGO D. YACOBACCIO. 2006. The domestication of South American camelids, a view from the south-central Andes. In: Melinda A. Zeder, Daniel G. Bradley, Eve Emshwiller, and Bruce D. Smith, eds. *Documenting Domestication: New Genetic and Archaeological Paradigms*. Berkeley: University of California Press. pp. 228–244.

MENZEL, DOROTHY, JOHN H. ROWE, AND LAWRENCE E. DAWSON. 1964. *The Paracas Pottery of Ica: A Study in Style and Time*. Berkeley: University of California Press. 399 pp. (University of California Publications in American Archaeology and Ethnology 50.)

MESÍA-MONTENEGRO, CHRISTIAN J. 2000. Anchucaya: aproximación teórica sobre un complejo con planta en U en el valle medio del río Lurín. *Arqueológicas* 24:45–52.

—2007. "Intrasite Spatial Organization at Chavín de Huántar During the Andean Formative: Three Dimensional Modeling, Stratigraphy and Ceramics" [dissertation]. Stanford: Stanford University. 298 pp. Order no. 3281903, https://search.proquest.com/docview/304812544?accountid=15172.

MIASTA GUTIÉRREZ, JAIME. 1979. *El Alto Amazonas, Arqueología de Jaén y San Ignacio, Perú*. Lima: Seminario de Historia Rural Andina, Universidad Nacional Mayor de San Marcos. 213 pp.

MILAN, CHRISTOPHER. 2012. "When Chavín came around: the Initial Period and Early Horizon occupation of Malpaso and its implications for the Central Coast of Peru"; paper presented at the 40th Annual Midwest Conference on Andean and Amazonian Archaeology and Ethnohistory; 2012 February 24–26; Chicago, Illinois. Schedule and abstracts. https://www.fieldmuseum.org/file/1003776.

—2014. "The Initial Period (1800–800 BC) Occupation of the Middle Lurín Valley: A Discussion on the Interactions between Early Civic-Ceremonial Centers on the Central Coast of Peru and Nearby Hamlets" [dissertation]. New Haven: Yale University, Department of Anthropology. 438 pp. Order no. 3580772, https:// search.proquest.com/docview/1542138941?accountid=15172.

MILLER, GEORGE R. AND RICHARD L. BURGER. 1995. Our father the Cayman, our dinner the llama: animal utilization at Chavín de Huántar, Peru. *American Antiquity* 60(3):421–458. https://doi.org/10.2307/282258.

MOHR CHÁVEZ, KAREN L. 1977. "Marcavalle: The Ceramics from an Early Horizon Site in the Valley of Cusco, Peru and Implications for South Highland Socioeconomic Interaction" [dissertation]. [Philadelphia]: University of Pennsylvania. 1209 pp. Order no. 7730181, https://search.proquest.com/docview/302832479 ?accountid=15172.

—1980. The archaeology of Marcavalle, an Early Horizon site in the valley of Cuzco, Peru. Part I. *Baessler-Archiv, Neue Folge* 28(2):203–329. https://www.digi-hub.de/viewer/image/1499936792234/211/LOG_0109/.

—1981a. The archaeology of Marcavalle, an Early Horizon site in the valley of Cuzco, Peru. Part II. *Baessler-Archiv, Neue Folge* 29(1):107–205. https://www.digi-hub.de/viewer/image/1499070598416/109/LOG_0048/.

—1981b. The Archaeology of Marcavalle, an Early Horizon site in the valley of Cuzco, Peru. Part III. *Baessler-Archiv, Neue Folge* 29(2):241–386. https://www.digi-hub.de/viewer/image/1499070598416/247/LOG_0086/.

MOORE, JERRY D. 1996a. *Architecture and Power in the Ancient Andes: The Archaeology of Public Buildings.* Cambridge: Cambridge University Press. 256 pp.

—1996b. The archaeology of plazas and the proxemics of power: three Andean traditions. *American Anthropologist* 98(4):789–802. https://doi.org/10.1525/aa.1996.98.4.02a00090.

—2005. *Cultural Landscapes in the Ancient Andes: Archaeologies of Place.* Gainesville: University of Florida Press. 270 pp.

—2010. Making a Huaca: memory and praxis in prehispanic far northern Peru. *Journal of Social Archaeology* 10(3):398–422. https://doi.org/10.1177/1469605310381550.

MORALES, DANIEL C. 1980. *El dios felino de Pacopampa.* Lima: Seminario de Historia Rural Andina, Universidad Nacional Mayor de San Marcos. 112 pp.

—1998. Investigaciones arqueológicas en Pacopampa, departamento de Cajamarca. In: Peter Kaulicke, ed. Perspectivas Regionales del Período Formativo en el Perú. *Boletín de Arqueología PUCP* 2(1998):113–126. http://revistas.pucp.edu.pe/index.php/boletindearqueologia/article/view/724.

MOSELEY, MICHAEL E. 1974. Organizational preadaptation to irrigation: the evolution of early water-management systems in coastal Peru. In: Theodore E. Downing and McGuire Gibson, eds. *Irrigation's Impact on Society.* Tucson: University of Arizona Press. pp. 77–82.

—1975. Prehistoric principles of labor organization in the Moche Valley, Peru. *American Antiquity* 40(2, pt. 1):191–196. https://doi.org/10.2307/279614.

MOSELEY, MICHAEL E. AND ERIC DEEDS. 1982. The land in front of Chan Chan: agrarian expansion, reform, and collapse in the Moche Valley. In: Michael E. Moseley and Kent C. Day, eds. *Chan Chan: Andean Desert City.* Albuquerque: University of New Mexico Press. pp. 25–43.

MOSELEY, MICHAEL E. AND LUIS WATANABE. 1974. The adobe sculpture of Huaca de los Reyes: imposing artwork from coastal Peru. *Archaeology* 27(3):154–161. http://www.jstor.org/stable/41685554.

MURAKAMI, TATSUYA. 2015. Replicative construction experiments at Teotihuacan, Mexico: assessing the duration and timing of monumental construction. *Journal of Field Archaeology* 40(3):263–282. https://doi.org/10.1179/2042458214Y.0000000008.

MURRA, JOHN V. 1972. El control vertical de un maximo de pisos ecologicos en la economia de las sociedades andinas. In: John V. Murra, ed. *Visita de la Provincia de León de Huanuco en 1562,* Volume 2. Huánuco, Peru: Universidad Nacional Herimilio Valdizan. pp. 429–476.

NAGAOKA, TOMOHITO, YUJI SEKI, WATARU MORITA, KAZUHIRO UZAWA, DIANA ALEMÁN PAREDES, AND DANIEL MORALES CHOCANO. 2012. A case study of a high-status human skeleton from Pacopampa in Formative Period Peru. *Anatomical Science International* 87(4):234–237. https://doi.org/10.1007/s12565-011-0120-z.

NEILL, DAVID. [2007a]. *Botanical Exploration of the Cordillera del Cóndor Region of Ecuador and Peru: Project Activities and Scientific Findings, 2004–2007* [online report]. St. Louis: Missouri Botanical Garden. http://www.mobot.org/MOBOT/Research/ecuador/cordillera/welcome.shtml.

—[2007b]. *Botanical Inventory of the Cordillera del Cóndor Region of Ecuador and Peru: Project Activities and Findings, 2004–2007* [final report]. St. Louis: Missouri Botanical Garden. 47 pp. http://www.mobot.org/MOBOT/Research/ecuador/cordillera/pdf/EntireEnglishReport.pdf.

NEIRA AVENDAÑO, MÁXIMO AND AUGUSTO CARDONA ROSAS. 2000–2001. El Período Formativo en el área de Arequipa. In: Mariusz S. Ziółkowski and Luis Augusto Belán Franco, eds. Proyecto arqueológico CONDESUYOS. *Andes: Boletín de la Misión Arqueológica Andina* 3:27–60. http://www.andes-online.org/images/andes/3/2.1.El%20Periodo%20Formativo%20en%20el%20area%20de%20Arequipa.pdf.

NESBITT, JASON. 2012a. "Excavations at Caballo Muerto: An Investigation into the Origins of the Cupisnique Culture" [dissertation]. New Haven: Yale University, Department of Anthropology. 461 pp. Order no. 3525307, https://search.proquest.com/docview/1039318323?accountid=15172.

—2012b. An Initial Period domestic occupation at Huaca Cortada, Caballo Muerto Complex. Research Reports. *Andean Past* 10(art. 14):279–284. https://digitalcommons.library.umaine.edu/andean_past/vol10/iss1/14.

—2016. El Niño and second-millennium BC monument building at Huaca Cortada (Moche Valley, Peru). *Antiquity* 90(351):638–653. https://doi.org/10.15184/aqy.2016.70.

NESBITT, JASON, BELKYS GUTIÉRREZ, AND SEGUNDO VÁSQUEZ. 2008 [2010]. Excavaciones en Huaca Cortada, complejo de Caballo Muerto, valle de Moche: un informe preliminar. In: Peter Kaulicke and Yoshio Onuki, eds. El Período Formativo: enfoques y evidencias recientes. Cincuenta años de la Misión Arqueológica Japonesa y su vigencia. *Boletín de Arqueología PUCP* 12(2008):261–286. http://revistas.pucp.edu.pe/index .php/boletindearqueologia/article/view/970.

NESBITT, JASON, YUICHI MATSUMOTO, MICHAEL D. GLASCOCK, YURI CAVERO PALOMINO, AND RICHARD L. BURGER. 2015. "Sourcing the obsidian from Campanayuq Rumi: implications for understanding Chavín interaction" [abstract]; paper presented at the 80th Annual Meeting of Society for American Archaeology; 2015 April 15–19; San Francisco, California. Symposium Abstracts. pp. 738–739.

NIELSEN, AXEL E. 2009. Pastoralism and the non-pastoral world in the late pre-columbian history of the southern Andes (1000–1535). *Nomadic Peoples* 13(2):17–35. http://www.jstor.org/stable/43123848.

NIMUENDAJÚ, CURT. 1946. *The Eastern Timbira*. Robert H. Lowie, translator. Berkeley: University of California Press. 357 pp.

NOWAK, ROLAND M. 1999. *Walker's Mammals of the World*. 6th ed. Baltimore: Johns Hopkins University Press. 2 vols.

OCHATOMA PARAVICINO, JOSÉ. 1985. "Acerca del Formativo en la sierra centro-Sur" [dissertation]. Ayacucho, Peru: Universidad Nacional de San Cristóbal de Huamanga, Facultad de Ciencias Sociales. 116 pp.

—1998. El período Formativo en Ayacucho: balances y perspectivas. In: Peter Kaulicke, ed. Perspectivas Regionales del Período Formativo en el Perú. *Boletín de Arqueología PUCP* 2(1998):289–302. http:// revistas.pucp.edu.pe/index.php/boletindearqueologia/article/view/784.

OLIVERA, QUIRINO. 1998. Evidencias arqueológicas del Período Formativo en la Cuenca baja del río Utcubamba y Chinchipe. In: Peter Kaulicke, ed. Perspectivas Regionales del Período Formativo en el Perú. *Boletín de Arqueología PUCP* 2(1998):105–112. http://revistas.pucp.edu.pe/index.php/boletindearqueologia/article /view/721.

—2013. Avance de las investigaciones arqueológicas en la alta Amazonía, nororiente de Perú. In: Francisco Valdez, ed. *Arqueología Amazónica: Las Civilizaciones Ocultas del Bosque Tropical*. Lima: Instituto Francés de Estudios Andinos. pp. 173–203. (Actes et Mémoires de l'Institut Français d'Études Andines 35.)

—2014. *Arqueología Alto Amazónica. El origen de la civilización en el Perú*. Lima: Apus Graph Ediciones. 278 pp.

ONUKI, YOSHIO. 1972. Pottery and clay artifacts. In: Seichi Izumi and Kazuo Terada, eds. *Andes 4: Excavations at Kotosh, Peru, 1963 and 1966*. Tokyo: University of Tokyo Press. pp. 177–248.

—1994. Las actividades ceremoniales tempranas en la cuenca del Alto Huallaga y algunos problemas generales. In: Luis Millones and Yoshio Onuki, eds. *El Mundo Ceremonial Andino*. Lima: Editorial Horizonte. pp. 71–95. (Etnología y Antropología 8.)

—1995. *Kuntur Wasi y Cerro Blanco: Dos sitios Formativo en el norte del Perú*. Tokyo: Hokusen-sha. 217 pp.

—2001. Una perspectiva del Período Formativo de la sierra norte del Perú. In: Guillermo Lohmann, ed. *Historia de la Cultura Peruana*, Volume 1. Lima: Fondo Editorial del Congreso del Perú. pp. 103–126.

—2011. Kuntur Wasi y los orígenes de la Civilización Andina. In: Yoshio Onuki and Kinya Inokuchi, eds. *Gemelos prístinos: El tesoro del templo de Kuntur Wasi*. Lima: Fondo Editorial del Congreso del Perú y Minera Yanacocha. pp. 15–50.

ONUKI, YOSHIO AND KINYA INOKUCHI. 2011. *Gemelos prístinos: El tesoro del templo Kuntur Wasi*. Lima: Fondo Editorial Congreso del Perú y Minera Yanacocha. 157 pp.

Onuki, Yoshio and Yasutake Kato. 1988. Las excavaciones en Cerro Blanco. In: Kazuo Terada and Yoshio Onuki, eds. *Las excavaciones en Cerro Blanco y Huacaloma, Cajamarca, Perú, 1985*. Tokyo: Universidad de Tokyo. pp. 1–30.

Onuki, Yoshio, Yasutake Kato, and Kinya Inokuchi. 1995. La primera parte: las excavaciones en Kuntur Wasi, la primera ctapa, 1988–1990. In: Yoshio Onuki, ed. *Kuntur Wasi y Cerro Blanco: Dos sitios del Formativo en el norte del Perú*. Tokyo: Hokusen-sha. pp. 1–125.

Orlove, Benjamin S., John C. H. Chiang, and Mark A. Cane. 2000. Forecasting Andean rainfall and crop yield from the influence of El Niño on Pleiades visibility. *Nature* 403:68–71. https://doi.org/10.1038/47456.

—2002. Ethnoclimatology in the Andes: a cross-disciplinary study uncovers a scientific basis for the scheme Andean potato farmers traditionally use to predict the coming rains. *American Scientist* 90(5):428–435. http://www.jstor.org/stable/27857722.

Paredes, María I. 1984. El complejo sur de la Meseta 2 de Montegrande. *Beiträge zur Allgemeinen und Vergleichenden Archäologie* 6:505–512.

Parsons, Jeffrey R., Charles M. Hastings, and Ramiro Matos M. 2000. *Prehispanic Settlement Patterns in the Upper Mantaro and Tarma Drainages, Junín, Peru*. Volume 1, The Tarma-Chinchaycocha Region, Parts 1 and 2. Ann Arbor: Museum of Anthropology, University of Michigan. 537 pp. (Memoirs 34.)

Patterson, Thomas C. 1983. The historical development of a coastal Andean social formation in central Peru, 6000 to 500 BC. In: Daniel H. Sandweiss, ed. *Investigations of the Andean Past: Papers from the First Annual Northeast Conference on Andean Archaeology and Ethnohistory*. Ithaca, NY: Latin American Studies Program, Cornell University. pp. 21–38. http://digitalcommons.library.umaine.edu/andean_past_special/3.

—1985. La Huaca La Florida, valle del Rimac, Perú. In: Christopher B. Donnan, ed. *Early Ceremonial Architecture in the Andes: A Conference at Dumbarton Oaks, 8th to 10th October 1982*. Washington, DC: Dumbarton Oaks Research Library and Collection. pp. 59–69.

Patterson, Thomas C., John P. McCarthy, and Robert A. Dunn. 1982. Polities in the Lurín Valley, Peru, during the Early Intermediate Period. *Ñawpa Pacha* 20(1):61–82. https://doi.org/10.1179/naw.1982.20.1.004.

Pauketat, Timothy R. 2004. The economy of the moment: cultural practices and Mississippian chiefdoms. In: Gary M. Feinman and Linda M. Nicholas, eds. *Archaeological Perspectives on Political Economies*. Salt Lake City: University of Utah Press. pp. 25–39.

—2007. *Chiefdoms and Other Archaeological Delusions*. Lanham: AltaMira Press. 257 pp.

—2013. *An Archaeology of the Cosmos: Rethinking Agency and Religion in Ancient America*. New York: Routledge. 230 pp.

Pauketat, Timothy R. and Susan M. Alt. 2003. Mounds, memory, and contested Mississippian history. In: Ruth M. Van Dyke and Susan E. Alcock, eds. *Archaeologies of Memory*. Malden, MA: Blackwell. pp. 151–179.

Peake, Harold and Herbert J. Fleure. 1927. *Peasants and Potters*. New Haven: Yale University Press. 152 pp.

Pimentel Spissu, Víctor. 1986. *Felszeichnungen im mittleren und unteren Jequetepeque-Tal, Nord-Peru* [*Petroglifos en el Valle Medio y Bajo de Jequetepeque, Norte del Perú*]. Munich: C. H. Beck. 143 pp. (Materialien zur allgemeinen und vergleichenden Archäologie 31.) [In German and Spanish.]

Porras, Pedro. 1987. *Investigaciones arqueológicas a las faldas del Sangay*. Quito: Tipton Sosa. 430 pp.

Pozorski, Sheila G. 1983. Changing subsistence priorities and early settlement patterns on the North Coast of Peru. *Journal of Ethnobiology* 3(1):15–38.

Pozorski, Shelia G. and Thomas G. Pozorski. 1979a. An early subsistence exchange system in the Moche Valley, Peru. *Journal of Field Archaeology* 6(4):413–432. https://doi.org/10.1179/009346979791489023.

—1979b. Alto Salaverry: A Peruvian Coastal Preceramic Site. *Annals of the Carnegie Museum of Natural History* 48(art. 19):337–375. https://biodiversitylibrary.org/page/52525529.

—1986. Recent excavations at Pampa de las Llamas-Moxeke, a complex Initial Period site in Peru. *Journal of Field Archaeology* 13(4):381–401. https://doi.org/10.1179/jfa.1986.13.4.381.

—1987. *Early Settlement and Subsistence in the Casma Valley, Peru*. Iowa City: University of Iowa Press. 149 pp.

—1990. Reexamining the critical Preceramic/Ceramic Period transition: new data from coastal Peru. *American Anthropologist* 92(2):481–491. https://doi.org/10.1525/aa.1990.92.2.02a00160.

—1992. Early civilization in the Casma Valley, Peru. *Antiquity* 66(253):845–870. https://doi.org/10.1017/S0003598X00044781.

Pozorski, Thomas G. 1975. El complejo de Caballo Muerto: los frisos de barro de la Huaca de los Reyes. *Revista del Museo Nacional* 41:211–252.

—1976. "Caballo Muerto: A Complex of Early Ceramic Sites in the Moche Valley, Peru" [dissertation]. Austin: University of Texas at Austin. 473 pp. Order no. 7626687, https://search.proquest.com/docview/288269644?accountid=15172.

—1980. The Early Horizon site of Huaca de los Reyes: societal implications. *American Antiquity* 45(1):100–110. https://doi.org/10.2307/279663.

—1982. Early social stratification and subsistence systems: the Caballo Muerto complex. In: Michael E. Moseley and Kent C. Day, eds. *Chan Chan: Andean Desert City*. Albuquerque: University of New Mexico Press. pp. 225–253.

—1983. The Caballo Muerto complex and its place in the Andean chronological sequence. *Annals of the Carnegie Museum of Natural History* 52(art. 1):1–40.

—1995. Huaca de los Reyes revisited: clarification of the archaeological evidence. *Latin American Antiquity* 6(4):335–339. https://doi.org/10.2307/971835.

Pozorski, Thomas G. and Shelia G. Pozorski. 1993a. Early complex society and ceremonialism on the Peruvian North Coast. In: Luis Millones and Yoshio Onuki, eds. *El Mundo Ceremonial Andino*. Osaka: National Museum of Ethnology. pp. 45–68. (Senri Ethnological Studies 37.)

—1993b. Review: *Chavín and the Origins of Andean Civilization* by Richard L. Burger. *Latin American Antiquity* 4(4):389–390. https://doi.org/10.2307/972077.

—2005. Architecture and chronology at the site of Sechín Alto, Casma Valley, Peru. *Journal of Field Archaeology* 30(2):143–161. https://doi.org/10.1179/009346905791072314.

—2012. Preceramic and Initial Period monumentality within the Casma Valley of Peru. In: Richard L. Burger and Robert M. Rosenswig, eds. *Early New World Monumentality*. Gainesville: The University Press of Florida. pp. 364–398.

—2018. Early complex society on the north and central Peruvian coast: new archaeological discoveries and new insights. *Journal of Archaeological Research* 26(4):353–386. https://doi.org/10.1007/s10814-017-9113-3.

Prieto, Gabriel. 2014. The Early Initial Period fishing settlement of Gramalote, Moche Valley: a preliminary report. *Peruvian Archaeology* 1:1–46.

Prieto, Gabriel and Erik E. Maquera. 2015. La arquitectura del sitio del Período Inicial de Menocucho: valle de Moche, costa norte del Perú. Uso de fotogrametría para el registro arqueológico. Alcances y potenciales. *Arkinka* 231:94–101.

Proulx, Donald. 1985. *An Analysis of the Early Cultural Sequence in the Nepeña Valley, Peru*. Amherst: University of Massachusetts, Department of Anthropology. 324 pp. (Research Report 25.)

Pulgar Vidal, Javier. 1981. Geografía del Perú: las ocho regiones naturales del Peru. 8th ed. Lima: Editorial Universo. 313 pp.

Quilter, Jeffrey and Luis J. Castillo B., eds. 2010. *New Perspectives on Moche Political Organization*. Washington, DC: Dumbarton Oaks Research Library and Collection. 388 pp.

Ramírez, Susan E. 1996. *The World Upside Down: Cross-cultural Contact and Conflict in Sixteenth-century Peru*. Stanford: Stanford University Press. 234 pp.

—2001. El concepto de "comunidad" en el siglo XVI. In: Héctor Noejovich Ch., ed. *América bajo los Austrias: Economía, Cultura y Sociedad*. Lima: Fondo Editorial de la Pontificia Universidad Católica del Perú. pp. 181–190.

Ramón, Gabriel. 2011. The swallow potters: seasonally migrant styles in the Andes. In: Simona Scarcella, ed. *Archaeological Ceramics: A Review of Current Research*. Oxford: Archaeopress. pp. 160–175. (British Archaeological Reports International Series 2193.)

Rathje, William L. 2002. The noveau elite potlatch: one scenario for the monumental rise of early civilizations. In: Marilyn A. Masson and David A. Freidel, eds. *Ancient Maya Political Economies*. Walnut Creek, CA: AltaMira Press. pp. 31–40.

RAVINES, ROGGER. 1981. *Mapa arqueológico del valle del Jequetepeque* [map]. 1:2000 scale, with text and illustrations. Lima: Instituto Nacional de Cultura, Proyecto Especial de Irrigación Jequetepeque-Zaña. 31 pp.

—1982. *Arqueología del valle medio del Jequetepeque*. Lima: Proyecto de Rescate Arqueológico Jequetepeque. 255 pp.

—1985a. Arquitectura monumental temprana del valle del Jequetepeque. In: Fernando Silva Santisteban, Waldemar Espinoza Soriano, and Rogger Ravines, eds. *Historia de Cajamarca*. Volume 1, Arqueología. Lima: Instituto Nacional de Cultura–Cajamarca, Corporación de Desarollo de Cajamarca. pp. 131–146.

—1985b. Early monumental architecture of the Jequetepeque Valley, Peru. In: Christopher B. Donnan, ed. *Early Ceremonial Architecture in the Andes: A Conference at Dumbarton Oaks, 8th to 10th October 1982*. Washington, DC: Dumbarton Oaks Research Library and Collection. pp. 209–226.

RAVINES, ROGGER AND WILLIAM H. ISBELL. 1976. Garagay: sitio ceremonial temprano en el valle de Lima. *Revista del Museo Nacional* 41:253–275.

RAYMOND, J. SCOTT. 1988. A view from the tropical forest. In: Richard W. Keatinge, ed. *Peruvian Prehistory: An Overview of Pre-Inca and Inca Society*. Cambridge: Cambridge University Press. pp. 279–300.

REINDEL, MARKUS AND JOHNY A. ISLA. 2009 [2010]. El Periodo Inicial en Pernil Alto, Palpa, costa sur del Perú. In: Peter Kaulicke and Yoshio Onuki, eds. El Período Formativo: enfoques y evidencias recientes. Cincuenta años de la Misión Arqueológica Japonesa y su vigencia. *Boletín de Arqueología PUCP* 13(2009):259–288. http://revistas.pucp.edu.pe/index.php/boletindearqueologia/article/view/1005.

REINDEL, MARKUS AND GÜNTHER WAGNER. 2008. *New Technology for Archaeology: Multidisciplinary Investigations in Palpa and Nasca, Peru*. Heidelberg: Springer. 512 pp.

RENFREW, COLIN. 1986. Introduction: Peer polity interaction and socio-political change. In: Colin Renfrew and John. F. Cherry, eds. *Peer Polity Interaction and Socio-political Change*. Cambridge: Cambridge University Press. pp. 1–18.

RICK, JOHN W. 2005. The evolution of authority and power at Chavín de Huántar, Peru. In: Kevin J. Vaughn, Dennis Ogburn, and Christina A. Conlee, eds. *Foundations of Power in the Prehispanic Andes*. Arlington, VA: American Anthropological Association. pp. 71–89. (Archaeological Papers of the American Anthropological Association 14.)

—2008. Context, construction, and ritual in the development of authority at Chavín de Huántar. In: William J. Conklin and Jeffrey Quilter, eds. *Chavín: Art, Architecture and Culture*. Los Angeles: Cotsen Institute of Archaeology, University of California. pp. 3–34. (Monograph 61.) https://doi.org/10.2307/j.ctvdmwx21.

RICK, JOHN W., CHRISTIAN MESIA, DANIEL CONTRERAS, SILVIA R. KEMBEL, ROSA M. RICK, MATTHEW SAYRE, AND JOHN WOLF. 2009 [2010]. La cronología de Chavín de Huántar y sus implicancias para el Período Formativo. *Boletín de Arqueología PUCP* 13(2009):87–132. http://revistas.pucp.edu.pe/index.php/boletindearqueologia/article/view/984.

RIDDEL, FRANCIS A. AND LIDIO M. VALDÉZ. 1987–1988. Hacha y la ocupación temprana del valle de Acarí. *Gaceta Arqueológica Andina* 16:6–10.

ROBINSON, ROGER W. 1994. Recent excavations at Hacha in the Acari valley, Peru. Andean Past 4(art. 5):9–37. https://digitalcommons.library.umaine.edu/andean_past/vol4/iss1/5.

ROE, PETER G. 1974. *A Further Exploration of the Rowe Chavin Seriation and Its Implications for North Central Coast Chronology*. Washington, DC: Dumbarton Oaks Research Library and Collection, Trustees for Harvard University. 80 pp. (Studies in Pre-Columbian Art and Archaeology 13.) https://www.jstor.org/stable/41263424.

ROJAS, PEDRO. 1961. *Informe Preliminar de la Exploración Arqueológica al Alto Marañon*, Volume 3. Lima: Museo Nacional de Antropología y Arqueología.

—1985. La "Huaca" Huayurco, Jaén. In: Fernando Silva Santisteban, Waldemar Espinoza Soriano, and Rogger Ravines, eds. *Historia de Cajamarca*. Volume 1, Arqueología. Lima: Instituto Nacional de Cultura–Cajamarca, Corporación de Desarollo de Cajamarca. pp. 181–186.

ROSAS LA NOIRE, HERMILIO AND RUTH SHADY SOLIS. 1970. *Pacopampa: un centro formativo de la sierra nor-peruana*. Lima: Seminario de Historia Rural Andina, Universidad Nacional Mayor de San Marcos. 104 pp. Reprinted 2017 in *ISHRA, Revista del Instituto Seminario de Historia Rural Andina* 2(3):145–209. https://doi.org/10.15381/ishra.v2i3.14820.

ROSTAIN, STÉPHEN. 1999a. Occupations humaines et fonction domestique de monticules préhistoriques d'Amazonie équatorienne. *Bulletin de la société Suisse des américanistes* 63:71–95.

—1999b. Secuencia arqueológica en montículos del valle del Upano en la Amazonia Ecuatoriana. *Bulletin de l'Institut Français d'Etudes Andines* 28(1):53–89. https://www.redalyc.org/articulo.oa?id=12628103.

ROSTAIN, STÉPHEN AND ESTANISLAO PAZMIÑO. 2013. Treinta años de investigación a las faldas del Sangay. In: Francisco Valdez, comp. *Arqueología Amazónica: Las Civilizaciones Ocultas del Bosque Tropical*. Lima: Instituto Francés de Estudios Andinos. pp. 55–82. (Actes et Mémoires de l'Institut Français d'Études Andines 35.) http://horizon.documentation.ird.fr/exl-doc/pleins_textes/divers17-06/010069918.pdf.

ROSTAIN, STÉPHEN AND GEOFFROY DE SAULIEU. 2013. *Antes: Arqueología de la Amazonía Ecuatoriana*. Quito: Instituto Francés de Estudios Andinos. 205 pp.

ROWE, JOHN HOWLAND. 1960. Cultural unity and diversification in Peruvian archaeology. In: Anthony F. C. Wallace, ed. *Men and Cultures: Selected Papers of the Fifth International Congress of Anthropological and Ethnological Sciences*. Philadelphia: University of Pennsylvania Press. pp. 627–631. http://www.jstor.org/stable/j.ctv4s7gkq.102.

—1962. Stages and periods in archaeological interpretation. *Southwestern Journal of Anthropology* 18(1):40–54. https://doi.org/10.1086/soutjanth.18.1.3629122.

—1967. Form and meaning in Chavín art. In: John Howland Rowe and Dorothy Menzel, eds. *Peruvian Archaeology: Selected Readings*. Palo Alto, CA: Peek Publications. pp. 72–103.

ROWLANDS, MICHAEL. 1993. The role of memory in the transmission of culture. *World Archaeology* 25(2):141–151. https://doi.org/10.1080/00438243.1993.9980234.

SAKAI, MASATO AND JUAN J. MARTÍNEZ. 2008 [2010]. Excavaciones en el Templete de Limoncarro, valle bajo de Jequetepeque. In: Peter Kaulicke and Yoshio Onuki, eds. El Período Formativo: enfoques y evidencias recientes. Cincuenta años de la Misión Arqueológica Japonesa y su vigencia. *Boletín de Arqueología PUCP* 12(2008):171–201. http://revistas.pucp.edu.pe/index.php/boletindearqueologia/article/view/965.

SAKAI, MASATO, SAWAKO TOKUE, EISEI TSURUMI, AND KOICHIRO SHIBATA. 2000. An archaeological reconnaissance in the North Coast of Peru, 1998 and 1999. *Journal of History, Geography and Cultural Anthropology, Yamagata University* 1:51–91. [In Japanese.]

SAKAI, MASATO, JUAN PABLO VILLANUEVA, YUJI SEKI, WALTER TOSSO, AND ARACELI ESPINOZA. 2007. Organización del paisaje en el centro ceremonial formativo de Pacopampa. *Arqueología y Sociedad* 18(2007):57–68. https://revistasinvestigacion.unmsm.edu.pe/index.php/Arqueo/article/view/13151.

SALAZAR, ERNESTO. 2008. Pre-Columbian mound complexes in the Upano River Valley, Lowland Ecuador. In: Helaine Silverman and William H. Isbell, eds. *Handbook of South American Archaeology*. New York: Springer. pp. 263–278.

SALAZAR, LUCY C. 2009. Escaleras al cielo: altares, rituales y ancestros en el sitio arqueológico de Cardal. In: Richard L. Burger and Krzysztof Makowski, eds. *Arqueología del Período Formativo en la Cuenca Baja de Lurín*, Volume 1. Lima: Fondo Editorial de la Pontificia Universidad Católica del Perú. pp. 83–94.

SALAZAR-BURGER, LUCY C. AND RICHARD L. BURGER. 1983. La araña en la iconografía del Horizonte Temprano en la Costa Norte del Perú. *Beiträge zur Allgemeinen und Vergleichenden Archäologie* 4(1982):213–253.

SANDOR, JON A. 1992. Long-term effects of prehistoric agriculture on soils: examples from New Mexico and Peru. In: Vance T. Holliday, ed. *Soils in Archaeology: Landscape Evolution and Human Occupation*. Washington, DC: Smithsonian Institute Press. pp. 217–247.

SAWYER, MICHAEL J. 1985. "An Analysis of Mammalian Faunal Remains from the Site of Huaricoto, PAN 3–35" [master's thesis]. Hayward: California State University, Department of Anthropology.

SCHEELE, HARRY G. 1970. "The Chavin Influence on the Central Coast of Peru" [dissertation]. Cambridge: Harvard University, Department of Anthropology. Order no. 0215499, https://search.proquest.com/docview/302403780?accountid=15172.

SCHORTMAN, EDWARD M. 1989. Interregional interaction in prehistory: the need for a new perspective. *American Antiquity* 54(1):52–65. https://doi.org/10.2307/281331.

SEKI, YUJI. 2006. *Kodai Andesu: Kenryoku no kōkogaku* [*Ancient Andes: Archaeolgy of Political Power*]. Kyoto: Kyoto Daigaku Gakujutsu Shuppankai. 315 pp. [In Japanese.]

—2014. La diversidad del poder en la sociedad del Periodo Formativo: una perspectiva desde la sierra norte. In: Yuji Seki, ed. *El Centro Ceremonial Andino—Nuevas Perspectivas para los Períodos Arcaico y Formativo*. Osaka: National Museum of Ethnology. pp. 175–200. (Senri Ethnological Studies 89.)

SEKI, YUJI AND MASATO SAKAI. 1998. Seinal oka (Holly hill). In: Yasutake Kato and Yuji Seki, eds. *Bunmei no sōzōryoku: Kodai undesu no shinden to shakai [The Invention of the Bunmei: Shinto Shrine and Society in the Ancient Andes]*. Tokyo: Kadokawa Shoten. pp. 95–162. [In Japanese.]

SEKI, YUJI, WALTER TOSSO MORALES, JUAN PABLO VILLANUEVA, AND KINYA INOKUCHI. 2006. Proyecto Arqueológico Pacopampa '05: avances y correlaciones regionales. *Arqueología y Sociedad* 17(2006):149–178. https://revistasinvestigacion.unmsm.edu.pe/index.php/Arqueo/article/view/13139.

SEKI, YUJI, JUAN PABLO VILLANUEVA, MASATO SAKAI, DIANA ALEMÁN, MAURO ORDÓÑEZ, WALTER TOSSO, ARACELI ESPINOZA, KINYA INOKUCHI, AND DANIEL MORALES. 2008 [2010]. Nuevas evidencias del sitio arqueológico de Pacopampa, en la sierra norte del Perú. In: Peter Kaulicke and Yoshio Onuki, eds. El Período Formativo: enfoques y evidencias recientes. Cincuenta años de la Misión Arqueológica Japonesa y su vigencia. *Boletín de Arqueología PUCP* 12(2008):69–95. http://revistas.pucp.edu.pe/index.php/boletindearqueologia /article/view/851.

SHADY, RUTH AND HERMILIO ROSAS. 1979. El complejo Bagua y el sistema de establecimientos durante el Formativo en la sierra norte del Perú. *Ñawpa Pacha* 17(1):109–142. https://doi.org/10.1179/naw.1979.17.1.006.

SHADY SOLIS, RUTH. 1973. "La Arqueología de la Cuenca Inferior del Utcubamba" [dissertation]. Lima: Universidad Nacional Mayor de San Marcos, Programa Académico de Antropología y Arqueología. 150 pp.

—1987. Tradición y cambio en las sociedades formativas de Bagua, Amazonas, Perú. *Revista Andina 10*, 5(2):457–488. http://www.revistaandinacbc.com/wp-content/uploads/2016/ra10/ra-10-1987-03.pdf.

—1999. Sociedades Formativas de Bagua-Jaén y sus relaciones Andinas y Amazónicas. In: Paulina Ledergerber-Crespo, ed. *Formativo Sudamericano: Una Revaluación*. Quito: Ediciones ABYA-YALA. pp. 201–211.

SHADY SOLIS, RUTH, JONATHAN HAAS, AND WINIFRED CREAMER. 2001. Dating Caral, a preceramic site in the Supe Valley on the Central Coast of Peru. *Science* 292(5517):723–726. http://www.jstor.org/stable/3083548.

SHIBATA, KOICHIRO. 2008 [2010]. El sitio de Cerro Blanco de Nepeña dentro de la dinámica interactiva del Período Formativo. In: Peter Kaulicke and Yoshio Onuki, eds. El Período Formativo: enfoques y evidencias recientes. Cincuenta años de la Misión Arqueológica Japonesa y su vigencia. *Boletín de Arqueología PUCP* 12(2008):287–315. http://revistas.pucp.edu.pe/index.php/boletindearqueologia/article/view/972.

—2011. Cronología, relaciones interregionales y organización social en el Formativo del valle bajo de Nepeña: esencia y perspectiva. In: Miłosz Giersz and Iván Ghezzi, eds. *Arqueología de la Costa de Ancash*. Lima: Centro de Estudios Precolombinos de la Universidad de Varsovia and Instituto Francés de Estudios Andinos. pp. 113–134.

—2014. Centros de "Reorganización costeña" durante el Período Formativo Tardío: un ensayo sobre la competencia faccional en el valle bajo de Nepeña, costa nor-central peruana. In: Yuji Seki, ed. *El Centro Ceremonial Andino—Nuevas Perspectivas para los Períodos Arcaico y Formativo*. Osaka: National Museum of Ethnology. pp. 245–260. (Senri Ethnological Studies 89.)

SHIMADA, IZUMI. 1994. *Pampa Grande and the Mochica Culture*. Austin: University of Texas Press. 323 pp.

SHIMADA, IZUMI, CARLOS G. ELERA, AND MELODY J. SHIMADA. 1982. Excavaciones efectuadas en el centro ceremonial de Huaca Lucía-Cholope, del Horizonte Temprano, Batán Grande, costa del Perú: 1979–1981. In: Ruth Shady and Izumi Shimada. *La Cultura Nievería y la Interacción Social en el Mundo Andino en la Época Huari*. Lima: Instituto Nacional de Cultura. pp. 109–208. (Arqueológicas 19.)

SHIMADA, IZUMI, CRYSTAL BARKER SCHAAF, LONNIE G. THOMPSON, AND ELLEN MOSLEY-THOMPSON. 1991. Cultural impacts of severe droughts in the prehistoric Andes: application of a 1,500-year ice core precipitation record. *World Archaeology* 22(3):247–270. https://doi.org/10.1080/00438243.1991.9980145.

SHIMADA, MELODY J. 1982. Zooarchaeology of Huacaloma: behavioral and cultural implications. In: Kazuo Terada and Yoshio Onuki, eds. *Excavations at Huacaloma in the Cajamarca Valley, Peru, 1979*. Tokyo: University of Tokyo. pp. 303–336.

SHIMADA, MELODY J. AND IZUMI SHIMADA. 1985. Prehistoric llama breeding and herding along north coast of Peru. *American Antiquity* 50(1):3–26.

SHIMIZU, MASAAKI, YASUTAKE KATO, AND MARINA SHIMIZU. 2007. Identification of the source of sodalite from Kuntur Wasi. In: Yasutake Kato, principal investigator. *Studies of the Process for the Formation of Ancient Andean Civilization. Report of Grant-in-Aid for Scientific Research (S) 2002–2006.* Project number 14101003. Tokyo: Japan Society for the Promotion of Science. pp. 159–168. [In Japanese.]

SHIMIZU, MASAAKI, M. NAKAJIMA, MARINA SHIMIZU, MEGUMI ARATA, AND YUJI SEKI. 2012. The Pacopampa archaeological site: the oldest smelting site in South America? In: Abstracts Issue of the Annual Meeting of the Korean Society for Geosystem Engineering. Jeju Island, South Korea. 53 pp.

SILVA, JORGE E. 1998. Una aproximación al Período Formativo en el valle del Chillón. In: Peter Kaulicke, ed. Perspectivas Regionales del Período Formativo en el Perú. *Boletin de Arqueología PUCP* 2(1998):251–268. http://revistas.pucp.edu.pe/index.php/boletindearqueologia/article/view/763.

SILVA, JORGE E. AND CECILIA JAIME TELLO. 2000. Pucará: un templo en "U" en la chaupiyunga del Chillón. *Arqueológicas* 24:27–44.

SILVERMAN, HELAINE. 1996. The Formative Period on the south coast of Peru: a critical review. *Journal of World Prehistory* 10(2):95–146. https://doi.org/10.1007/BF02221074.

SPIELMANN, KATHERINE A. 2002. Feasting, craft specialization, and the ritual mode of production in small-scale societies. *American Anthropologist* 104(1):195–207. https://doi.org/10.1525/aa.2002.104.1.195.

—2007. Ritual and political economies. In: E. Christian Wells and Karla L. Davis-Salazar, eds. *Mesoamerican Ritual Economy: Archaeological and Ethnological Perspectives.* Boulder: University Press of Colorado. pp. 287–300.

SPLITSTOSER, JEFFREY, DWIGHT D. WALLACE, AND MERCEDES DELGADO. 2009 [2010]. Nuevas evidencias de textiles y cerámica de la época Paracas Temprano en Cerrillos, valle de Ica, Perú. In: Peter Kaulicke and Yoshio Onuki, eds. El Período Formativo: enfoques y evidencias recientes. Cincuenta años de la Misión Arqueológica Japonesa y su vigencia. *Boletín de Arqueología PUCP* 13(2009):209–235. http://revistas.pucp.edu.pe/index.php/boletindearqueologia/article/view/1001.

STAHL, ANNE BROWER. 2004. Political economic mosaics: archaeology of the last two millennia in tropical sub-saharan Africa. *Annual Review of Anthropology* 33(2004):145–172. http://www.jstor.org/stable/25064849.

STINER, MARY C. 1991. An interspecific perspective on the emergence of modern human predatroy niche. In: Mary C. Stiner, ed. *Human Predators and Prey Mortality.* Boulder, CO: Westview Press. pp. 15–30, 149–185.

STRATHERN, ANDREW. 1971. *The Rope of Moka: Big-men and Ceremonial Exchange in Mount Hagen, New Guinea.* Cambridge: Cambridge University Press. 254 pp. (Cambridge Studies in Social Anthropology 4.)

SWENSON, EDWARD R. 2006. Competitive feasting, religious pluralism and decentralized power in the Late Moche Period. In: William H. Isbell and Helaine Silverman, eds. *Andean Archaeology III: North and South.* Boston: Springer. pp. 112–142.

TAM, MANUEL AND IRIS AGUIRRE. 1984. El Complejo Sur-Este de la Meseta 2 de Montegrande. *Beiträge zur Allgemeinen und Vergleichenden Archäologie* 6:513–519.

TELLENBACH, MICHAEL. 1986. *Die ausgrabungen in der formativzeitlichen siedlung Montegrande, Jequetepeque-Tal, nord-Peru.* Munich: C. H. Beck. 302 pp. (Materialien zur Allegemeinen und Vergleichenden Archaologie 39.)

TELLO, JULIO C. 1922. *Introducción a la Historia Antigua del Perú.* Lima: Sanmarti y Cia., Impresores. 48 pp. https://hdl.handle.net/2027/mdp.39015061393347.

—1939. Sobre el descubrimiento de la cultura Chavín del Perú. In: Congrèso Internacional de Américanistas. *Vigesimoséptimo Congrèso Internacional de Américanistas: actas de la primera sesión, celebrada en la ciudad de México en 1939,* Volume 1. [Mexico]: Instituto Nacional de Antropología e História. pp. 231–252.

—1940. Origen y desarrollo de las civilizaciones prehistóricas Andinas. In: *Congrèso Internacional de Américanistas, XXVII sesión, 1939,* Volume 1. Lima: International Congress of Americanists. pp. 589–720.

—1943. Discovery of the Chavín culture in Peru. *American Antiquity* 9(1):135–160. https://doi.org/10.2307/275457.

—1960. *Chavín, cultura matriz de la civilización andina (primera parte).* Lima: Universidad Nacional Mayor de San Marcos. 425 pp. (Publicación Antropológica del Archivo Julio C. Tello 2.)

—2005. *Arqueología del Valle de Nepeña: Excavaciones en Cerro Blanco y Punkurí.* Transcribed and edited by Víctor Paredes Castro and Wilbert Salas Egúsquiza. Lima: Universidad Nacional Mayor de San Marcos, Museo de Arqueología y Antropología. 184 pp. (Cuadernos de Investigación del Archivo Tello 4.)

Terada, Kazuo and Yoshio Onuki. 1982. *Excavations at Huacaloma in the Cajamarca Valley, Peru 1979.* Tokyo: University of Tokyo Press. 351 pp.

—1985. *The Formative Period in the Cajamarca Basin, Peru: Excavations at Huacaloma and Layzón, 1982.* Tokyo: University of Tokyo Press. 345 pp.

Tilley, Christopher. 1994. *A Phenomenology of Landscape: Places, Paths, and Monuments.* Oxford: Berg. 221 pp.

Topic, Theresa Lange. 2009. The meaning of monuments at Marcahuamachuco. In: Joyce Marcus and Patrick Ryan Williams, eds. *Andean Civilization: A Tribute to Michael E. Moseley.* Los Angeles: Cotsen Institute of Archaeology, University of California. pp. 241–255. (Monograph 63.) https://doi.org/10.2307/j.ctvdmwx3h.16.

Torero, Alfredo. 1986. Deslindes lingüísticos en la costa norte peruana. *Revista Andina 2,* 4(2):523–548. http://www.revistaandinacbc.com/wp-content/uploads/2016/ra08/ra-08-1986-07.pdf.

—1990. Procesos lingüísticos e identificación de dioses en los Andes centrales. *Revista Andina 15,* 8(1):237–263. http://www.revistaandinacbc.com/wp-content/uploads/2016/ra15/ra-15-1990-09.pdf.

Tsurumi, Eisei. 2008 [2010]. La secuencia cronológica de los centros ceremoniales de la Pampa de las Hamacas y Tembladera, valle medio de Jequetepeque. In: Peter Kaulicke and Yoshio Onuki, eds. El Período Formativo: enfoques y evidencias recientes. Cincuenta años de la Misión Arqueológica Japonesa y su vigencia. *Boletín de Arqueología PUCP* 12(2008):141–169. http://revistas.pucp.edu.pe/index.php/boletindcarqueologia/article/view/964.

—2012. A preliminary report on the survey in three valleys of Northern Peru. *América Antigua* 15:65–74. [In Japanese.]

—2014. El estudio de agrupaciones espaciales de centros ceremoniales Formativos: el caso del Complejo Hamacas del valle medio de Jequetepeque. In: Yuji Seki, ed. *El Centro Ceremonial Andino: Nuevas Perspectivas para los Períodos Arcaico y Formativo.* Osaka: National Museum of Ethnology. pp. 201–223. (Senri Ethnological Studies 89.)

—2016. El Período Formativo en el valle medio de Jequetepeque, norte del Perú. *Nayra Kunan Pacha, Revista de Arqueología Social* 1(1):175–186. http://www.zonacaral.gob.pe/downloads/publicaciones/previo-nayra-kunan-pacha.pdf.

Tsurumi, Eisei and Carlos A. Morales Castro. 2012. Plataforma con petroglifo del Periodo Formativo en Pampa de Mosquito, valle medio de Jequetepeque. *Arqueológicas* 29:19–35.

— 2013. Un gato con muchas vidas: un petroglifo Arcaico Tardío en el valle medio de Jequetepeque (Perú). *Mundo de Antes* 8:141–157. http://www.mundodeantes.org.ar/pdf/revista8/07Tsurumi%20y%20Morales.pdf.

Ulbert, Cornelius. 1994. *Die Keramik der formativzeitlichen siedlung Montegrande, Jequetepequetal, nord-Peru.* Mainz am Rhein: Verlag Philipp von Zabern. 205 pp. (Materialien zur Allegemeinen und Vergleichenden Archäologie 52.)

Urton, Gary. 1981. *At the Crossroads of the Earth and the Sky.* Austin: University of Texas Press. 248 pp.

—1984. Chuta: el espacio de la práctica social en Pacariqtambo, Perú. *Revista Andina 3,* 2(1):7–56. http://www.revistaandinacbc.com/wp-content/uploads/2016/ra03/ra-03-1984-01.pdf.

Urton, Gary and Anthony Aveni. 1983. Archaeoastronomical fieldwork on the coast of Peru. In: Anthony Aveni and Gordon Brotherston, eds. *Calendars in Mesoamerica and Peru.* Oxford: British Archaeological Reports. pp. 221–234. (BAR International Series 174.)

Uzawa, Kazuhiro. 2008 [2010]. La difusión de los camélidos domesticados en el norte del Perú durante el Período Formativo. In: Peter Kaulicke and Yoshio Onuki, eds. El Período Formativo: enfoques y evidencias recientes. Cincuenta años de la Misión Arqueológica Japonesa y su vigencia. *Boletín de Arqueología PUCP* 12(2008):249–259. http://revistas.pucp.edu.pe/index.php/boletindearqueologia/article/view/969.

Valdez, Francisco. 2007. Mayo-Chinchipe: the half-open door. In: Daniel Klein and Iván Cruz Cevallos, eds. *Ecuador: The Secret Art of Precolumbian Ecuador.* Milan: 5 Continents Editions. pp. 320–349.

—2008. Inter-zonal relationships in Ecuador. In: Helaine Silverman and William H. Isbell, eds. *Handbook of South American Archaeology*. New York: Springer. pp. 865–888.

—2011. La cerámica Mayo Chinchipe, el Formativo Temprano de la ceja de selva oriental. Francisco Valdez, ed. *Revista Nacional de Cultura: Letras, Artes, y Ciencias del Ecuador* 15–16(3):685–708.

—2013a. Mayo Chinchipe: hacia un replanteamiento del origen de las sociedades complejas en la civilización Andina. In: Francisco Valdez, comp. *Arqueología Amazónica: Las Civilizaciones Ocultas del Bosque Tropical. Actas del coloquio internacional Arqueología Regional en la Amazonía Occidental: Temáticas, Resultados y Políticas*. Lima: Instituto Francés de Estudios Andinos. pp. 99–146. (Actes et Mémoires de l'Institut Français d'Études Andines 35.) https://doi.org/10.4000/books.irdeditions.18758.

—2013b. *Primeras Sociedades de la Alta Amazonía: La Cultura Mayo Chinchipe-Marañón*. Quito: Institut de Recherche pour le Développement. 84 pp. https://doi.org/10.4000/books.irdeditions.18159.

VAN DYKE, RUTH M. AND SUSAN E. ALCOCK. 2003. Archaeology of memory: an introduction. In: Ruth M. Van Dyke and Susan E. Alcock, eds. *Archaeologies of Memory*. Malden, MA: Blackwell. pp. 1–13.

VEGA-CENTENO SARA-LAFOSSE, RAFAEL. 2007. Construction, labor organization, and feasting during the Late Archaic Period in the Central Andes. *Journal of Anthropological Archaeology* 26(2):150–171. https://doi.org/10.1016/j.jaa.2006.07.002.

VRADENBERG, JOSEPH A. 2009. Biología ósea de una población del Periodo Inicial tardío: Cardal, Perú. In: Richard L. Burger and Krzysztof Makowski, eds. *Arqueología del Periodo Formativo en la Cuenca Baja de Lurín*, Volume 1. Lima: Fondo Editorial de la Pontificia Universidad Católica del Perú. pp. 161–183.

WALLACE, DWIGHT T. 1962. Cerrillos, an early Paracas site in Ica, Peru. *American Antiquity* 27(3):303–314. https://doi.org/10.2307/277797.

WATANABE MATSUKURA, LUIS. 1976. "Sitios Tempranos en el Valle de Moche (Costa Norte del Peru)" [dissertation]. Lima: Universidad Nacional Mayor de San Marcos. 274 pp.

WHEELER, JANE C. 1984. On the origin and early development of camelid pastoralism in the Andes. In: Juliet Clutton-Brock and Caroline Grigson, eds. *Animals and Archaeology*. Volume 3, Early Herders and Their Flocks. Oxford: British Archaeological Reports. pp. 395–410. (BAR International Series 202.)

—1995. Evolution and present situation of the South American Camelidae. *Biological Journal of the Linnean Society* 54(3):271–295. https://doi.org/10.1111/j.1095-8312.1995.tb01037.x.

WHEELER PIRES-FERREIRA, JANE, EDGARDO PIRES-FERREIRA, AND PETER KAULICKE. 1977. Domesticación de los camélidos en los Andes centrales durante el período precerámico: un modelo. *Journal de la Société des Americanistes* 64:155–165. https://doi.org/10.3406/jsa.1977.2152.

WIEGEND, MAXIMILIAN. 2002. Observations on the biogeography of the Amotape-Huancabamba zone in northern Peru. *Botanical Review* 68(1):38–54. http://www.jstor.org/stable/4354410.

WIESSNER, POLLY. 2002. The vines of complexity: egalitarian structures and the institutionalization of inequality among the Enga. *Current Anthropology* 43(2):233–269. https://doi.org/10.1086/338301.

WILLEY, GORDON R. 1945. Horizon styles and pottery traditions in Peruvian archaeology. *American Antiquity* 11(1):49–56. https://doi.org/10.2307/275530.

—1951. The Chavín problem: a review and critique. *Southwestern Journal of Anthropology* 7(2):103–144. https://doi.org/10.1086/soutjanth.7.2.3628619.

WILLEY, GORDON R. AND PHILIP PHILLIPS. 1958. *Method and Theory in American Archaeology*. Chicago: University of Chicago Press. 269 pp.

WILLIAMS, CARLOS. 1980. Complejos de pirámides con planta en U, patrón arquitectónico de la costa central. *Revista del Museo Nacional* 44:95–110.

—1985. A scheme for the early monumental architecture of the central coast of Peru. In: Christopher B. Donnan, ed. *Early Ceremonial Architecture in the Andes: A Conference at Dumbarton Oaks, 8th to 10th October 1982*. Washington, DC: Dumbarton Oaks Research Library and Collection. pp. 227–240.

WING, ELIZABETH S. 1972. Appendix 4, Utilization of animal resources in the Peruvian Andes. In: Seichi Izumi and Kazuo Terada, eds. *Andes 4: Excavations at Kotosh, Peru, 1963 and 1966*. Tokyo: University of Tokyo Press. pp. 327–352.

Wolf, Eric R. 1990. Distinguished lecture: facing power—old insights, new questions. *American Anthropologist* 92(3):586–596. https://doi.org/10.1525/aa.1990.92.3.02a00020.

Yamamoto, Atsushi. 2007. El reconocimiento del Valle de Huancabamba, Jaén, Cajamarca, Perú. *ARKEOS. Revista Electrónica de Arqueología PUCP* 2(2):1–12. http://revistas.pucp.edu.pe/index.php/arkeos/article/view/1259/1214.

—2008 [2010]. Ingatambo: Un sitio estratégico de contacto interregional en la zona norte del Perú. In: Peter Kaulicke and Yoshio Onuki, eds. El Período Formativo: enfoques y evidencias recientes. Cincuenta años de la Misión Arqueológica Japonesa y su vigencia. *Boletín de Arqueología PUCP* 12(2008):25–52. http://revistas.pucp.edu.pe/index.php/boletindearqueologia/article/view/1404.

—2011. Contacto intercultural entre el sur de Ecuador y el norte del Perú. *Revista Nacional de Cultura* 15–16(2):399–408. https://downloads.arqueo-ecuatoriana.ec/ayhpwxgv/bibliografia/Yamamoto_2012-RNC.pdf.

—2013. Las rutas interregionales en el Período Formativo para el norte del Perú y el sur de Ecuador: una perspectiva desde el sitio Ingatambo, valle de Huancabamba. *Arqueología y Sociedad* 25(2012):9–34. https://revistasinvestigacion.unmsm.edu.pe/index.php/Arqueo/article/view/12353/11063.

Yasuda, Yoshinori. 1989. Indasu Bunmei no seisui to Jōmon bunka [The rise and fall of the Indus civilization and the Jomon culture]. *Japanese Studies: Bulletin of International Research Center for Japanese Studies* 1:205–272. [In Japanese.] https://doi.org/10.15055/00000957.

Yoffee, Norman. 2005. *Myths of the Archaic State: Evolution of the Earliest Cities, States, and Civilizations.* Cambridge: Cambridge University Press. 277 pp.

Yomoda, Shinsuke. 2002. "Application of Mineral Sciences to the Archaeological Samples of Pre-Andes Civilization" [master's thesis]. Toyama: University of Toyama, Graduate School of Science and Engineering. [In Japanese.]

Young, Kenneth and Carlos Reynel. 1997. Huancabamba region, Peru and Ecuador. In: Stephen D. Davis, Vernon H. Heywood, O. Herrera-MacBryde, J. Villa-Lobos, and Alan C. Hamilton, eds. *Centres of Plant Diversity: A Guide and Strategy for their Conservation.* Volume 3, The Americas. Gland, Switzerland: World Wide Fund for Nature; International Union for Conservation of Nature and Natural Resources. pp. 465–469.

Zaro, Gregory. 2007. Diversity specialists: coastal resource management and historical contingency in the Osmore Desert of southern Peru. *Latin American Antiquity* 18(2):161–179. https://doi.org/10.2307/25063102.

Zoubek, Thomas. A. 1997. "The Initial Period Occupation of Huaca El Gallo/Huaca La Gallina, Virú Valley, Peru and Its Implications for Guañape Phase Social Complexity" [dissertation]. New Haven: Yale University, Department of Anthropology. 558 pp. Order no. 9817424, https://search.proquest.com/docview/304383519?accountid=15172.

—1998. Archaeological evidence of Preceramic/Initial Period ancestor worship and its relevance to early Andean coastal social formations. *Journal of the Steward Anthropological Society* 26(1–2):71–112.

INDEX

Mollake Chico ceramics, 185
mollusks
  Caballo Muerto Complex, 11
  Kuntur Wasi site, 84
monochrome friezes, 59
monoliths
  anthropomorphic figures,
    126–127
  Kuntur Wasi site, 83, 84
  Pacopampa archaeological site,
    124–125
  significance, 125–127
montane forests, 150, 151
Montegrande architectural
    complex
  archaeological excavations, 20
  architectural axes, 23
  architectural features, 22, 23,
    152–153, 167
  burial practices, 166
  flash floods, 26, 27
  Hamacas Phase, 22, 25, 27–28
  location shifts, 27–28
  pottery artifacts, 21
  residential dwellings, 28
Montegrande Valley, 25, 26
Montegrande (village), 19, 25, 28
Montículo Laguna, 112
monumental architecture
  architectural axes, 145
  architectural layouts, 145–146
  Chavín de Huántar, 141
  early construction, 1–2
  Kuntur Wasi Phase, 83–84
  Pacopampa archaeological site,
    137–138, 142–146
  renovations, 142–143, 147
  social memory construction, 121
  See also civic-ceremonial centers
Moro canal system, 3
mortars, 164
mortuary practices
  leadership authority and power,
    127, 194
  social memory construction, 124
  See also burial artifacts; burials
Mosquito Plain, 19–20, 30–32
mounds
  architectural axes, 17, 72, 73
  Caral complex, 17
  Cardal archaeological complex,
    49, 53–60, 62–65
  Cerro Blanco site, 36–37, 39
  early public architecture, 2
  Hamacas Complex, 23
  Huaca Cortada, 6–9, 11
  Huaca Herederos Grande, 9–10
  Huaca Partida, 31, 35, 37, 39
  Ingatambo site, 169
  lateral arms, 57–59, 62–63, 64
  multi-mound settlements, 16, 17
  Nuer territory, Africa, 15
  religious ceremonies, 11, 13

Upano Valley, 167
U-shaped complexes, 49, 52–60,
    62–65
  See also Caballo Muerto
    Complex; Montegrande
    architectural complex;
    Pacopampa archaeological
    site
Mount Fila Caraneros, 30
multicolored painted walls, 111
multi-mound settlements, 16, 17
mural decorations, 31
mural paintings, 111, 121
Museo Larco Herrera, 125
Muyu Moqo Phase ceramics, 175,
    177

N

National Museum of Ethnology of
    Japan, 110
natural terraces, 71, 76, 78, 79
Nazca Valley, 175, 181, 183, 185
necked jars, 157, 161, 164, 169
necklaces, 163, 164, 166, 168
neckless jars/ollas
  Anchucaya, 69, 73, 76, 79
  Cerro Blanco site, 39
  Huayurco complex, 157, 164, 169
  South Coast, 175
needles
  Huayurco complex, 157, 159, 164
  Pacopampa archaeological site,
    119, 124
negative painting technique, 175,
    181
Nepeña Phase
  architectural features, 41
  chronology, 36
  construction techniques, 37
Nepeña Valley, 41
nicked appliqué bands, 158
nonreinforced rims, 163, 165
Norte Chico complex, 17
North Coast
  architectural features, 40
  ceramic styles, 175
  cultural continuities, 188
  influence, 83, 84
  interregional interactions, 109
  kenning, 41
Northern Highlands
  camelid domestication, 99
  coastal vacancy, 104
  cultural continuities, 188
  hunting-to-herding shift, 97–98
  leadership authority, 109
  pottery artifacts, 169
  See also Kuntur Wasi site;
    Pacopampa archaeological
    site
North Platform (Cerro Blanco), 39
Nuer territory, Africa, 15

O

observatories, astronomical,
    133–134, 138–139, 141, 144,
    146, 147
obsidian
  Campanayuq Rumi, 183–184
  interregional interactions, 153,
    169–170, 177–178, 183–184,
    187–188, 191, 196
  Kuntur Wasi site, 104
  Pacopampa archaeological site,
    111
  provenience, 188
Odocoileus virginianus, 101
Old Adult category, 100, 101, 102
oncilla, 168
ornaments
  Campanayuq Rumi, 183
  Huayurco complex, 164,
    168–169
  Pacopampa archaeological site,
    119, 124
ornithopomorphic figures, 42

P

pacas, 159, 164, 167
Pachacamac, 41
Pacific Ocean, 136
Pacopampa I Phase
  access control, 114, 115, 195
  architectural axes, 145, 147
  construction activity, 110, 129,
    138–140, 145
  leadership authority and power,
    142, 145
  monumental architecture,
    137–138
  pottery artifacts, 121, 126, 137,
    148
  reused stone materials, 121
  subdivisions, 110, 129
Pacopampa II Phase
  access control, 115, 195
  construction activity, 112–113,
    119, 129, 136–138, 143–144
  leadership authority and power,
    142
  pottery artifacts, 119, 137
  reused stone materials, 121
  ritual practices, 124
  social differentiation and
    complexity, 116–117, 119
  stone monoliths, 125
  subdivisions, 110, 129
Pacopampa Archaeological Project,
    110, 129
Pacopampa archaeological site
  access control, 114–115, 127,
    144–146, 147
  archaeoastronomy, 129, 134, 135,
    137, 139–147, 195